D0176679

FAIR USE, FREE USE AND USE BY PERMISSION

How to Handle Copyrights in All Media

Lee Wilson

ALLWORTH
PRESS
NEW YORK

09 08 07 06 05   5 4 3 2 1

Published by Allworth Press
An imprint of Allworth Communications, Inc.
10 East 23rd Street, New York, NY 10010

Cover design by Derek Bacchus
Interior design by Joan O'Connor
Page composition/typography by Integra Software Services

ISBN: 1-58115-432-1

Library of Congress Cataloging-in-Publication Data

Wilson, Lee, 1951-
    Fair use, free use, and use by permission: using and licensing copyrights in all media/by Lee Wilson.
        p.   cm.
    Includes index.
1. Copyright—United States—Popular works.   2. Fair use (Copyright)—United States.   I. Title.

    KF2995.W477 2005
    346.7304'82—dc22

                                                                    2005026429

Printed in Canada

This book is dedicated
to my very good friend Carolyn Taylor Wilson,
whose personal life has been dedicated
to her family and friends and
whose professional life has been dedicated
to book lovers.
If there were more people like Carolyn
in the world, there would be far fewer problems.

CONTENTS

© Part III
Permissions and Licenses 135

© Part IV
Appendixes 175

PREFACE

THIS BOOK IS DESIGNED TO FUNCTION SOMETHING like the casebooks used in most law school courses. After all, those books and this one are designed for the same purpose—to teach. Casebooks present series of digest versions of actual appeals court decisions. Law students are supposed to read these and, after considering the facts in each case and the written opinion of the court in deciding the case, learn how the law applies to various fact situations. For the most part, the situations described in the examples given in this book are fictitious. However, they are realistic and because they are written specifically to demonstrate how application of the law regarding fair use of copyrights depends greatly on the specific facts in any situation, they are even more instructive than most real-life cases. They demonstrate an important basic principle of copyright fair use: that two situations—identical except for one circumstance—may lead to opposite results. One set of facts may amount to a fair use of a copyrighted work while another nearly identical use may constitute infringement. These examples are meant to teach you how to decide correctly for yourself, in most instances, whether a proposed use is a fair use.

You'll notice a lot of lawyers in these examples. That's because they are true-to-life examples of situations involving questions of copyright infringement. In real life, such situations usually involve lawyers, often even if the suspected infringer proves not to have trespassed on anyone's rights. And those lawyers almost always charge high hourly fees, between about $175 and $400 per hour, to evaluate the circumstances surrounding the claimed infringement. This means that even being accused of infringement can be expensive. One of the best ways to avoid infringement claims is to educate yourself sufficiently to be able to decide correctly when you need permission to use a copyrighted work. It's not too hard, especially if you begin the fair-use analysis with respect for the copyright rights of others. That respect, and the ability to read and apply the guidelines contained in this book, ought to keep you out of trouble in most situations and help you avoid the need for a lawyer. Think of it this way: The imaginary lawyers throughout this book can substitute for a real lawyer who charges you for his opinion. Save the money you'd otherwise have to spend on legal fees for a rainy day. Lawyers already profit sufficiently from disputes Americans can't or don't avoid; they don't need *your* hard-earned paycheck, too.

But why respect copyright, especially if no one will ever know you "borrowed" someone else's copyright? It has to do with more than the probability of getting caught (or not getting caught). Deciding whether to respect the copyrights of others is an ethical decision. For most creative people, it's not a hard decision to make; they respect the copyrights of others because they hope that others will respect *their* copyrights. It doesn't necessarily work this way, of course—there's no guarantee that your copyrights are safe because you decline to steal from other creators—but we must remember that any group is made up of its members and that the actions and attitudes of any group are made up of the actions and attitudes of the individuals in it. If you believe that copyright benefits society, as our founding fathers planned, then you must, for the sake of consistency, recognize the boundaries copyright imposes.

Furthermore, as with many ethical decisions, respecting copyright leads to self-respect. Any person who enjoys the ability to create something is not so desperate for the necessities of life that he must steal from others. Art is a bourgeois activity only possible after the immediate needs of life are met. But so are ethics—the fine points of who owns what is usually a consideration only when everyone's tummy is full.

And respecting copyright law is one of many small stones in the wall we as a society erect against chaos. It's an important part of the current social contract. We shall see that copyright is really an incentive to encourage the creators among us to produce the art and literature—and lesser works—that we all depend on. American culture, and especially American popular culture, is perhaps our main export. For better or for worse, we influence the world. To enhance our own lives and to protect our influence worldwide, we should all respect and protect copyright. If you love art and culture, popular culture, or just the wonderful American system that lets almost anyone say—or write—almost anything at almost any time, you should understand that, along with the First Amendment, it was all created by, and is supported by, our copyright system. It's a long-held tradition in this country to speak out and to allow others to do the same; when you consider it, respecting copyright is patriotic and ethical and essential for an informed life in a free society. This book can tell you how to respect the copyright rights of others while making the maximum allowable use of works created by others. Like democracy, it's not a perfect system. But, again like democracy, it's the best anyone has come up with. Knowledge is power—read on!

PART I.

Understanding Copyright

CHAPTER 1

Copyright Basics

THE MEN WHO WROTE OUR CONSTITUTION acted to ensure the production of the works of art and intellect necessary to create and promote culture and learning in our infant nation. In Article I, Section 8, Clause 8 of the main body of the original, unamended Constitution, they gave Congress the power "to Promote the Progress of Science and useful Arts, by securing, for limited Times to Authors and Inventors, the exclusive Right to their respective Writings and Discoveries." Congress carried out this mandate by passing the first U.S. copyright statute in 1790 (and also by enacting a succession of patent statutes). You may think from reading the language of the Constitution that only authors of books are protected by copyright law, but that is not the case.

Historically, American copyright law has interpreted broadly the "writings" granted constitutional protection. At the time of the enactment of the first copyright statute, only "maps, charts, and books" were protected. In the intervening the two centuries, U.S. copyright statutes (there have been several) and court decisions have extended copyright protection to new subjects of copyright as previously nonexistent classes of works emerged, needing protection. U.S. copyright statutes have successively embraced, among other new technologies, photography, motion pictures, and sound recordings.

This system of enumerating the classes of "writings" protected by copyright worked well enough until it became obvious that new methods of expression were being created faster than courts and lawmakers could amend the then-current copyright statute to include emerging technologies within the scope of copyright protection. The present U.S. copyright statute abandons the effort to enumerate every class of work protected by copyright and simply states that "copyright protection subsists . . . in original works of authorship fixed in any tangible medium of expression, now known or later developed, from which they can be perceived, reproduced, or otherwise communicated, either directly or with the aid of a machine or device." This language allows copyright to grow automatically, extending protection to new forms of expression. This is fortunate, because the revolution in communications that characterized the last half of the twentieth century shows no sign of abating. Indeed, it may have reached warp speed.

By recognizing property rights in creative works and awarding ownership of those rights to the creators of the works, our copyright statute encourages expression in every art form and medium. It balances the interests of creators against those of the public. Creators reap the profits from their works for the duration of copyright protection by limiting access to their creative works to those who pay for the privilege of using them. The public immediately enjoys controlled access to the works that artists, writers, and composers create, and eventually, those works become public property, available for use by anyone. This is precisely what the founding fathers had in mind; James Madison cited copyright as an instance in which the "public good fully coincides with the claims of individuals."

So, the United States gives its citizens the right to say almost anything at all and rewards that expression, whether meritorious or mundane, by bestowing upon it a copyright. But what, exactly, is a copyright? It is a set of rights that the federal copyright statute grants to the creators of literary, musical, dramatic, choreographic, pictorial, graphic, sculptural, and audiovisual works and sound recordings. Copyright law rewards creators by granting them the exclusive right to exploit and control their creations. With few narrow exceptions, only the person who created the copyrighted work or someone who has been sold the copyright in the work or given permission to use the work is legally permitted to reproduce it, to prepare alternate or "derivative" versions of it, to distribute and sell copies of it, and to perform or display it publicly. Any unauthorized exercise of any of these rights is called "copyright infringement" and is actionable in federal court.

Before you can begin to understand copyright—that invisible but powerful and infinitely expandable concept that governs so many of our dealings with each other—you must first learn what it is *not*. Two of the things that copyright is not are trademarks and patents. The three forms of intellectual property are more like cousins than triplets, but many people, even lawyers and judges, confuse them.

Copyrights Compared to Trademarks and Patents

Although all three protect products of the human imagination, copyrights, trademarks, and patents are distinct but complementary sorts of intellectual property. Each is governed by a different federal law. The U.S. patent statute originates in the same provision of the Constitution that gives rise to our copyright statute. Our federal trademark statute originates in the "commerce clause" of the Constitution, which gives Congress the power to regulate interstate commerce. Only the federal government regulates copyrights; copyright registrations are granted by the Copyright Office, which is a department of the Library of Congress. Similarly, only the federal government can grant a patent. However, although the federal government grants trademark registrations, so do all the fifty states.

Copyrights

Since January 1, 1978, in the United States, a copyright is created whenever a creator "fixes" in tangible form a work for which copyright protection is available. Under most circumstances, a copyright will endure until seventy years after the death of the creator of the copyrighted work; after copyright protection expires, a work is said to have fallen into the "public domain" and anyone is free to use it. Registration of a copyright enhances the rights that a creator automatically gains by the act of creation, but it is not necessary for copyright protection. The chief limitation on the rights of copyright owners is that copyright protects only particular *expressions* of ideas rather than the ideas themselves. This means that several people can create copyrightable works based on the same idea; in fact, there is no infringement, no matter how similar one work is to another unless one creator copied another's work.

Trademarks

Trademarks are words or symbols that identify products or services to consumers. Unlike a copyright, in which the creator has protectable rights from the inception of the copyrighted work, rights in a trademark accrue only by use of the trademark in commerce. They then belong to the company that applies the mark to its products rather than to the person who came up with the name or designed the logo that becomes the trademark. Roughly speaking, a company gains rights in a trademark in direct proportion to the duration and the geographic scope of its use of the mark; ordinarily, the company that first uses a mark gains rights in that mark superior to those of any other company that later uses it for the same product or services. Unauthorized use of a trademark is "trademark infringement."

As is the case with copyrights, registration enhances rights in trademarks but does not create them. It is generally easy to register a mark within a state, whereas federal trademark registration, which confers much greater benefits, is more difficult to obtain. Trademark rights last indefinitely; as long as a mark is used in commerce, its owners have protectable rights in it.

(For more information about trademarks, see *The Trademark Guide*, by Lee Wilson, published by Allworth Press.)

Patents

A patent is a monopoly granted by the U.S. Patent Office for a limited time to the creator of a new invention. A utility patent may be granted to a process, machine, manufacture, composition of matter, or improvement of an existing idea that falls into one of these categories. For example, a utility patent would be granted to the inventor of a new industrial or technical process or a new chemical composition. Utility patents endure twenty years after the patent application was filed. Plant patents are issued for new asexually or sexually reproducible plants and last seventeen years from the date of issue. Design patents are granted for ornamental designs used for nonfunctional aspects of manufactured items. An example of this would be a lamp base in the shape of a caryatid; the caryatid would visually enhance the appearance of the lamp but would not improve the function of the lamp base—that is, elevating the bulb and shade portions of the lamp. A design patent lasts fourteen years from the date it is issued. An inventor must meet very strict standards before the Patent Office will grant a patent for his invention; then, he can stop everyone else from manufacturing the invention without permission or even importing an infringing invention into the United States, even if the infringer of the patent independently came up with the same invention.

No product name is protectable by patent law; a product name is a trademark, and trademark protection is earned in the marketplace rather than being awarded like a patent. And no song, story, painting, or play can be patented; copyright gives writers and artists the right to keep others from copying their works, but not a complete monopoly on the creation or importation of similar works. (For a more detailed discussion of patent law, see *The Patent Guide*, by Carl Battle, published by Allworth Press.)

Requirements for Copyright Protection

Under the U.S. copyright statute, a work must satisfy three conditions to qualify for copyright protection. Each of these requirements must be met in order for the work to come under the copyright umbrella.

The three statutory prerequisites for protection are:

1. The work must be "original" in the sense that it cannot have been copied from another work
2. The work must embody some "expression" of the author, rather than consisting only of an idea or ideas
3. The work must be "fixed" in some tangible medium of expression

Originality

The originality condition for protection leads to the apparent anomaly that two works identical to each other may be equally eligible for copyright protection. So long as neither of the two works was copied from the other, each is considered "original." In the sense that it is used in the copyright statute, "originality" means simply that a work was not copied from another work rather than that the work is unique or unusual. Judge Learned Hand, a jurist who decided many copyright cases, summarized the originality requirement with a famous hypothetical example: "[I]f by some magic a man who had never known it were to compose anew Keats's *Ode on a Grecian Urn*, he would be an 'author,' and, if he copyrighted it, others might not copy the poem, though they might of course copy Keats's." For copyright purposes, the similarities between two works are immaterial, as long as they do not result from copying.

Expression

The current copyright statute restates the accepted rule, often enunciated in copyright decisions, that copyright subsists only in the expression embodied in a work and not in the underlying ideas upon which it is based. The statute says: "In no case does copyright protection for an original work of authorship extend to any idea, procedure, process, system, method of operation, concept, principle, or discovery, regardless of the form in which it is described, explained, illustrated, or embodied in such work." This rule plays an important role in copyright infringement cases, because a judge often must determine whether the defendant has taken protected expression from the plaintiff or merely "borrowed" an unprotectable idea (or "procedure, process, system," etc.).

Fixation

The U.S. copyright statute protects works eligible for protection only when they are "fixed in any tangible medium of expression, now known or later developed, from which they can be perceived, reproduced, or otherwise communicated, either directly or with the aid of a machine or device." The statute deems a work fixed in a tangible medium of expression "when its embodiment in a copy or phonorecord, by or under the authority of the author, is sufficiently permanent or stable to permit it to be perceived, reproduced, or otherwise communicated for a period of more than transitory duration."

This third requirement for copyright protection sometimes surprises people, who may not realize, for instance, that a new song performed at an open-mic "writers' night" or a dance routine presented in a talent show, although it may be original and contain a high proportion of protectable expression, is not protected by copyright until it is "fixed" within the definition of the copyright statute and can be legally copied, word for word or move for move, by anyone who witnesses its performance. A song can be "fixed" by recording any intelligible version of its music and lyrics on a cassette or CD or by reducing its melody to written musical notation that also includes its lyrics. Any piece of choreography can be "fixed" by videotaping it in sufficient detail to record the movements of the dancers or by use of a written system of choreographic notation such as Labanotation.

What Is Protected

Most people realize that copyright protects works of art like poems and short stories, photographs, paintings and drawings, and musical compositions. It may be less obvious that copyright also protects more mundane forms of expression, including such diverse materials as advertising copy, instruction manuals, brochures, logo designs, computer programs, term papers, home movies, cartoon strips, and advertising jingles. Artistic merit has nothing to do with whether a work is protectable by copyright; in fact, the most routine business letter and the most inexpertly executed child's drawing are just as entitled to protection under our copyright statute as bestselling novels, hit songs, and blockbuster movies.

However, copyright does not protect every product of the human imagination, no matter how many brain cells were expended in its creation. In fact, any discussion of copyright protection must be premised on an understanding of what copyright *does not* protect.

Idea Versus Expression

It is such an important principle of copyright law that it bears repeating: Copyright protects only particular *expressions* of ideas, not the ideas themselves. This means, of course, that if the guy sitting behind you on the bus looks over your shoulder and sees, comprehends, and remembers your sketches for a necklace formed of links cast in the shape of sunflowers, he is legally free to create his own sunflower necklace so long as it isn't a copy of yours. It may be *unethical* for him to steal your idea, but it's neither illegal nor actionable in court. Although this may seem unjust, if you think about it, the logic is clear. Our Constitution empowered Congress to pass a copyright statute granting the creators among us property rights in the products of their imaginations so that American society could benefit from their creations. Because ideas are the building blocks for creations of any sort, and because one idea may lead to thousands of expressions of that idea, granting control over an idea to any one person would have the effect of severely limiting creative expression; no one else would be able to use the idea as the basis for a new creation. Therefore, copyright protects only your particular *expression* of an idea, not idea itself. Similarly, copyright protection is denied to procedures, processes, systems, methods of operation, concepts, principles, or discoveries, because these products of the imagination are really all particular varieties of ideas.

This means that your *idea* of printing grocery coupons right on the brown paper bags used in your supermarket can be copied by anyone, even a competing grocery store, although the particular expression of your idea—your copy and artwork for the bags and the advertisements publicizing the promotion—may not.

And your *system* of giving your customers double the face-value discount of any coupon if they use it to buy two items at the same time is not protectable by your copyright in your coupon-promotion materials and can be employed at any time by anyone, without your permission.

Furthermore, if you print recipes on your grocery bags in addition to discount coupons, you cannot, of course, stop anyone from using the *method* outlined in the Low-Fat Meatloaf recipe to create a low-fat meatloaf. Nor can you stop anyone, even a competitor, from employing your *concept* of using a low-fat meatloaf recipe to sell the food products used in the recipe or from employing the marketing *principle* behind your promotion—that food shoppers are likely to purchase particular brands of food products that are specified by name in an interesting recipe. And even if you were the first person in the universe to come up with a technique for lowering the fat content of the finished dish, once you disclose your *discovery* to the public, you can't stop anyone from passing it on to others. You can't even stop anyone from using the *information* outlined in your recipe to create his or her own recipe for low-fat meatloaf. (See the discussion of functional works below.)

Unprotectable Elements

A few categories of products of the imagination are too close to being mere unembellished ideas for copyright protection to apply. In other words, these categories of "creations" lack sufficient expression to be granted copyright protection. There are several commonly occurring unprotectable elements of various sorts of works from which the copyright statute or courts have withheld protection, including:

- Literary plots, situations, locales, or settings
- *Scènes à faire*, which are stock literary themes that dictate the incidents used by an author to express them
- Literary characters, to the extent that they are "types" rather than original expressions of an author, as opposed to pictorial characters, the visual representation of which adds considerable protectable expression to the characters
- Titles of books, stories, poems, songs, movies, and so forth, which have been uniformly held by courts not to be protected by copyright (although a title may gain protection under the law of unfair competition if it becomes well known and associated in the public mind with one author)
- Short phrases and slogans, to the extent that they lack expressive content, the determination of which is aided by the length of the phrase or slogan, very short phrases and slogans being more likely to constitute the equivalent of an unprotectable idea than long ones
- The rhythm or structure of musical works
- Themes expressed by song lyrics
- Short musical phrases
- Arrangements of musical compositions, unless an arrangement of a musical composition really amounts to an alternate version of the composition, in which case the arrangement infringes the underlying composition unless it was written with the permission of the copyright owner in that composition (The exception to this is an arrangement of a public-domain song. Since you

9

can use a public-domain composition any way you want, it's legal to make a detailed arrangement of such a song, and the arrangement is protectable. The same is true for any derivative work based on a public-domain work; the derivative work is protectable.)

- Social dance steps and simple routines, which are not copyrightable as choreographic works because they are the common property of the culture that enjoys them
- Uses of color, perspective, geometric shapes, and standard arrangements dictated by aesthetic convention in works of the visual arts (However, an artist's *arrangement* of these elements may be protectable expression.)
- Jewelry designs that merely mimic the structures of nature, such as a jeweled pin that accurately replicates the form of a honeybee
- Names of products, services, or businesses (However, these are protected under trademark law from use without permission on similar products or services.)
- Pseudonyms or professional or stage names (These may also be protected under trademark law or the law of unfair competition.)
- Mere variations on familiar symbols, emblems, or designs, such as typefaces, numerals, or punctuation symbols, and religious emblems or national symbols
- Information, research data, and bare historical facts (Although many compilations of such information or data and extended expressions based on historical facts are protectable by copyright.)
- Blank forms, such as account ledger page forms, diaries, address books, blank checks, restaurant checks, order forms, and the like (These record information rather than conveying it.)
- Measuring and computing devices like slide rules or tape measures, calendars, height and weight charts, sporting event schedules, and other assemblages of commonly available information that contain no original material

Utilitarian Aspects of Design

In addition, protection is specifically denied in the copyright statute to "utilitarian elements of industrial design." Pictorial, graphic, and sculptural works are, of course, protectable, but only insofar as their forms, the "mechanical or utilitarian aspects" of such designs, are not protected. The reasoning behind this provision is that if such aspects of otherwise decorative objects are to be protected at all, they must meet the rigorous requirements for a utility patent.

The question of what features of utilitarian objects are protected by copyright is most prevalent in the case of objects that have little ornamentation and consist mostly of a simple design that is largely determined by the function of the object. For instance, in the case of a ceramic lamp base decorated with painted ferns, the fern design has nothing to do with the function of the base—that of elevating the bulb and shade of the lamp to a height sufficient to illuminate the area surrounding the lamp—and is protectable by copyright.

However, a cylindrical brass lamp base fixed to a square marble foundation would embody no elements that were not primarily functional and would be unprotectable under the copyright statute. If a marble caryatid were substituted for the lamp's cylindrical brass base, the sculpture of the draped female figure would be protectable because of its more decorative and less utilitarian nature, even though it would still serve to elevate the lamp's bulb and shade. This principle of copyright law is easier to remember if you consider the general rule of copyright that the more elaborate and unusual the expression embodied in the work, the more protection the work is given (provided, of course, that the work is not copied from any other work).

Functional Works

Similarly, courts treat functional works like recipes, rules for games and contests, architectural plans, and computer programs somewhat differently from works that have no inherent functional aspects. Although they are eligible for copyright protection, protection for functional works is somewhat narrower than for other sorts of works because the intended function of such a work dictates that certain standard information, symbols, etc., be included in the work and that certain protocols be followed for the ordering and presentation of the information such works contain.

For example, copyright in recipes is very limited. Copyright does not protect any list of ingredients, because such lists consist of information only and embody no protectable expression. A particular expression of recipe instructions *may* be protectable, at least from word-for-word copying, but probably only to the extent that the explanation of the steps in making the dish embodies expression that is not dictated by the necessary technique or inherent chemistry of the process. Courts have also held the view that very short explanations of concepts, such as game rules and recipes, are *not* copyrightable, because granting copyright in them would effectively prevent any other recounting of such rules or recipes.

Copyright in Real Life

All this has a practical application. It may be that anyone is free to use the beautiful new typeface design that you worked nights and weekends to perfect, even though you intended it to be used only in a hand-lettered story you wrote for your niece's birthday. Or that great new slogan that you came up with to advertise your company's product may soon be on everyone's lips, in contexts that don't help your sales for the quarter at all.

The good news is that if you design a poster calendar for your sporting goods company, you may copy from any other calendar all the information you need concerning the days of the week on which the dates fall and the dates of holidays and any information about the year's sporting events from schedules published in newspapers or by colleges, sports magazines, or anyone else. And when you compose the copy for ads for your business, you can make free use of slogans and catchphrases from popular culture without obtaining permission from the copyright owner of the work from which the slogan was taken; otherwise, you'd have to call up (and most likely, *pay*) Edgar Rice Burroughs' heirs to use "Me Tarzan, You Jane," or George Lucas to use "May the Force Be with You," in an ad.

However, a famous phrase or slogan of this sort may become so associated in the public's mind with its originator that it may not be used to sell products or services without the real threat of a suit for unfair competition. This means that the originator of a famous phrase or slogan could sue on the ground that your use of that phrase or slogan to market your product or service might cause consumers to associate your product or service with the originator of the phrase or slogan. Be very careful in employing a well-known phrase or slogan in any manner that displays it more prominently than, say, a line of text from a book or fragment of dialogue from a movie.

Copyright law treats facts of all sorts like ideas; the only thing relating to facts that is protectable under copyright law is the particular expression of those facts. You may write a movie script based on the historic facts surrounding the battle of the Alamo; those facts are free for use by anyone who cares to gather them at the library or from other sources. However, if you believe that it's time for another movie about the Alamo and that Hollywood will buy your script, you may want to think twice before you mention your project to your cousin the screenwriter, since she is free to recognize your idea as a good one and write her own competing script based on the very facts you planned to use.

The same is true of plots. Shakespeare's *Romeo and Juliet* has spawned many works based on the plot of his play: the play *Abie's Irish Rose,* the movie *The Cohens and The Kellys*—now both forgotten except for the well-known copyright infringement suit concerning their similar plots—the famous musical *West Side Story,* the old television series *Bridget Loves Bernie,* and the 1969 Zeffirelli film *Romeo and Juliet,* which was only one in a long line of movies based on the Shakespeare play.

And if you think of the innumerable love songs written about heartbroken, jilted lovers, you will realize that themes are not protectable by copyright, either: each of the 2,438,954 songs written about somebody's broken heart is a perfectly legitimate use of that theme. No doubt there will be more, similar uses as long as popular music exists.

Public-Domain Materials

The largest category of literary and artistic material that is not protected by copyright is "public-domain" material. Most public-domain material is material for which copyright protection has expired. Examples of this are the works of "dead poets"—literary gentlemen who have been dead a long time, like Shelley, Keats, and Shakespeare. The trick is to make sure that the author whose work you want to use has been dead long enough.

Herman Melville died in 1891. More important for purposes of determining the copyright status of his works is the fact that his books were written before 1891, which means that any rights Melville or his heirs had in them expired some time ago. This means that you may freely use Melville's *Moby-Dick* characters and story in your screenplay. The same is not true of, for example, Tennessee Williams; even though he is just as dead as Melville, his plays are still protected. Williams's estate owns the copyrights in those plays and collects royalties from performances of them. All this applies to painters and composers, too, as well as to lesser mortals like you and me whose creations are not quite great literature or art but are valuable to us nevertheless.

However, figuring out whether a work is in the public domain is not simply a matter of determining whether the author has been dead a while, since the creators of many still-valid copyrights expired a long time before their copyrights will. Unless you know for sure that the copyright in a work has expired, you must investigate the copyright status of the work before reprinting it or adapting it or otherwise exercising any right reserved to the owners of valid copyrights.

U.S. copyrights have been, for most of our history, considerably shorter than they now are. The last enlargement of the term of copyright granted to U.S. authors occurred with the passage of the 1998 Sonny Bono Copyright Term Extension Act. This Act amended the U.S. copyright statute to extend the duration of U.S. copyrights until seventy years after the death of an author (as opposed to the life-plus-fifty-years provided before the passage of the Act). This change was made in order to bring the United States into conformity with the longer term adopted by the countries of the European Union. This most recent extension of the term of U.S. copyrights was challenged in court by people who believed that extending the term of copyright rewarded rich copyright owners like entertainment giants Walt Disney and AOL-TimeWarner. However, the Supreme Court recognized that Congress had the power to grant longer protection to copyright owners and that it was immaterial that some of them were rich companies that had acquired, rather than created, the copyrights they own. Justice Ruth Bader Ginsburg said, from the bench, that the Constitution "gives Congress wide leeway to prescribe 'limited times' for copyright protection and allows Congress to secure the same level and duration of protection for all copyright holders, present and future." In other words, she knew that U.S. copyright law protects all copyright creators and other owners equally, the starving songwriter who owns only his guitar as well as the giant corporation that has acquired libraries of famous movies.

The best way to begin to determine whether a work is still protected by copyright is to consult the Copyright Office circular called *How to Investigate the Copyright Status of a Work*, which is reprinted in appendix B. This pamphlet will give you the information you need to either figure out the copyright status of a work yourself or get help in doing so. You may also be able to determine the copyright status of a work by accessing one of the copyright duration charts mentioned at the end of chapter 3.

Copyright Notice

Copyright notice is an important tool in copyright protection. It is like a "No Trespassing" sign—notice to the world that you claim ownership of the copyright in the work to which it is affixed. The three elements of copyright notice, which should appear together in close proximity, are:

- **The word "Copyright" (that is C-O-P-Y-R-I-G-H-T, *not* "copywrite"), the abbreviation "Copr.," or the © symbol (or, in the case of a sound recording, the ℗ symbol).** Even though it is often used by people who attempt to create the © symbol on a typewriter, the symbol (C) is *not* the equivalent of the © symbol. If you can't produce the © symbol, use the word "Copyright" instead of the © symbol or draw the c-in-a-circle symbol by hand, but don't use parentheses in lieu of the circle—it's not the same. Because some countries do not recognize the word "Copyright" and the abbreviation "Copr." as valid elements of copyright notice, it is preferable to use the © symbol if your work is distributed, or may be in the future, outside the United States.
- **The year of "first publication" of the work.** "Publication" is "the distribution of copies of a work to the public by sale or other transfer of ownership, or by rental, lease, or lending." For compilations or derivative works, the year of first publication of the compilation or derivative work should be used. However, the year-date of first publication may be omitted from copyright notice when a pictorial, graphic, or sculptural work, with any accompanying text, is reproduced on greeting cards, postcards, stationery, jewelry, dolls, toys, or other useful articles.
- **The name of the owner of the copyright or an abbreviation or alternate name by which that copyright owner is generally recognized.** For example, International Business Machines, Incorporated, can call itself "IBM" for purposes of copyright notice. However, when in doubt, use the form of your legal name that you commonly use for other formal purposes—for example, "Aaron L. Bowers" rather than "Sonny Bowers." If two or more people or other entities own the copyright, use all their names: "© 2005 Charles Dennis Wile and Christopher Lawrence Fort." Furthermore, bear in mind that the *author* of the work may no longer be the *owner* of copyright in it.

In the United States, proper copyright notice consists only of some combination of the three elements mentioned above. All the following forms are correct: "Copyright 2005 Natalie Marie Wilson," "© 2005 N. M. Wilson," and for a sound recording, "℗ 2005 Natalie M. Wilson."

Countries that are signatories to the Buenos Aires Convention (see the discussion of copyright treaties) require that "a statement of the reservation of the property right" in a work appear on or in the work for copyright protection. This means that for complete protection in Buenos Aires Convention countries, a statement asserting your ownership of your copyright and your reservation of the rights in it should be used in addition to the copyright notice described by the U.S. copyright statute that is also acceptable in Universal Copyright Convention countries. The most familiar form of such "reservation of rights" language is the phrase "All rights reserved." This means that the form of copyright notice that guarantees the fullest protection available throughout the world is: "© 2005 Paul Clifford, All rights reserved." You should use this form of notice, even if you do not anticipate that your work will be distributed outside the United States. Ink is cheap, and proper copyright notice can offer valuable benefits and protections.

Occasionally, copyright owners will add to the title page of a book or magazine something like this:

No portion of this publication may be reproduced or transmitted in any form or by any means, electronic or mechanical, including by photocopying, recording, or use of any information storage and retrieval system without express written permission from Bifocal Book Publishers.

Here's an even scarier notice of authorship:

This photograph is a print prepared by Wile Studio under the supervision of the photographer Dennis Wile. The copyrighted image embodied in this photograph is owned by Dennis Wile and may not be reproduced by any means whatever for any use, personal or otherwise, by any person or entity without specific written permission from Dennis Wile. Any unauthorized reproduction of this image constitutes copyright infringement as defined by U.S. law and subjects the infringer to such penalties as are prescribed by the federal copyright statute (17 U.S.C. section 101, *et seq.*, including, where appropriate, fines and other criminal penalties) and enforceable under international treaties. The legal owner of this print has the right to display it in a private setting and by law acquires no right to reproduce the print in any form or for any purpose. Any other use of this print is a copyright violation unless advance written permission is secured from Wile Studio for any such additional use.

Besides scaring off some potential copyright infringers who may not know or appreciate the full significance of copyright notice, added language of this sort has no effect and *is not a substitute for proper copyright notice.* However, nothing in copyright law says that you cannot use some language of this sort near your copyright notice to make more explicit your claim of ownership of copyright in your work.

The important thing to remember is that *there is no legal substitute for proper copyright notice.* It costs nothing to use, and you don't need permission from anyone to use it. Not using notice on any work that leaves your hands is foolish.

When Notice Is Required

Foolish though it may be to fail to use copyright notice, it must be said that copyright notice is not *required* for any work published after March 1, 1989, which is the date that the United States' entry into the Berne Convention became effective. The Berne Convention is a very old and widespread copyright treaty, but, for a variety of complicated reasons, the United States became a signatory to it only in late 1988. One of these reasons is that Berne Convention signatory countries may not require as a condition to copyright protection any "formalities," such as using copyright notice. However, confusingly enough, the copyrights in works published before January 1, 1978, the effective date of the current copyright statute, may be *lost* in the United States if notice is not used.

Benefits of Using Notice

The short of this long story is that you cannot now lose copyright protection for any work published after March 1, 1989, even if you fail to use copyright notice. However, in order to encourage the use of copyright notice in the United States, the law provides a valuable procedural advantage in infringement lawsuits to copyright owners who do use it. Specifically, an infringer cannot successfully claim that he or she did not know that his or her act constituted copyright infringement if the copyright owner has used proper copyright notice. Being able to prove that a defendant willfully ignored such clear evidence that the plaintiff's work was protected by copyright effectively increases the potential damages award available to a plaintiff, since courts are typically much harder on defendants who have intentionally violated the rights of plaintiffs.

That takes care of people dishonest enough to ignore copyright notice. Using copyright notice also precludes the possibility that honest people, seeing no copyright notice, will believe that your work is free for anyone to use. Even after Berne, copyright notice remains one of the most useful tools for copyright protection.

Placement of Copyright Notice

Copyright notice does not have to be obtrusive. Copyright Office regulations specify only that notice be placed, in a durable form affixed in a permanent manner, in a location on the work where it is reasonably easy to discover.

For works published in book form, acceptable locations for copyright notice include the title page, the page following the title page, either side of the front or back cover, and the first or last page of the main body of the book.

For motion pictures and other audiovisual works, notice should be embodied in the film or tape as a part of the image itself so that it will appear whenever the work is played, broadcast, or otherwise performed. It may be located with or near the title or credits or immediately following the beginning of the work or at or immediately preceding the end of the work.

If the audiovisual work last sixty seconds or less, copyright notice may appear in any of the locations specified above or on the leader of the film or tape immediately preceding the work if the notice is embodied there electronically or mechanically (that is, not simply written by hand on the leader). For audiovisual works or motion pictures distributed to the public for private use, such as movie videotapes or DVDs, notice may also appear on the permanent container for the work.

For pictorial, graphic, or sculptural works embodied in two-dimensional copies, copyright notice should be affixed directly, durably, and permanently to the front or back of the copies or to the backing, mounting, or framing to which the copies are attached. For such works embodied in three-dimensional copies, notice should be affixed directly, durably, and permanently to any visible portion of the work or any base, mounting, framing, or other material to which the copies are attached. If, because of the nature of the work, it is impractical to affix notice to the copies directly or by means of a durable label, notice may appear on a tag or durable label that is designed to remain attached to the copy.

For copies of sound recordings, such as audiotapes, cassettes, CDs, and records, copyright notice should appear on the surface of the copy of the sound recording and on the container of the copy, so as to give reasonable notice of the claim of copyright ownership.

There are other sorts of works for which the Copyright Office prescribes placement of copyright notice. Further and more detailed information concerning copyright notice and placement is available in the free Copyright Office pamphlet *Copyright Notice*, and in the Copyright Office circulars, also free, *Methods of Affixation and Positions of the Copyright Notice on Various Types of Works* and *Copyright Notice*. These publications and many more are available free from the Copyright Office; you may print them from the Copyright Office Web site or call the Copyright Office Forms Hotline to have copies mailed to you. The Copyright Office Web site is at *www.copyright.gov*; the Copyright Office Forms Hotline, which operates every day around the clock, is (202) 707-9100.

Geographic Limits of Protection

All rights of U.S. copyright owners are granted to them by the U.S. copyright statute, which is a federal law—that is, a law passed by Congress that governs copyright matters throughout the United States. The provisions of the federal copyright statute are interpreted by court decisions. These decisions become another segment of United States copyright law, because they are used by other courts in deciding later copyright cases.

It is important to realize that all this law skids to a halt at the geographic boundaries of the United States because, of course, U.S. laws have no jurisdiction outside the fifty states and possessions of the United States. Other countries grant more or less reciprocal recognition to U.S. copyrights under the various copyright treaties to which the United States is a party.

There are two situations in which geography and copyright combine to concern average creators or copyright owners. These situations involve the protection of U.S. copyrights outside the United States and the circumstances under which the work of foreign nationals working in the United States are granted copyright protection by the U.S. copyright statute.

International Copyright Relations

Most other countries have their own copyright laws with provisions that may diverge considerably from those of our statute. For example, the terms of copyright in other countries are not necessarily the same as those in the United States. Copyright treaties get around the fact that no country's law has any effect outside that country by documenting the agreements between countries that each will give the same recognition to the others' copyrights that it gives to its own citizens.

The United States is now a signatory to the principal copyright treaties, which are basically agreements among several nations that each treaty signatory will accord the same respect to the rights of copyright owners who are citizens of the other signatory countries as it does to those of its own citizens. In addition to the Berne Convention, which is the most important copyright treaty and offers the most protection to copyright owners, the United States is a signatory to the Universal Copyright Convention and the Buenos Aires Convention. With the exception of China and Russia, most industrialized nations are signatories to one or more of the principal copyright treaties. To ensure protection for United States copyrights in countries that are not signatories to these copyright treaties or that ignore the rights of U.S. copyright owners, the United States has, where possible, entered bilateral treaties—that is, treaties that are signed only by the United States and the other nation.

Copyrighted works such as books, movies, television shows, and computer programs are important exports of the United States. However, intellectual-property rights have been given little or no respect in countries where domestic problems of poverty, disease, or war take precedence over the intellectual-property rights of citizens of other nations, and in countries that are still unfamiliar with the ideas of capitalism and private property, such as China and the territories that once combined to form the Soviet Union. Protection against unauthorized use of copyrighted works in any particular country depends basically on the laws of that country; where the law is lax, unenforced, or non-existent, U.S. companies suffer. For example, China is reputed to have the highest incidence of copyright piracy in the world, and infringers there have cost U.S. companies hundreds of millions of dollars annually in recent years, largely as a result of pirated compact discs, DVDs, and computer software.

Perhaps these problems will be solved or ameliorated as a result of the United States' efforts to normalize trade relations with such renegade countries—better trade relations may bring those nations into the world intellectual-property community and increase their observance of the copyright rights of U.S. citizens. The leaders of countries that make an industry of infringing U.S. copyrights are yielding to pressure from the United States to stop counterfeiters, who previously may have operated openly and without government interference. Increasingly, the U.S. government has enforced its citizens' copyright rights (as well as trademark and patent rights) by means of trade sanctions to punish nations that ignore U.S. intellectual-property rights. Like the 800-pound canary, the United States wields considerable clout. Some of this clout comes from provisions affecting the recognition of intellectual-property rights in trade agreements such as the North American Free Trade Agreement (NAFTA) and the General Agreement on Tariffs and Trade (GATT). Most of the United States' ability to coerce cooperation from other countries stems from the power of its collective pocketbook; many countries produce goods—or want to—for the U.S. market.

Such cooperation is necessary because no U.S. copyright owner can sue in the United States for copyright infringement that occurs elsewhere. If an American CD is counterfeited in China and sold there or in another country, the only recourse the U.S. copyright owner may have is to lobby the U.S. government to impose trade sanctions on China, to compel it to shut down the infringer's operation. Similarly, some developing countries, although they are signatories to one or more of the world's copyright treaties, do not impose meaningful penalties on infringers of foreign copyrights. This can make suing in one of these countries expensive and futile, because the only law that applies to infringements in other countries is the law of the country where the infringement occurs.

But if a foreign company brings its infringement to the United States, the U.S. copyright owner can sue here. For example, a U.S. copyright owner cannot sue profitably in Somalia to stop the manufacture of infringing products, because Somalia is not a signatory to any copyright treaty with the United States. However, if the infringing products are imported into the United States, the copyright owner can sue and can ask for seizure and destruction of the infringing products and any other remedy available under the U.S. copyright statute.

Foreign National Authors

A related question is that of the copyright status of authors who are not U.S. citizens. Under certain conditions, the copyright statute limits the right of some foreign nationals to enjoy the protection of U.S. copyright law even if they create their otherwise copyrightable works within the United States.

The copyright statute says that published works of foreign nationals are protected if one of the following is true:

•   On the date of first publication, one or more of the authors is a national or domiciliary of the United States, or of a foreign nation that is a party to a copyright treaty to which the United States is also a party, or is a stateless person, wherever that person may be domiciled

- The work is first published in the United States or in a foreign nation that, on the date of first publication, is a party to the Universal Copyright Convention
- The work is first published by the United Nations or any of its specialized agencies, or by the Organization of American States
- The work is a Berne Convention work
- The work comes within the scope of a presidential proclamation that extends protection to works of which one or more of the authors is, on the date of first publication, a national, domiciliary, or sovereign authority of a country that protects U.S. works on substantially the same basis as it protects works of its own citizens

Any unpublished work is protected by U.S. copyright law, regardless of the citizenship of the author or in what country he or she resides.

U.S. citizens may register their copyrights in other countries, but such registration is not usually necessary. Protection for any U.S. work—to the same extent as is given to works of citizens of that country—is by operation of law granted to U.S. works by any country that is a signatory to one of the copyright treaties to which the United States is a party. Circular 38a, *International Copyright Relations of the United States*, is available from the Copyright Office Forms Hotline or you can print it from the Copyright Office Web site. This free publication contains general information about the treaties to which the United States is a signatory and specifies to what treaties each country of the world is a party. However, because copyright relations between the many countries of the world and the United States are in a constant state of flux and because new government regimes in some countries can quickly change policies toward U.S. copyrights, if you are planning to market a valuable copyrighted work in a particular country or countries, it is a good idea to consult a copyright lawyer before you publish the work.

You can find out more about copyright by consulting *The Copyright Guide*, by Lee Wilson, published by Allworth Press. And you can read the actual copyright statute, which is informative and relatively simple to understand, at *www.copyright.gov/title17/index.html*. This site will also allow you to read either PDF or text versions of its individual chapters as well as the amendments to the statute that have been enacted since it was originally passed by Congress in 1976.

CHAPTER 2

Copyright Infringement

COPYRIGHT OWNERS ARE JUSTIFIABLY CAREFUL with the rights the copyright statute gives them and they usually don't hesitate to complain—often in federal court—if they feel that someone is stepping on their rights. If you create copyrightable works yourself or use the works of others, you need to understand copyright infringement. Having to sue someone for copyright infringement is no fun, but it's even less fun being sued yourself.

Defining Infringement

The federal copyright statute defines copyright infringement with a simple statement: "Anyone who violates any of the exclusive rights of [a] copyright owner . . . is an infringer of . . . copyright." Because it is a violation of rights granted under federal law, copyright infringement is actionable in federal court; that is, any copyright infringement lawsuit must be filed in one of the federal district courts found throughout the country.

The question of just *what* actions are sufficient to violate the rights of a copyright owner is left for the courts to answer as they evaluate the circumstances in each case of claimed infringement. The body of law made up of court decisions in copyright infringement cases is called copyright "case law." Copyright case law is the source for the test for copyright infringement and the standard for applying the test to the facts in particular copyright infringement cases.

Only the creator of a copyrighted work (or someone to who has given permission to use the work) is legally permitted to reproduce it, perform or display it, distribute copies of it, or create variations of it. Any of these exclusive rights of copyright may be infringed. However, as a practical matter, copyright infringement suits most often claim that the defendant copied the plaintiff's work in some manner without first securing permission.

Sometimes an infringer *has* intentionally copied the copyright owner's song or book or painting in an effort to steal the successful features of that work and profit from them. However, many copyright infringement lawsuits are brought because the plaintiff wrongly believes that someone who has created a *somewhat* similar work has infringed the plaintiff's copyright. Understanding the most common form of copyright infringement claim—unauthorized copying—means understanding the test that courts use in evaluating whether accusations of copying are true.

The Infringement Test

Assuming that the copyright in the work that is said to have been infringed is valid and that the work was created *before* the work accused of infringing it, and in the absence of any admission by the defendant author that he or she *did* copy the plaintiff's work, the courts ordinarily judge copyright infringement by a circumstantial evidence test. The circumstantial evidence test for copyright infringement has three parts:

1. Did the accused infringer have *access* to the work that is said to have been infringed, so that copying was possible?
2. Is the defendant actually guilty of *copying* part of the plaintiff's protectable expression from the plaintiff's work?
3. Is the accused work *substantially similar* to the work the plaintiff says was copied?

If you can remember and understand these three parts of the test for copyright infringement—access, copying, and substantial similarity—you should always be able to decide correctly for yourself whether a work of yours infringes someone else's work or vice versa.

Access to the "Infringed" Work

"Access" simply means what it says. Did the accused infringer have access to the "infringed" work before creating the "infringing" work? It's important to remember that the action for which the copyright statute prescribes penalties is *copying*, not the mere *coincidental creation* of a work that is similar or even nearly identical to a preexisting work. In most cases, access is not presumed but must be proved before the questions of copying and substantial similarity are addressed.

Let's say you write a piece for a local alternative newspaper on the continuing economic fallout from the failure of so many startup dot-com companies in your city in recent years and some other journalist writes an article on the same subject (addressing the same issues and coming to the same conclusions your piece did) for a regional magazine that hits the newsstands soon after. In this case, *each* of you owns a valid copyright in your own article.

This is easier to understand if you remember that our copyright statute rewards the act of creation. You own the copyright in a product of your own imagination as long as your imagination—and not that of another author— really is the source of your work. This is true regardless of what anybody else in the world comes up with before at the same time or after you create your work.

If you are a freelancer, the obvious implication of the access requirement in proving copyright infringement is that good documentation of your attempts to sell your novel or song or screenplay to those who are in position to exploit it can be critically important in the event someone decides your work is good enough to steal. If you know where your manuscript or demo or script has been, you may be able to prove that an infringer had "reasonable opportunity" (which is usually sufficient proof of access) to copy your work.

Copying of Protectable Expression

The circumstantial evidence test for copyright infringement is like a three-legged stool. All three legs of the test are necessary to support a claim of copyright infringement, and the absence of one of the three parts of the test means an infringement suit will fail. Proving the second element of copyright infringement—copying of protected subject matter—is just as important as proving access and substantial similarity, but would-be plaintiffs often gloss over this requirement in the mistaken assumption that *any* copying is sufficient to support an infringement suit.

To understand what constitutes copying of protected expression, you must consider what elements of your work are not protected. The copyright statute specifically excludes from protection "any idea, procedure, process, system, method of operation, concept, principle or discovery." And, as we discussed in chapter 1, there are numerous elements of copyrightable works, some of them important to the overall quality of a work, that are not protected by copyright.

If you review the list of *exceptions* to the general rule that copyright protects what you create, you can better apply the second part of the test for copyright infringement: *Does the material suspected to have been copied from the "infringed" work include protectable expression?* If your answer is "yes" and it can be proved that the accused infringer had access to the work that is said to have been infringed, you must then evaluate whether the theft was substantial.

Substantial Similarity

The third part of the test for copyright infringement is determining whether the infringing work is "substantially similar" to the infringed work. Substantial similarity is hard to define. Even the courts have never been able to come up with a hard-and-fast test for determining substantial similarity. This may be because no such test is possible—each copyright infringement case must be decided entirely on the facts of *that* case, and what happened in a similar suit has no real bearing on the question of whether *this* defendant's work is substantially similar to *this* plaintiff's work. The test for copyright infringement is like the system one Supreme Court justice once said he used for determining whether a work was obscene: "I can't define it," he said, "but I know it if I see it."

Although it's not possible to pinpoint the border between infringing and non-infringing similarity, a map of the danger zone between the two exists in the form of copyright case law. The courts do not require plaintiffs to demonstrate that their defendants' works are nearly identical to their own works in order to prove substantial similarity. However, the courts will not interpret even several small, unimportant similarities between the works in question as substantial similarity. In short, "substantial similarity" is just that: substantial. The *sort* of similarity between two works is just as important as the *degree* of similarity—the judgment of substantial similarity is both *qualitative* and *quantitative*.

Furthermore, although plaintiffs in copyright infringement suits routinely hire expert witnesses—usually people who are very familiar with the sort of work that is the subject of litigation—to testify as to what similarities exist between the works at issue, the courts decide whether those similarities are substantial by the "ordinary observer" test, which is a sort of "man on the street" view of the effect of those similarities. The courts try to decide whether an ordinary observer, reading or hearing or seeing two similar works for the first time, would believe that the infringing work and infringed work are the same. If so, substantial similarity exists. This means that you probably have the equipment you need—your own eyes and ears—to decide for yourself whether someone's work infringes yours.

Examples of Substantial Similarity

Some examples of actions that will always result in infringement if the work copied is not a public-domain work will help you grasp the difficult concept of substantial similarity.

Outright duplication of significant portions of a work obviously results in substantial similarity; this sort of substantial similarity has been characterized as taking the fundamental substance of another person's work and is the sort of copying that is often called simply "plagiarism."

Another sort of substantial similarity has been called "comprehensive literal similarity." This occurs when, as a whole, the accused work tracks the pattern of expression of the work said to have been infringed and uses the same theme or format. Close paraphrasing of an entire protected work or significant portions of it would produce this variety of substantial similarity.

A third variety of substantial similarity is the taking of portions of a work that are important to its impact and character but do not amount to a large portion of the infringing work. This sort of infringing substantial similarity points up the fact that what is important is the quantity and importance of the material taken from the infringed work rather than simply the portion of the infringing work that the stolen material constitutes. In other words, an infringer cannot escape responsibility for his or her infringing actions by pointing out how much of the infringing work was *not* stolen.

Striking Similarity

The situation in which one part of the copyright infringement test need not be proved is the existence of "striking similarity" between two works. Essentially, this is just a specialized application of the three-part infringement test. In cases where the similarity between the two works at issue is so striking that the only feasible explanation for such overwhelming similarity is that one work was copied from the other, the courts say that access may be assumed and the circumstances that made the infringement possible need not be reconstructed by the plaintiff. The "striking similarity" approach to proving infringement is rarely allowed by the courts, which prefer to see plaintiffs prove every element of their cases.

Creator Beware

Copyright infringement is an area of real danger for creative people. Consequently, anyone who aspires to earn a living by exploiting the products of his or her imagination needs to know enough about copyright infringement to steer clear of danger. People think that writing plays or songs or advertising copy is a nice, safe job that can't get anyone in trouble. In reality, what you do with your computer or guitar or pad and pencil in your own little workspace can land you in federal court, where you will be asked to explain just *what* you did and *why* and *when* you did it.

Plaintiff Versus Defendant

The only thing worse than being a plaintiff in a lawsuit is being a defendant. At least a plaintiff has the choice of filing the suit or not and can choose, to some extent, when and where the suit is filed and what issues are involved. A defendant has none of these choices. In a suit brought on meritorious grounds, a plaintiff has some justifiable hope of winning the suit, collecting an award of damages and, possibly, an award of the attorney fees and costs he has incurred in pursuing the suit.

If someone sues you for copyright infringement, the best that you can hope for is to have the court rule in your favor, in which case you can pay your own (probably) enormous legal fees and go home (although since 1994, the courts may, in their discretion, award attorney fees and costs to a prevailing defendant in copyright infringement suits). And even if the case is settled before it goes to trial, you may still have to pay a cash settlement to the plaintiff, as well as your lawyer's fees for handling the case to the point of settlement. If the court finds that an infringement took place, it may award the plaintiff an injunction to halt further sales, distribution, or dissemination of the infringing work and you could be forced to pay a substantial judgment, including any profits you have made from the infringement and possibly the plaintiff's attorney fees. The legal fees you will incur in defending a copyright infringement suit through trial can be enormous, even if the judgment against you isn't. Finding yourself on the receiving end of these remedies for infringement will make you regret that you were ever so fool-ish as to trifle with the plaintiff's copyright. Sometimes plaintiffs come out ahead in lawsuits; defendants almost never do, even if the judgment is in their favor.

In determining whether your work infringes someone else's copyright, let your conscience be your guide; if you think that you have taken more than inspiration from a copyrighted work, you could very well have stepped over the meandering boundary between permissible use of another's work and "substan-tial similarity."

Is It Infringement?

Q You decide to launch your career as a playwright by writing a three-act play about your hometown's only real hero, a local farm boy who became an internationally famous war correspondent during World War II. You pore over the only biography ever published about him, an out-of-print book called *From Cornfield to Battlefield: The Life of Walter Swenson*. You take lots of notes to make sure your play is accurate and finish it in time to offer it to your hometown Rotary Club for their annual fundraising program. The Rotary Club board members who read your play love it. Plans are made to present the play over three nights at the local high school. You are ecstatic, especially since the Rotarians ask you to direct the play yourself.

You buy a black beret to wear to the dress rehearsal, but no one is there to appreciate it because no one shows up but the Rotary board chairman, who tells you that plans to present your play have been cancelled. It seems that the Rotary Club has received a letter from a New York lawyer claiming that your play *Foreign Correspondent* infringes the copyright in the book *From Cornfield to Battlefield: The Life of Walter Swenson* and threatening a lawsuit if the play is presented. You splutter that you wrote *every word* of your play and that you don't know *what* the lawyer could mean.

You slink back home, where you find a copy of the lawyer's letter in your own mailbox. You remove your beret and call your college drama professor, who tells you to call Mr. Donaldson, another New York lawyer and also a former student of your drama professor. You take a deep breath and make the call. When you get Donaldson on the phone, you ask, "Is it infringement?"

A You don't like what Donaldson tells you. After asking you a few perti-nent questions, he says that you have indeed infringed the rights of the author of the Swenson biography because what you have done is to prepare from that book something he calls a "derivative work." "But," you say, "plays and movies are based on books all the time!" "That's true," he replies, "but those playwrights and screenwriters did one thing you didn't do—*they got permission* to adapt the books on which their plays and screenplays were based." "Oh," you say, feeling small. Then another thought hits you. "But Walter Swenson was a famous man," you say. "There were lots of articles in the local newspaper about him, especially the year he won the Pulitzer Prize."

Donaldson is not convinced. He asks, "Did you consult any sources besides *From Cornfield to Battlefield* when you wrote your play? Did you read any of those old newspaper articles? Did you examine Swenson's papers in some university library? Did you interview people who knew him?" You tell the lawyer that you did not conduct any interviews. As he questions you further, you are forced to admit that your play tracks the structure of the biography practically scene by scene, that you used as characters in your play the contemporaries of Swenson who were interviewed by the biographer, and that most of the dialogue in your play came directly from interviews conducted *by the biographer*. Donaldson says, "So, basically, your entire play came directly from the Swenson biography, right?" It seems pretty harsh put into those words, but what he says is true.

By this time, you're feeling pretty defeated, but you raise one last point. "But *From Cornfield to Battlefield* is out of print!" you say. Donaldson explains that "out of print" is *not* the same as "out of copyright" and that, in fact, since the Swenson biography was published in 1979 and its author, John Jennings, is still alive, the copyright in the biography won't expire for at least seventy years.

You ask him what you can do. He tells you that the only course open to you other than locking the play in your bottom dresser drawer and abandoning plans to produce it is to approach the author of the biography, who is probably the owner of copyright in it, for permission to do what you have already done, i.e., create a play based on the book. Donaldson tells you that Jennings is not required to grant you the right to base a play on the book but that he may consider it if he likes your play and if he hasn't previously sold the same right to someone else. Then Donaldson tells you to let him know if you have any *paid* work for him—because he has other clients waiting.

You are depressed for three days and spend your time eating junk food and watching old, bad movies. On the fourth day, you force yourself to sit at your computer, where you write a letter to Mr. Jennings, in care of his lawyers, asking for the right to write and produce a play based on his book. You explain the situation, apologize for your mistake, and emphasize your admiration for Swenson and for Jennings' biography of him. You also enclose a copy of your play.

When you have just about given up hope, you get a phone call from Mr. Jennings himself. He sounds rather old, but he is very nice. He tells you that he will allow the play to be produced if you will include him as co-author and donate any proceeds from the production to the local library. You realize that you could never have written the play without Jennings' book and all the interviews and research he did for it, and you feel certain that the Rotary Club will have no problem supporting your local library, so you say yes and ask him to send the documents necessary to grant the permission you need.

Jennings comes for the opening night of the play, along with his literary agent, who tells you that he may be able to help you get the play produced off-Broadway. The audience loves the play, the library makes some money, and you vow never again to ignore the rights of another writer.

Q You start a small publishing company in your spare bedroom. Your first project is a calendar called "Impressionists Month by Month" that uses as illustrations twelve famous Impressionist paintings. You scan photos of the paintings into your computer from an Art Institute of Chicago guidebook and copy the monthly calendar grids from an old Hallmark calendar. You are pleased with the result of your efforts and are sending your project out for printing bids when your best friend asks you whether it took a long time to get permission to use the photos and the calendar grid. You tell her "no" because, of course, you haven't spent any time at all getting permissions from anyone. Then you take your prototype calendar to your lawyer because you need some clarification. You ask your lawyer, "Is it infringement?"

A Your lawyer asks a lot of questions before she answers your question. She also makes you go home and bring back the Art Institute of Chicago guidebook and the Hallmark calendar. Then she says, "There's good news and there's bad news." It seems that you are not going to get in trouble for using the old Hallmark calendar. Your lawyer tells you that because you have taken nothing from the Hallmark calendar but the calendar grid with numbers corresponding to the dates for each month and the typeset names of each month, you have not infringed any copyright rights of Hallmark. She explains that, according to copyright law, a calendar is a "measuring or computing device" that is the common property of everyone in society and is not subject to copyright protection. Because what you copied contains no original material but, rather, simply depicts in written form our society's method of computing the days and months of the year, you have not taken from Hallmark anything that belongs to Hallmark and are not guilty of copyright infringement.

You start grinning when you hear this, but then your lawyer gives you a stern look and tells you that you can't go around blithely scanning things into your computer without getting into trouble sooner or later and that the "bad news" part of her evaluation of your calendar is proof of that. Your grin vanishes when she tells you that using the photos of Impressionist paintings in your calendar will infringe the copyright rights of the Art Institute of Chicago. You tell her that although you may have acted without considering the question of copyright when you assembled the elements of your calendar, you're pretty sure that all the Impressionists are dead and that their paintings are no longer protected by copyright. She says that although this is true, it's not the point. The point is, she says, that you scanned photos from an Art Institute of Chicago guidebook into your computer and planned to use those photos in your calendar without obtaining permission to do so. "Where do you think those photos came from?" she asks. "You don't think the Impressionists took them, do you?" You are forced to admit that you had not considered the fact that there were one or more photographers between you and the Impressionists. Your lawyer looks at the copyright date of the guidebook and informs you that the photos of the paintings probably have several decades of copyright protection left.

Then she explains that you must get permission to use those photos from the Art Institute or the photographers who took them. She says that although the copyrights in the paintings themselves, most of which were painted in the late 1800s, have expired, the Art Institute controls access to the paintings it owns and, therefore, no one can produce photos of them without its permission. In addition, she says that the Art Institute probably hired the photographers to take the photos in the guidebook and will either own the copyrights in those photos or can direct you to the photographers who do. Then she gives you a quarter and suggests that you make a phone call to the Art Institute of Chicago. "Ask for their 'permissions administrator,'" she says. You thank her for the quarter on your way out the door. She says, "Oh, that's all right. I'll add it to your bill."

Q Your boss put you in charge of writing the sales training manual that will be sent out to all the branch offices of your company. You are a fan of Mark McCormack's book *What They Don't Teach You at Harvard Business School* and decide to paraphrase two chapters of this bestseller as sections of your training manual. You proudly present the finished manual to your boss, who takes it home to read over the weekend. You are chagrined and surprised when he demands to see you first thing Monday morning. It seems that your boss is also a fan of Mr. McCormack and has recognized the source material for the two paraphrased sections of the manual. He says that you and your company could be sued by McCormack and his publisher. You are almost sure that paraphrasing McCormack's material is all it takes to eliminate the threat of any lawsuit. Is it infringement?

A Yes, of the most blatant sort. While it is permissible to quote authorities in any field ("McCormack believes that . . .") or even to cite their theories without attribution ("Many business theorists hold that . . ."), using whole chunks of their writings violates their rights and the rights of their publishers, to whom they have assigned the exclusive right to reproduce and disseminate their works. When you paraphrased McCormack's chapters, you followed them line by line and simply changed the way his ideas were expressed. Although no one's *ideas* are protected by copyright, their expressions are protected. Your paraphrasing was a bodily theft of McCormack's expressions of his *ideas*. The fact that you changed McCormack's words makes little difference since the sections of your training manual based on his book are simply reworded duplications of his statements. That's copying of protected expression. *And* substantial similarity.

Your boss is also correct that both you *and* your employer can be sued for copyright infringement. As a full-time employee, you are an agent of your company, and any action that you take during the course of performing your duties as an employee is attributable to your company. You timidly ask, "Can't we just get permission to, uh, paraphrase the chapters I used?" Your boss explains to you that it is highly unlikely that McCormack's publisher would allow any such use in your training manual, that if the use were allowed, it would cost your small company much more than it could afford to pay, that it would be much cheaper to simply buy a copy of McCormack's book for each member of your sales staff, and that because it is your job to come up with the training manual, anyway, he's not even going to consider asking for such a permission.

You say, "I guess I need to get back to work." He says, "I guess you do." Your boss is one smart guy. Maybe that's why he's the boss. Next time, if you can't come up with your own material, either hire someone on a work-for-hire basis to write your manual or copy *The Prince* by Niccolo Machiavelli, written in 1513, or *The Art of War* by Sun Tzu, written more than 2,500 years ago. But be very careful with the work of anyone who ever saw an electric light bulb.

Q You are the program director for the annual weekend convention of Girl Scout troops in your area. Most of your work goes into planning the grand finale, which will feature a choir of one hundred and fifty girls, wearing pastel dresses in five different colors, singing a selection of songs from recent Broadway shows. You will have only one afternoon to rehearse all the girls, so you photocopy the six tunes the girls will sing and send a packet of sheet music to each troop leader whose Scouts will participate.

The rehearsal goes well and so does the performance, but your pleasure in your accomplishment is spoiled by something one of the Scout leaders, a woman named Marjorie, tells you after the second curtain call. She tells you that her husband is a lawyer and that he says that you should not have photocopied the sheet music for the songs performed. Marjorie tells you that your actions amount to copyright infringement, which is a violation of federal law, and that neither she nor her husband feels that you have set a good example for the Scouts who sang in the choir. This is all news to you, but you take Marjorie's husband's business card and promise to call him on Monday. When you get him on the phone, you ask, "Is it infringement?"

A Marjorie's husband confirms what she told you. He explains that by making one hundred and fifty or more copies of the sheet music for the six Broadway tunes you had the Scouts perform, you have violated the copyright rights of the writers and publishers of those songs because one of the rights reserved to copyright owners is the right to prepare copies of their works. He tells you that the publishers of the sheet music you copied purchased the right to publish the songs from the writers of the songs in return for a promise to pay those writers a royalty on sales of the sheet music. "But I bought a copy of the sheet music for *every one* of the songs we performed," you say. He scoffs, "That's just the problem! You bought *a* copy of the sheet music—and then you made one hundred and fifty photocopies of it. You deprived the music publisher and songwriter of one hundred and fifty sales of the music for each song." "But the Girl Scouts are a non-profit organization," you say. "Isn't there some sort of exception for nonprofit organizations?"

Marjorie's husband tells you that there are special rules for non-profit organizations, and that under the principle of "fair use" nonprofit organizations are allowed to make and use very small numbers of copies of copyrighted works. But, he adds, "The number of copies you made far exceeds this small exception. A very important factor in determining whether such copying is permissible is whether potential sales for the copied work are affected." You say, "But I couldn't have asked each of the girls to pay for sheet music for six separate songs! That would have cost too much!"

He tells you that you are making his case about the sheet music publishers' lost income and says that perhaps you should have considered this problem when you planned the choral program. "You could have presented a program of older songs, perhaps folk songs from one widely available—and inexpensive—songbook," he says, and adds, "Often you can even find copyright-free sheet music on the Internet." You ask the question you've been afraid to ask, "Am I going to be sued?" His answer makes you feel a little better. "Probably not. But it's still not right to do what you did, and it does set a bad example for the girls. And I suggest that you destroy the photocopies you made of the songs that were performed. You don't want illegal copies floating around." You are so relieved to hear that neither you nor the Scouts are going to be sued that you shred and then burn the infringing photocopies that same afternoon. Then you call Marjorie and ask her to book her husband for a short seminar for your older Scouts on respecting the copyrights of others. And you start collecting copies of public-domain songs for next year.

Q You are appointed a Resident Advisor for your college dorm the first term of your junior year. This means that in exchange for helping ride herd on the students who live in the dorm, you get to live there for free. You also think that having served in such a responsible position even before you are out of college will make prospective employers after college view you with interest. The first couple of months of your tenure as an RA go well—it's mostly a matter of telling the other students to turn down their stereos on a nightly basis. Then, the Dorm Manager has to be out of town over one winter weekend and you are left in control.

You plan a big gathering for Saturday night—you're going to have a movie party in the dorm common area. You buy some popcorn and soft drinks, rent three new DVDs from Blockbuster, and make posters to advertise the event ("Movies in the dorm! Come in your jammies!"). The party is a wild success—the dorm residents think it's cool to be able to party in the dorm in their pajamas. You charge $3 a head and collect nearly $200—which leaves a profit of more than $150 after you deduct the cost of the movie rentals and the refreshments. You have to throw out two guys who try to sneak in some beer, but otherwise, there are no problems. Not until Monday, at least.

On Monday, you get a note in your mailbox from Ms. Willoughby, legal counsel for the college, who requests, in somewhat stern language, to see you in her office at your earliest convenience. You bite the bullet and walk directly over to the administration building, wondering all the way what on earth she wants to talk to you about. You realize that you're failing your calculus course, but you don't think that the college's legal counsel is concerned with your grades. You hurry to ask her, "What's the problem?"

A As you find out, the problem is infringement. Ms. Willoughby asks you several questions about your movie party. In particular, she wants to know just which movies you screened and whether and how much you charged for admission to the party. After she weighs your answers to her questions, she expounds for a few minutes on what seems to be your gross lack of judgment. She doesn't raise her voice, but before she is finished you feel as if you are a member of a jury that is probably going to vote *guilty*. It seems that you are in danger of being sued for copyright infringement by three movie studios. Ms. Willoughby is blunt: "Your 'movie party' was an unauthorized public display of the movies you screened. The right to publicly display a copyrighted work is one of the rights reserved to owners of copyright—in this case, the movie studios. You have usurped the role of movie theaters, which pay a lot to the studios to be able to show those same movies to their audiences— substantially more than you paid to *rent* the movies. Blockbuster rents movies for home viewing—*not* public screenings. You didn't pay enough for a public screening, *nor* did you have the right to hold one. Movie studios don't like to see such unauthorized displays of their properties, and sometimes they sue to stop them. And you do realize, don't you, that because you are an employee of the college your actions within the scope of your job are attributable to the college? That means the college would be sued, too."

You *didn't* realize this. It makes you squirm in your seat. Then you get the courage to ask, "Am I—I mean, we—are *we* going to be sued?" Ms. Willoughby says that you are probably not going to be sued, especially because you are going to sign a letter to the movie studios that she will write for you. In this letter, you will confess your unwitting infringement, promise never to do anything of the sort again, and enclose the profits you earned. "I'd say fifty dollars per studio will do it," she says. You lay your $150 in her outstretched hand and promise to come back by her office that afternoon to sign the letter. Then you walk to the library and bury yourself in your calculus textbook. And you decide that your adventure as a movie impresario is one activity that you *won't* mention to prospective employers.

Q Armed with a brand-new diploma in hotel-restaurant management, you go to work for your Uncle Vito, helping him run his restaurant, Vito's. Driving to the restaurant on your second day of work, you hear on your favorite oldies station the Billy Joel standard "My Italian Restaurant." You get the great idea to use the song as the background for the new radio and television spots you talked your uncle into the day before. You buy a copy of the Billy Joel album that includes "My Italian Restaurant," get your uncle to narrate the spots, and rush to get them on the air. Your uncle loves the spots and you begin to think about asking for a raise.

Then one morning, Uncle Vito receives by certified mail a "cease and desist" letter from a New York law firm representing Billy Joel's record company and music publishing company. The letter informs your uncle that his use of the Billy Joel recording of the song "My Italian Restaurant" in ads for Vito's is an infringement of the copyright rights of both the record company, which owns the copyright in the recording of the song, and the music publishing company, which owns the copyright in the song itself. Your uncle calls you and wakes you up to ask, "Is it infringement?"

A Yes. The New York lawyers are right. They demand that your Uncle Vito immediately cease use of the recording or song and desist from any additional use of either and they offer to forego filing suit if your uncle pays a settlement of $20,000 within thirty days, in lieu of the licensing fees they would have charged had he contacted them before using the song and recording. The lawyer you and your uncle consult brushes aside your arguments that, since no more than sixty seconds of the recording were used in any spot, your use of the song and recording does not constitute infringement and that, in any event, your uncle shouldn't be sued, since neither you nor he *intended* to trespass on anyone's rights.

Your lawyer informs you that any broadcast of any recording of a copyrighted song in a *commercial* context is infringement if it is made without the permission of the owners of the copyrights in the recording and in the song because it is a violation of the copyright owners' exclusive right to control performances of their copyrighted recording and song. He says that using sixty seconds or thirty seconds or even ten seconds of a three-minute recording is more than sufficient to eliminate any argument that Vito's use of "My Italian Restaurant" was merely an incidental, "fair" use of the song and recording. He tells you that it is immaterial that you did not realize that your actions amounted to infringement, since copyright infringement is judged by evaluating the quantity, quality, and context of the use of the copyrighted work, *not* by gauging the wrongful intent of the accused infringer.

When you make your brilliant argument that you know for a fact (because you once had a summer job as a deejay) that radio stations do not call up record companies and music publishing companies to ask permission before playing each recording they broadcast, your lawyer reminds you that radio stations (and other users of copyrighted recordings) pay license fees each year to the performing rights organizations that collect such fees on behalf of songwriters and publishers. Uncle Vito settles. You are out of bright ideas, as well as a job.

Copyrights—or Not

If none of this information about copyright infringement sounds familiar, you may, in actuality, be dealing with a trademark. Trademarks (and patents) are often confused with copyrights, even by people who should know better, so don't feel alone if you have made this common error. If you want to use the name of a product in a literary project, ad, or song lyrics—or in just about any other way—it *is* likely that you will have problems if you don't get permission before you use the trademark. Using someone's copyright without permission can cause big problems, but using a trademark without permission may be an even quicker way to end up as a federal-court defendant in a lawsuit for infringement. Whether you want to use a trademark in a parody or in a flattering way or to compare your product with theirs, don't proceed without first determining that your use won't be simply the grounds for a lawsuit. (Again, for more information about trademarks, see *The Trademark Guide*, by Lee Wilson, published by Allworth Press.) And if you still have doubts about whether you can use someone else's trademark as you have planned without first obtaining permission, get advice from an attorney experienced in trademark law.

CHAPTER 3

Copyright Duration

CREATIVE PEOPLE OFTEN BELIEVE THAT copyright law is a dark mystery, accessible only to lawyers, and that the mechanisms of copyright protection are incredibly complex. Fortunately, they're wrong.

"Copyright protection" means the protection the law gives copyright owners from unauthorized use of their works. As a general rule, the U.S. copyright statute protects all varieties of literary, musical, dramatic, choreographic, pictorial, graphic, sculptural, audiovisual works, and sound recordings as soon as they are fixed in what the statute calls any "tangible medium of expression." Copyright protection lasts a very long time. Copyrights in works created today may not expire until well into the next century and many copyrights in works dating from the early decades of the twentieth century are still valid. The period of time during which the law offers copyright protection to a particular work is called the "term of copyright."

Determining Copyright Duration

There are two primary reasons why you may want to determine the copyright status of a work: 1) you want to determine whether the copyright in the work has expired, thereby transforming the work into a public-domain work, which means that you may use it in any way without permission from anyone; and 2) you want to contact the owner of copyright in a work that is still protected to ask permission to use it.

Determining the term of copyright for a work is not hard if you know a few things about when, by whom, and under what circumstances the work was created. The initial question to ask in determining the copyright status of any work is whether it was created before or after January 1, 1978. Copyright protection for any work created *before* that date, which is when the current United States copyright statute went into effect, is governed by the provisions of the previous copyright statute, the Copyright Act of 1909. Protection for any work created on or after January 1, 1978 is governed by the present copyright statute, the Copyright Act of 1976. (The present statute was voted into law in 1976; it became effective January 1, 1978.)

Copyright protection for any eligible work created on or after January 1, 1978 commences at the moment the work is first "fixed" in any tangible form. This protection is automatic; no action by the author of the work is necessary to begin it; the mere act of creating a work that qualifies for copyright protection triggers that protection. How long copyright protection endures for any such work depends largely upon its author or authors. For purposes of determining the duration of copyright, the copyright statute divides works into basic categories and specifies a term for each category of work. These categories of works and their corresponding terms are discussed below.

Works Created by Individual Authors

Copyright in a work created by an individual author vests in that author from the inception of his or her work. The copyright in a work created by an individual author will endure until seventy years after his or her death. This rule for determining the duration of copyright protection for a work by an individual author applies even if the author assigns or licenses the copyright in the work to someone else.

The Copyright Office maintains records concerning the deaths of authors of copyrighted works. In addition, in order to facilitate the determination of the expiration dates of copyrights, the copyright statute provides that "any person having an interest in a copyright" may notify the Copyright Office that the author of the work embodying that copyright has died or is still living. Information is also gathered from Copyright Office records and from other sources.

Anyone seeking information about an old copyright in a work by an obscure author may obtain a certified report from the Copyright Office stating that nothing in the records of the Copyright Office indicates that the author is living or has died within the previous seventy years. Anyone who uses a work that, in reliance on such a report, he or she in good faith believes to have fallen into the public domain may use the report as a defense if the author of the work, or the author's heirs, brings suit for copyright infringement, because any such lawsuit would be premised on an assertion that the copyright in the work is still valid.

Under the present statute, all copyright terms expire at the end of the calendar year. This means that if you write a short story in 2005, copyright protection begins as soon as you have written your story, whether it is handwritten, typed on a typewriter, entered into a computer, or even recorded onto a cassette or CD. Copyright protection for your story will expire at the end of the seventieth year after your death; if you die in January 2053, your story will be protected by copyright through December 31, 2123.

Joint Works

The copyright statute says that if two or more people create a work "with the intention that their contributions be merged into inseparable or interdependent parts of a unitary whole," those people are "joint authors," and the work they create is a "joint work." To qualify as one of the joint authors of a work, a person must contribute copyrightable expression to the work; someone who contributes only an unembellished idea to a work is not a joint author of the work.

Joint authors share equally in any profits created by an exploitation of the work unless the authors agree otherwise at the time of the creation of the work. With the limitation that he or she may not grant an exclusive license to use the work without permission from the other author or authors, a joint author may exploit the work without the permission of any other joint author. However, the exploiting author must share the profits derived from any such exploitation with the other joint author or authors. The copyright in a joint work endures until seventy years after the death of the last surviving author.

Anonymous and Pseudonymous Works

The copyright statute says that an anonymous work is a "work on the copies or phonorecords of which no natural person is identified as author." A pseudonymous work is defined as a "work on the copies or phonorecords of which the author is identified under a fictitious name." The status of a work as an anonymous or pseudonymous work has an important effect on the duration of its copyright protection. The term of copyright for an anonymous or pseudonymous work is ninety-five years from the year of first publication of the work, or one hundred and twenty years from the year of its creation, whichever expires first. Even if the identity or, in the case of pseudonymous works, the real identity, of the author of an anonymous or pseudonymous work is known, unless the real name of the author appears on the copies or phonorecords of the work, the work will be treated as an anonymous or pseudonymous work.

The status of a work as an anonymous or pseudonymous work has an important effect on the duration of copyright protection for the work. The term of copyright for an anonymous or pseudonymous work is ninety-five years from the year of first publication of the work, or one hundred and twenty years from the year of its creation, whichever expires first. However, the copyright statute also provides that any person having an interest in the copyright in an anonymous or pseudonymous work may convert the term of copyright protection for the work to a term measured by the life or lives of the author or authors of the work plus seventy years. This is accomplished by simply filing with the Copyright Office, at any time before ninety-five years after the work's publication or one hundred twenty years after its creation, a statement that identifies the authors or one of the authors of the work. This has the effect of converting the term of copyright for the work to the life-plus-seventy-years measurement that applies to individual works.

The new copyright statute has not been in effect long enough to allow the heirs or assigns of any anonymous or pseudonymous author who disclosed his or her real name to the Copyright Office during his or her lifetime to determine if, by that action, the term of copyright in the formerly anonymous or pseudonymous work was enlarged. However, depending upon the age at which an author creates an anonymous or pseudonymous work and how many years the author lives thereafter, disclosing the author's name to the Copyright Office may, indeed, have the effect of prolonging copyright protection for the work. Therefore, this provision of the copyright statute is something that should be kept in mind by any anonymous or pseudonymous author and anyone who acquires the copyright in an anonymous or pseudonymous work.

Although most authors are proud to affix their names to their works, in some circumstances the anonymity of an author is desirable. Perhaps the most common example of this is the ghostwritten celebrity "autobiography." Virtually anyone who thinks about it will readily realize that the movie star, rock star, athlete, or statesman whose autobiography is the newest addition to the bestseller list did not personally spend six months of eight-hour days in front of a computer and that the hard work of researching and writing the book was performed by someone else.

However, it is often the case that only the celebrity's name appears on the book's dust jacket or copyright page. The ghostwriter for the book may be mostly responsible for the book's appeal and cohesiveness and may be contractually entitled to a fat fee for writing the book and/or a generous share of the royalties produced by its sale, but, in the same contract that entitles him or her to be paid, may have agreed to keep his or her role in creating the book a secret.

Works Made for Hire

Works made for hire are the only category of work in which the copyrights do not initially vest in the creators of those works. The most common variety of works made for hire are those prepared by employees within the scope of their employment. The present copyright statute also specifies nine categories of specially commissioned works created by independent contractors that are appropriate for works made for hire, provided that the person or company who commissions the work and the freelancer who creates it agree in writing that the work is to be considered a work made for hire. (See *The Copyright Guide*, by Lee Wilson, for a more detailed discussion of works made for hire.)

The term of copyright for a work made for hire is ninety-five years from the year of its first publication, or one hundred and twenty years from the year of its creation, whichever expires first.

Pre-1978 Works

Determining whether a work created before January 1, 1978 (while the 1909 copyright statute was still in effect) is protected by copyright may be a complicated undertaking.

Under the 1909 copyright statute, a work was entitled to an initial twenty-eight-year term of copyright protection. This initial term was measured from the date the work was first published with copyright notice. At the end of the first twenty-eight-year term of protection, copyright could be renewed for an additional twenty-eight years, for a total of fifty-six years of copyright protection. If renewal was not made, the copyright in the work was lost and the work fell into the public domain. This sometimes led to the unfortunate result that some authors earned nothing in old age from their years of creative labor because the copyrights in their works had expired.

In drafting the present copyright statute, our legislators tried to remedy this situation by eliminating the renewal concept for works created on or after January 1, 1978. In addition, they extended copyright protection for works created under the previous copyright statute that were still protected by copyright (under the old statute) when the new statute went into effect. Copyright protection for works that were in their renewal terms on January 1, 1978 was extended by nineteen years; this meant that the term of protection for those works was enlarged to a total of seventy-five years. Works that were in their initial twenty-eight-year term of protection on January 1, 1978 still had to be renewed at the end of that term; they, too, were granted extended renewal terms of forty-seven years for a total of seventy-five years of protection.

In spite of this bonanza for the owners of pre-1978 copyrights, many of these older copyrights continued to be lost because of the failure to renew them. A very large percentage of pre-1978 works therefore entered the public domain after only twenty-eight years of copyright protection.

To even things up a bit between the owners of pre-1978 copyrights and copyrights created under the present statute, the law was changed in 1992. The new law, the Copyright Renewal Act of 1992, made renewal automatic for pre-1978 works first published between January 1, 1964 and December 31, 1977. With the passage in late 1998 of the Sonny Bono Copyright Term Extension Act, which generally increased copyright terms twenty years across the board, the renewal term for pre-1978 copyrights was increased to sixty-seven years (twenty-eight plus nineteen plus twenty years). Owners of pre-1978 copyrights may still file renewal forms and, in fact, are encouraged to do so, but no such action is *required* to secure the forty-seven additional years of protection granted to these older works. Certain benefits, such as the presumption that the statements made in the renewal certificate are valid, accrue to those who do file in a timely manner.

If no renewal was made for works published *before* 1964, those works have fallen into the public domain, which is an irrevocable state of copyright outer darkness that no one can alter.

Unpublished Works

Unpublished works created before January 1, 1978 fall into a special class of works regarding the term of copyright protection.

The current copyright statute provides that works created prior to 1978 that have neither been published nor registered for copyright will be protected in the same way as post-1977 works. That is, the term of copyright protection for such a work created by an individual is the life of the author plus seventy years (or the life of the last surviving author plus seventy years, for joint works). If the work is anonymous, pseudonymous, or a work made for hire, the term of protection is ninety-five years from the year of first publication of the work, or one hundred and twenty years from the year of its creation, whichever expires first.

The present copyright statute provides that protection for works created prior to 1978 but published only *after* January 1, 1978 could not expire before December 31, 2002. Furthermore, if such a pre-1978 work was published before December 21, 2003, its copyright cannot expire before December 31, 2047. These periods of protection are not affected by the dates of death of the authors of such works.

This provision has interesting implications for anyone who has an ancestor who kept a diary, wrote novels, or composed music. Old manuscripts and other works that would have entered the public domain many years ago had they been published prior to 1978 may be eligible for copyright protection for several decades to come.

Circular 15a

If you want another, more detailed explanation of copyright duration in all its forms, the best course is to get it direct from the horse's mouth, so to speak. The Copyright Office publishes a circular on the topic, Circular 15a. It says all there is to be said on the matter, and includes explanations of some complicated calculations for determining the duration of copyrights that fall into oddball categories because of when or how they were created or their status when amendments to the basic copyright statute were created. Circular 15a is, like all Copyright Office publications, available to be printed out for free, twenty-four hours a day, from the Copyright Office Web site at *www.copyright.gov*. You can ask the Copyright Office to mail the circular to you by calling the Copyright Office Forms Hotline, which also operates twenty-four hours a day, at (202) 707-9100.

Tools for Figuring Copyright Duration

If you create, own, or use copyrights, you need to know how to reliably determine their duration. Such determinations are really not outside the reach of anyone who can use one or both of the tools that are available without charge. The first of these tools is the Copyright Office pamphlet *How to Investigate the Copyright Status of a Work*. This pamphlet, written specifically to offer guidance in determining whether a work is still protected by copyright or has fallen into the public domain, is reprinted in its entirety in appendix B. It should be the basis of any determination you make about the status of a copyright.

Another useful tool for determining the copyright status of a work is a copyright duration chart. Anyone can access these duration charts without payment and they are easy to use after you get the hang of them. Several are readily available on the Internet; any such chart found on the Web site of a major university is probably accurate and reliable. One of the best and most current is found at *www.copyright.cornell.edu/training/Hirtle_Public_Domain.htm*. If you use both the information in the Copyright Office pamphlet reprinted in appendix B and a good copyright duration chart, such as the one mentioned above, you should be able to decide whether the work you want to use is in the public domain or requires permission to use. And if you plan to spend any significant amount of time or money on a project that depends to any great degree on the availability of a work created by someone else, use the belt-and-suspenders approach: Consult a lawyer who is well versed in copyright after you make your initial determination. A consultation fee is preferable to a lawsuit any day.

After the Verdict

Once you have definitely determined the copyright status of a work, your actions should be dictated accordingly.

If you find that the copyright in the work you want to use is still valid, you must do one of two things:

1. Make sure that your use of the work qualifies as a "fair" use; that is, that the use itself and the circumstances surrounding it are such that the use does not amount to copyright infringement but is permitted under the law even without the consent of the copyright owner; or
2. Request from the owner of the copyright in the work you want to use permission to use the work in the manner you have planned. Finding the owner of copyright in a work (as opposed to the *author* of the work, who may no longer own the copyright in the work) may be easy or difficult, depending on the circumstances.

The chapters in Part II discuss in detail fair use and the process of finding copyright owners and getting permissions. The next chapter clarifies what "public domain" really means.

CHAPTER 4

Public-Domain Materials

IN THIS CHAPTER, WE'LL DISCUSS MATERIALS you don't need permission to use—those materials and works that are in the public domain.

If you are certain that the copyright in the work has expired, you may safely use the work in any way, including exercising any of the rights reserved to owners of valid copyrights. This means that you can adapt Charlotte Brontë's novel *Jane Eyre* for a screenplay; set Ben Jonson's poem "Though I Am Young and Cannot Tell" to music; reprint all or any portion of Ralph Waldo Emerson's essay on self-reliance; adapt and record Johann Pachelbel's *Canon* for use as a film soundtrack; print and sell reproductions of Leonardo da Vinci's famous painting, *Mona Lisa*; create a poster from a photograph by the very early photographer Julia Margaret Cameron; or create and sell copies of Michelangelo's sculpture *David*.

If you think about it, the public domain is a fascinating subject. In fact, public-domain materials are like a treasure trove of the best that the world's creators have manufactured out of their imaginations with a little paint, ink, and sweat. (OK—sometimes copyright protects the *worst*, too, since copyright protects good and bad art and literature equally.) If you remember the rationale behind copyright, which is that copyright is the system the framers of our Constitution instituted to reward creators, you'll realize that public-domain materials are your payoff for copyright. You—and everybody else—are free to use any public-domain work in any way whatever after the limited monopoly—the copyright—in it has expired and the creator of the work or owner of the copyright in it is no longer the only person or entity who is permitted to exercise the exclusive rights of copyright. However, before you make use of any public-domain work, you need to make sure that your evaluation of the work as a public-domain work is accurate. There are several evaluations that you must make to ensure that you don't mistakenly tread on someone's rights when you use what you believe is a public-domain work.

Expired Protection

The first evaluation is obvious, but not as simple as it seems: Determine whether the work is protected by copyright. With some works, this is easy and simple. Anything Nathaniel Hawthorne wrote is now in the public domain, not because he is dead, but because his works were written so long ago that any copyright protection they once enjoyed has now expired. Today, works created as long ago as the early twentieth century may still be protected by copyright; however, it may be hard to determine whether the copyrights in those works are still valid. And somewhat more recent works may or may not be protected by copyright, depending on such technicalities as whether copyright notice was used when they were first published and whether renewals of copyright were filed in a timely manner. Often these questions can be answered and the copyright status of a work can be determined by carefully evaluating the facts surrounding the work in terms of the information on copyright duration given in chapter 3 and by consulting the Copyright Office circular *How to Investigate the Copyright Status of a Work* reprinted in appendix B.

Never-Protected Materials

Besides works for which copyright has expired, the largest body of public-domain material is that which was never protected by copyright to begin with. One kind of never-protected material is the sort of material (often *elements* of copyrighted works) discussed in chapter 1 as unprotectable by copyright. Another kind of never-protected material is the sort of work that is sometimes available on the Internet and elsewhere as a "copyright-free" work. Any such copyright-free status results from an overt declaration by the owner of the work that he or she does not claim ownership of the copyright in the work. Either sort of never-protected work is safe to use *if* you are sure that no copyright protection applies to it and *if* you are careful not to include any protected material in your use. The third sort of never-protected material is U.S. government works.

Works created by officers or employees of the U.S. government as a part of their government jobs are not protected by copyright. These works are in the public domain because the government has chosen not to claim copyright in works created at the taxpayers' expense. This means that you may quote the entire text of a government publication on how to buy a car in your handbook for consumers without any special permission from the government. However, if your end creation consists predominantly of material produced by the government, it's only honest that your copyright notice should acknowledge the fact, as in: Copyright 2005 Wilson St. Charles, except material reproduced on pages 21–40 and 64–89, which was taken from U.S. Government Publications 306A, *New Car Buying Guide*, and 303A, *Buying a Used Car*.

Public-Domain Pitfalls

Some works require a more detailed appraisal to determine their copyright status and/or the safety of using them. Two of the primary pitfalls with public-domain works are discussed below. However, other problems can arise from using the works of others, and it may be that if you encounter any such problems, those problems can be eliminated. If you plan any big project around an existing work, even if you are sure that it is a public-domain work, it's a good idea to enlist the advice and help of an intellectual-property lawyer—your real-estate lawyer won't be very helpful:

- **Pseudo-U.S. government works**: Before you use material from a government publication, you should make sure that the material you want to use was prepared by the U.S. government proper and not by some private or semi-private agency of the government or a government contractor. You can probably do this by simply looking at the title page of the government publication or by calling the department or organization that published it. Anything published by the U.S. Government Printing Office or offered through the Consumer Information Catalog is almost certainly public-domain material. However, the "government" may be merely an agency of the federal government; for instance, the materials produced by the United States Postal Service are not public-domain materials, because the USPS is an independent agency of the U.S. government rather than a branch of the government itself. There are more than a few of these quasi-government entities around. Investigating the actual status of the entity that publishes a work (and therefore the copyright status of the work) is only reasonable—you can save yourself a lot of trouble by eliminating a non-public-domain work from your plans before you build an entire project around it. And remember that, almost without exception, publications and other works produced by *state* and *local* governments are protected by copyright.
- **Derivative works of public-domain works**: As we have seen, public-domain works are available for use by anyone in any way. Lots of people know this. For example, the composer Claude-Michel Schönberg and the librettist Alain Boublil knew that Victor Hugo's classic 1862 novel of the French Revolution was a public-domain work *before* they based *Les Misérables* (the 1980 musical) on *Les Misérables* (the 1862 book). In addition, there were several movies based on Hugo's book during the twentieth century.

    Despite the movies and the musical, anyone can base any new work of any sort on the novel without any copyright problems. However, any creator who plans to use public-domain work must avoid a challenge to the new work by avoiding any use at all of works *derived from* the public-domain work. Such derivative works—like the 1980 musical *Les Miserables*—add original expression to the underlying public-domain work. This original expression, as embodied in the new, derivative work, is protected by copyright. All this means that, if you consider using a public-domain work as the basis for or part of a new work, be sure that what you are using is the original work—the work that is now in the public domain—rather than a more recent, still-protected derivative work.

This distinction between public-domain works and later works derived from them has important implications. It means, for example, that although the first of the A.A. Milne *Winnie-the-Pooh* books (published in 1926) will become a public-domain work in a few years, available for use by anyone, the Disney Studios *Winnie-the-Pooh* movies based on the Milne books—the first of which was the 1977 feature-length animated film *The Many Adventures of Winnie the Pooh*—will not fall into the public domain for many years. Although anyone will be able to republish versions of the original Milne books once the copyright protection has expired, no one can make use of the Disney movies or the Disney visual depictions of the Milne characters without incurring the wrath of Disney. Its "Winnie-the-Pooh" characters, movies, and products are second only to Mickey Mouse in popularity.

And the derivative-work trap for those who want to use public-domain works exists with *every* sort of work. For example, while anyone can use the melody or the lyrics or both of a song for which copyright protection has expired, original arrangements of public-domain songs are new, derivative works of those songs and are fully protected by copyright. The same is true for a translation of a public-domain work—whereas copyright protection for the original work may have expired, the translation of that work into English (or any other language) may still be protected by copyright. It pays to be sure that, once you have determined that a work is actually in the public domain, you use the *original* version of the work rather than someone else's later version, which may amount to a derivative work that is protected by copyright.

Is It Infringement?

Q The summer you finally finish your PhD dissertation, you run across a couple of interesting old novels in the top of a big box of old books at an auction. You buy the whole box for fifty dollars and haul it home. When you sort through the contents of the box, you find two bundles of old letters at the bottom. You can hardly believe your luck when you discover that they are love letters between the famous poet Marian Crenshaw and her paramour, the equally famous novelist Harding Smythe. You feel very privileged to be able to read these letters, written nearly forty years ago, and feel that almost anyone interested in twentieth-century literature would also like to read them. You spend the last two weeks before you start your first teaching job writing a proposal to publish the letters as a book, edited by you. You feel certain that publishers will compete to publish your book and that you will set a land-speed record for gaining tenure in your department. You send out your proposal to several publishers and spend your spare time deciphering the handwritten letters and transcribing them into your computer. When you approach your boss, the chairman of the English department, to ask him to consider writing a foreword for your book, something he says stops you in your tracks. After you tell him how the letters came into your possession, he asks a question you haven't considered. He wants to know, "Is it infringement?"

A Your department chair sends you, and your question, to the intellectual-property professor at your university's law school. You find out from this professor that your book project may be considerably more difficult than you thought it would be. Professor Harris tells you that although you do legally own the Crenshaw-Smythe letters by virtue of having purchased them at the auction, your ownership extends only to the physical objects themselves. "You can do anything you like with the letters themselves," he says, "because you own them. But your ownership of the paper and ink that comprise the letters does *not* mean that you own the words themselves."

"That's silly," you say. "What are the words if not ink on paper?"

"They are the property of Ms. Crenshaw and of Mr. Smythe," he says. *"They* own their words, regardless of the ownership of the physical objects that embody them. It's a concept we call copyright, and the ownership of a copyright is *not* included in the ownership of a book or tape recording or photograph or painting that embodies the copyright."

"But Ms. Crenshaw and Mr. Smythe are dead," you say. "Don't their copyrights die with them?" Professor Harris asks when the letters were written and what years Crenshaw and Smythe died; then he does a little figuring on his desk blotter.

"Copyrights don't die with their owners," he says, while giving you a look that clearly conveys his opinion that you are old enough to know this by now. "What you have here are *unpublished* letters," he continues. "The copyrights in an unpublished work created before January 1, 1978, will endure until seventy years after the death of the author. If Ms. Crenshaw died in 1991, the copyrights in her unpublished letters will not expire until 2061. Mr. Smythe died in 1995, so the copyrights in his unpublished letters will not expire until 2065." Then he tells you that you cannot publish the letters without the permission of the estates of the two authors and that book publishers' first question will be whether you have permission to publish from the executors of those estates.

The wind is out of your sails. You admit that you had not considered these complications. Professor Harris advises you to write the last publishers of the two writers to locate the executors for their estates so that you can then seek permission to reprint the letters. And he tells you not to send out any press releases about your book just yet, because the executors are under no obligation whatsoever to allow publication of the letters and that there is no way that you can compel them to allow the letters to be published if they choose not to do so. "Then again," he says, "maybe the executors will let you publish the letters because they think that your book would revive interest in the writers." As soon as you get home, you start researching the publishers to whom you will write. You hope that you can publish your book; you also hope that you won't have to sit on the letters for sixty years before you can do so.

Q You decide to turn the old Anglo-Saxon poem *Beowulf* into a radio play with a narrator and actors playing the parts of Beowulf, Grendel, and so forth. You don't think a play in the original Old English would draw a big audience, so you use the translation of the epic poem by the Nobel Prize–winning poet Seamus Heaney. You hire actors and book a recording studio and rehearse your part as narrator. Things go well during the first day of recording, but halfway through the second day one of the actors tells you that he is leaving because he himself is a poet and refuses to participate in the infringement of the copyright in Mr. Heaney's work. You and the other actors think he's a crank because you, a former English lit major, know for a fact that a) *Beowulf* was written several centuries ago and b) no one knows who wrote it, anyway. You state these reasons that you are practically sure that your radio play is not infringing any right of Seamus Heaney's. But right after you shut down production for the day because you have no one else to take the place of the departing actor, you call your lawyer. What you ask her is, "Is it infringement?"

A Your lawyer doesn't take long to give you an answer, but you don't like it much. When you get your lawyer on the phone you make your best point, which is that there can't be any copyright protection for the poem because, as everybody knows, the author of *Beowulf* is anonymous and the epic itself is centuries old. She tells you that the anonymity of an author has nothing whatever to do with copyright protection—that there are many works that are protected by valid copyrights even though their authors are anonymous. "But that's not the point," she says. Then she asks you a few questions. "You're using a *translation* of *Beowulf*, right?" she asks. "Just where did you get the translation?"

"At Barnes & Noble," you answer. "The famous poet Seamus Heaney was the translator. He won something called the Whitbread Award for Poetry for it. It says so right here on the back of the book."

"And what does it say on the front of the book?" your lawyer asks. "Who published the Heaney *Beowulf*?"

"Uh, Farrar, Straus & Giroux published it in the U.K. in 2000," you reply. "Then W.W. Norton & Company published it in the U.S. in 2002. Hey! I think they're the ones who publish *The Norton Anthology of English Literature*! I used that book in college. That's so cool! Now I'm doing a play of *Beowulf*!"

Your lawyer is not so excited. "No, it's *not* cool," she says. "Because by recording the Heaney translation of *Beowulf*, you have infringed the rights of Mr. Heaney, of Farrar, Straus & Giroux, and of W.W. Norton & Company." You can't believe that your little radio play has transgressed the rights of so many august literary personages. And you don't think your lawyer has been paying attention, so when you answer her, you speak very slowly and distinctly.

"How is it possible to infringe the copyright in a poem that has been around since the twelfth century?" you ask.

"Tenth or eleventh century, actually," she says. "And it *isn't* possible to infringe the copyright in *Beowulf*. You're right about that much, at least. *Beowulf* itself is in the public domain. However, you have disregarded the very important fact that it *is* possible to infringe the copyright in Seamus Heaney's *translation* of the poem, which is a new, derivative work of the Old English original. And because the translation of the old poem is a new work—fully protectable by copyright—you need the permission of the author or maybe one of the publishers of the translation to turn it into a play."

"Does this mean that I'll have to ask them before I can air the play?" you ask.

She says, "If you're smart, you'll cut your losses, cancel the rest of your recording sessions, and tell the actors you'll call them in a month or so—maybe. *Then* ask for permission to turn the Heaney translation into a play—*before* you spend any more money on the project. And bear in mind that they may say no."

"But it's a good play!" you protest.

"Maybe so," she says, "but remember that no one is compelled to let you record the Heaney translation—they may have plans to produce a recorded version of the translation themselves, in fact—and they would at least want a share of any money you made off your play."

"Can't you just write a really persuasive letter to them to get whatever permission I need?" you say.

"I can write a letter for you, but you could write it yourself and save some money. There's nothing I can say that will make them grant the permission you need if they don't want to give it."

"Oh," you say. "Does this mean that I just lost the $2,000 I spent on recording sessions and actors?"

"The only way to find out is to write that letter," she says. "I'll send you my bill." You do write the letter. The one you get in return politely tells you that Mr. Heaney himself has recorded his translation of *Beowulf*, that the publishers of his translation will not license the right to write a play based on it "unless a producer of greater reputation desires to prepare such a dramatic version of the translation." Which does not mean you, you figure. You know that you could base your play on one of the many other existing translations of *Beowulf*—one in which copyright protection has expired, but you are out $2,000 for a partial recording that you can't use at all and you still haven't paid your lawyer for her advice on the phone, so you decide to wait at least until your bank account is in better shape. And while you are waiting for your bank account to recover its health, you become very conscious of the copyright dates in the front of the books you read.

Q You are a graphic designer who works for an ad agency, but you want to quit your job. You're tired of being in a service business because the agency's clients drive you crazy and you have a new boss who must have transferred in from hell. You decide that you want to put your great taste and eye for design to use in a less stressful endeavor, so you incorporate a small company you call Tabletops, Inc. to manufacture and market boutique table linens. You work after hours in your spare bedroom creating the artwork for your prototype linens. Your first products are colorful tablecloths and napkins based on the U.S. Postal Service's "Greetings from America" first-class series of fifty stamp designs—one for each state in the United States. You scan a "pane" of all fifty stamps into your computer to produce artwork and end up with colorful cotton tablecloths and napkins printed with the stamp design. You are lucky enough to sell your table linens to the big retail chain HomeStuff and spend most of your savings having them manufactured. When you receive the first check from the HomeStuff you photocopy it so that you can frame it for the wall of your office and compose a letter resigning your job at the ad agency.

Then you get a call from the buyer for HomeStuff. You think she's calling to place a new order, but she's not. Instead, she's irate because she has just been notified that her company has been sued for copyright infringement by the United States Postal Service and because some federal marshals have just confiscated all the "Greetings from America" tablecloths and napkins in the HomeStuff warehouse. She says that she is calling as a courtesy to let you know that the HomeStuff accounting department has already stopped payment on the check it sent you. You have never heard anyone be "courteous" in such a loud voice and you are stunned. And you can't believe that the U.S. government is suing you over *table linens*! You assure the HomeStuff buyer that there has been a mistake and that you will get back to her as soon as you have straightened it out. Then you call your lawyer to ask, "Is it infringement?"

As you describe your predicament, your lawyer groans. You think that this is a bad sign. "Hold on a minute," he says. "My assistant has brought me something that was just delivered." It turns out that what was just delivered was *your* copy of the complaint for the federal court copyright infringement lawsuit that the HomeStuff buyer is so exercised about; because your lawyer is the registered agent for Tabletops, Inc., the lawsuit documents were sent to him on your behalf.

He scans the complaint and tells you what you already know—that you've been sued for copyright infringement. You say, "That's impossible! I only copied postage stamp designs, and the U.S. government doesn't claim copyright in what it produces. I remember that from art school." Your lawyer says that he will have to investigate the matter further and that he will talk to Jones, the head of his firm's intellectual-property law section, that afternoon. You tell him to go ahead, but you start to realize it's going to cost you some money.

Your lawyer calls back the following day. "I'm afraid the news is not good," he says. "You're right that the U.S. government doesn't claim copyright in works that are created by its employees, but Jones says that the U.S. Postal Service *isn't* the U.S. government per se, and is, rather, an independent agency of the U.S. government. That means that the USPS *does* own a valid copyright in the stamp designs and it *can* enforce its copyrights in court. Apparently, you should have done a little more homework before you launched this project by copying the stamp designs."

You ask, "What does this mean? Can I just pay a fine or something and get them to leave me alone? How soon can I get my table linens back in the hands of HomeStuff?"

Again your lawyer has bad news. "It's not that simple. You can't pay a fine to settle a civil suit, which is what this is. And even though I haven't yet talked to the USPS lawyers, I would be very surprised if they *ever* let you sell your tablecloths and napkins again, at HomeStuff or anywhere."

You are incensed. "What?! That's outrageous! Can they just *do* that? I thought this was a free-enterprise society, but you tell me that the U.S. government can just stop my new venture cold! How can that be fair?"

Your lawyer tells you to stop yelling. Then he repeats what he said earlier, since, he says, you must not have been listening. "As I told you, the USPS is *not the U.S. government*. And this *is* a free-enterprise society, but that doesn't mean that you can do whatever you want without penalty. In this case, it means that you cannot simply appropriate for your own use the stamp designs that the USPS has commissioned and owns. And the Postal Service isn't so much stopping your new venture as it is enforcing its own rights. That's allowed under the law and even predictable. You just didn't do your due diligence before you started manufacturing your little table doilies, or whatever."

"Table linens. They are 'table linens,' not 'doilies,'" you say.

"Whatever you call them," your lawyer says, "you'll probably never see them again because the USPS has asked that all the 'infringing items' be impounded and destroyed. The judge has already agreed to allow them to be impounded—that's what the marshals did when they confiscated them from the warehouse. And you can pay me to argue that they shouldn't be destroyed, but I'll lose and you still won't have your merchandise. My advice to you is to settle. Authorize me to write a letter that says that if they drop their suit, you will let them keep the, uh, table linens, and will cease any use of their designs whatsoever. That way, you may get out of this with only having to pay my fees. But if you fight the suit, you could end up paying damages to the USPS and a lot more in legal fees."

"Do it," you say, miserably. "My savings are almost gone and I don't want to have to mortgage my house to pay for a bunch of lawyers." You hang up the phone. Then you retrieve your resignation letter from the outgoing mail basket and call your manufacturer to tell him to destroy the plates for printing your "Greetings from America" tablecloths and napkins. That evening, you start working on your next project, linens printed with a design of oak leaves; you begin the project by photocopying a selection of fallen leaves from your backyard, which, you reflect, are not and have never been protected by copyright.

Q While helping your grandmother clean out her attic, you run across a tattered little book called *The Collins Guide to American Wildflowers* that is filled with beautiful pen-and-ink outline drawings of wildflowers. The front cover and the first ten pages of the book are missing, but the rest of the book, with its beautiful illustrations, is intact. Your grandmother says that she doesn't remember where it came from and that you can keep the book. When you get home, you carefully take apart the stitching of the little volume so you can scan a dozen of the drawings into your computer. You size the drawings for notecards and have them printed on heavy white paper.

Then you turn your dining table into a factory. Every night you paint all the cards that are illustrated with a particular flower—tonight coneflowers, tomorrow night dwarf crested iris—until you and your watercolors have turned every notecard into a hand-painted master-piece. After your cards have dried, you sort them into sets of twelve with envelopes and offer them to local stationery stores. The stores love them because their customers love them and you are thinking that you may have to go back to press. Then your cousin Rodney comes for a long visit. On his way to the refrigerator for the second time one Saturday, Rodney pauses at your dining-table factory, picks up a notecard, and says, in the snide tone he always uses, "*You* didn't draw these. Aren't you worried that Mr.—let's see—*Collins* will sue you for using his drawings? I can't believe that *you*, president of the student body, homecoming queen, and general all-round Miss Know-It-All, would make such a dumb mistake! Collins will put a halt to this little business. You'll be selling shoes again!" While Rodney is making himself a ham sandwich, you call your brother the lawyer to ask, "Is it infringement?"

A The first thing your brother wants to know is the date in the copyright notice in the front of your little old book. "I don't know," you say. "The first few pages of the book were missing when I found it. But it was pretty tattered and looked really old."

"That's not enough," he says. "Tell me the exact name of it again and I'll look it up on ABE." You recite the name of the book to your brother and ask him, "What's ABE? Some sort of search engine for lawyers?"

"ABE is AbeBooks.com. It's for everybody," he replies. "It's a search engine for used, old, and rare books. It includes the stock of dealers from all over the world." You hear him typing on his keyboard. "O.K., here's your book."

"You found it already?" you ask.

"Yeah. It doesn't take long if you have the title of the book or part of it or the name of the author. Your little book was published in 1899 by something called Adams-Jones Publishing."

"That's good to know," you say. "But level with me, bro, is Rodney right? Am I in trouble?"

"I don't think you have anything to worry about except Rodney," your dear brother says. "Grandma's wildflower guide was published so long ago that any copyright protection it once had has now expired. That means that everything in it—the descriptions, the drawings, everything—is now in the public domain. Anyone can use them for any project. You can reprint and sell the book, turn it into wildflower wallpaper or gift wrap—or hand-painted notecards—without violating anyone's rights. But, sis, you really should have figured this out before now. I can't believe you're getting legal advice from Rodney."

You tell your brother that you can't believe you're getting *any* kind of advice from Rodney and that you'll never put yourself in that position again. Then, because you're afraid somebody else will use your public-domain wildflower book for a competing project, you gather up the pages and lock them in a file cabinet. And you tell Rodney that if he's going to continue to live in your guest room, he's going to have to help you paint your notecards. "Those who don't work, don't eat, Rodney. It's an old American principle." While he's packing his suitcase, you get an order for fifty more sets of notecards. But you don't mind having to interrupt your work to drive Rodney to the airport; that way you'll know he has actually gone.

Q You are a member of the fundraising committee for the athletics programs at the middle school your two children attend. During a meeting to consider ways to raise money for new uniforms for the basketball team, you suggest that your committee compile and sell a cookbook. You outline your methods: All the children in the school will ask their parents for a favorite recipe; the recipes will be collected and sorted into categories; and someone (probably you, since you work as a newsletter editor) will choose the recipes to be included and ready them for the printer.

The fundraising committee members love the idea—no one has ever done anything like it before in the history of the school and they are sure that students' parents will be glad to participate. The letters asking for recipes go out and, within a week, you are inundated. Most of the favorite recipes are photocopies of handwritten recipe cards; there are also photocopies of cookbook pages and magazine articles and a few labels and back-of-the-box recipes. You sort the recipes one weekend and give them to another committee member for input into her computer. She is a very good typist; when you proof the computer printout for the book, you find that she has reproduced each recipe word for word.

You work late several nights getting the book ready for press but your effort pays off because cartons of the finished cookbooks are delivered to the school just before Thanksgiving. By Christmas vacation, five hundred copies of the book have been sold. The basketball team has plenty of money for new uniforms and you anticipate that you will receive a special award at the spring athletics banquet.

Then, in January, one of the other committee members calls you. "I showed your little cookbook to my sister over the holidays," he says. "She wondered where you got your recipes. I told her that the parents sent in all kinds of stuff—pages from cookbooks and magazines, handwritten recipe cards, even recipes off the back of packages. She was horrified. She's a law student, you know, and she thinks that your whole cookbook may be one giant example of copyright infringement. I just thought you ought to know." You terminate the phone call with as much grace as possible. After you get over wondering when the committee's cookbook became "your" cookbook, you call your own sister, who has been out of law school for some time. What you ask her is, "Is it infringement?"

A Your sister, who is usually the most decisive—even opinionated—member of your family, gives you a less-than-definite answer. "Maybe," she says. "I can't be sure until I compare the source material to the finished book. I can drop by after I leave the office, if you like." You gather the recipes the school parents submitted for the cookbook and arrange them in the order in which they appear in the book. Then you wait for your sister. She doesn't look at the recipes and the cookbook long before she tells you that probably neither you nor the school will be sued for copyright infringement.

"You lucked out with this project," she says. "But it could have caused you and the school some problems. Let's start at the top, because this is a complicated analysis. Recipes are, to some extent, not subject to copyright protection because they fall into the 'idea, method, or system' category of unprotectable material. However, although the list of ingredients in a recipe is completely unprotectable, the *instructions* for assembling those ingredients *are* protectable, at least to the extent that they embody original expression more than is necessary to communicate the system that is essential for assembling the ingredients into the finished dish. Still following me? O.K. This means that there may be a little protectable expression in each recipe. Since your typist copied the recipes exactly from your source material, you may have infringed the rights of the original authors of those recipes—but ever so slightly. And since it appears that your recipes came from numerous sources, you have not simply replicated the contents of any one cookbook or magazine article, which would be infringement because of the substantiality of the material taken. And I don't think the analysis is any different for the recipes you took from labels or box backs—those don't enjoy any more protection than any other recipe and it's arguable that they were printed on the product containers expressly for the purpose of allowing people to save and use them, so none of the companies are likely to complain if you simply further promulgate their recipes." She pauses. "That smells like your meatloaf—can I stay for dinner?"

You tell your sister that she can eat as much meatloaf as she wants and give her a big hug, because she has just taken away your throbbing headache and relieved your mind. You call the guy on the committee the next day and give him the news. He admits that his sister hasn't taken an intellectual-property law course yet and that maybe she overstated things just a little. You are kinder to him than you want to be because you like his young son and because you realize that, for all you knew before publishing the cookbook, you and the school could have been in copyright trouble. You vow to follow your sister's parting advice. "Next time, look before you leap," she said. "Like most lawyers, I prefer to see my clients *before* they do something dumb to get themselves in trouble."

Q You are a freelance writer for "shelter" magazines. Every month, in order to earn enough to pay the rent, you have to come up with a household-hints column and at least two feature articles. You have trouble coming up with new topics and it seems that the time it takes to research your columns and feature articles increases every month. Then you get what seems like a great idea. You devote a couple of hours to reading old copies of women's magazines in the basement of the local university library. You find articles in early copies of several magazines that are similar to the pieces you write.

After hours in the dusty stacks of the library, you settle on three articles that have the most potential as sources for your writing—a piece on planting tulip bulbs from a 1913 issue of *The Garden*; an article on furniture arrangement from a 1917 issue of *House and Garden*; and a piece on handmade Christmas gifts from a 1942 issue of *American Home*. You photocopy the three articles and head home to your computer. As you type your byline at the start of your "Handy Tips for the Home" column, it occurs to you that you could simply update the language used in the 1917 *House and Garden* article on furniture arrangement and use it without further alteration. Because your deadline is less than twenty-four hours away and because you also have to come up with two more pieces by the end of the week, you decide that this is what you will do. It isn't hard to adapt the 1917 article—the aesthetics of furniture arrangement haven't changed much since then. In an hour, you e-mail "your" column to *Happy Homes* magazine. Your editor writes back the next day, praising your column. That's all it takes to convince you that the other two magazine editors would also probably like slightly adapted versions of the other two old pieces from the library.

You turn in "your" pieces on handmade Christmas gifts and planting tulip bulbs early and are excited to get messages praising the pieces from each of the two editors. You receive your checks in due course, you pay the rent, and you vow to spend more time in the library from now on. Then you get a call from the *Happy Homes* editor.

It seems that one of the magazine's copy editors thinks that your column on furniture arrangement is simply a reprint of an older piece because some of the language in it is archaic. The copy editor says that no one refers to a sofa as a "davenport" anymore and that using large fringed shawls to decorate pianos went out with the Model T. You are forced to admit that you lifted your column from an old magazine and dig up your photocopy of the original article to give your editor the specifics. She says, tersely, that she'll talk to the in-house counsel for *Happy Homes* and that either she or he will call you back. It appears that she's going to ask him, "Is it infringement?"

You force yourself to answer the phone when it rings. As you feared, your caller is the in-house lawyer for *Happy Homes*, a Mr. McIntosh. He doesn't sound angry, but he doesn't sound happy, either. "Are you aware that *House and Garden* magazine still publishes?" he asks.

"Of course," you say, although this concept never entered your crowded brain until the moment he mentioned it. "But, uh, they'll never know that I, uh, used some of their 1917 article, will they?" you say in a voice that, you notice with annoyance, sounds pretty wimpy and tentative.

"Maybe not," McIntosh says, "but *we* know. But what really worries me is the issue of copyright infringement. Did you even consider that?"

"No," you say in an even more cowardly tone. "Is that a problem? I mean, I found that copy of *House and Garden* in the far reaches of the stacks—it's so out of print that it's probably a collector's item!" You laugh nervously. McIntosh concedes that your copying of a 1917 magazine article will not result in a copyright infringement suit.

"Actually, it's out of copyright. It's in the public domain. Even if they knew about it, *House and Garden* couldn't sue because its rights in the article have expired."

"Great! It's such a relief to know that there's no problem! Thank you!" you say.

"Oh, I didn't say there was no problem," he replies. "I just said that there was no problem with copyright infringement."

"What do you mean?" you ask, in your very small voice again.

"I mean that we pay you to write original articles, not to try to pass off something you have plagiarized as your own work," he says. "And you have shown a shocking lack of judgment in attempting to use someone else's work as your own. Do you realize that if this article had been just a few years newer we could be sued for publishing it?"

"No, I didn't," you admit. "You mean that you could be sued for something I wrote—well, sort of wrote—even if you didn't know that the piece was, uh, adapted from another magazine?"

"That's exactly what I mean," he says. "And that's exactly why we are terminating our arrangement with you. From now on, the 'Handy Tips for the Home' column will be written in-house. And don't call us, we'll call you." Then he hangs up. You are devastated. You're also very nervous about the other two articles you "wrote." You rush back to the library, where you throw yourself on the mercy of the reference librarian, who helps you access the U.S. Copyright Office Web site, where you learn by reading a publication called *Duration of Copyright: Provisions of the Law Dealing with the Length of Copyright Protection* that your use, without permission, of the 1913 article *can't* get you sued—not for copyright infringement, anyway—but that using the 1942 article *could* result in a copyright infringement suit, since it may still be protected by copyright. You are almost certain that the magazine that published the 1942 article, *American Home* magazine, is no longer published, but the reference librarian tells you that it was bought out by another company, so you figure that *someone* owns the copyright in the article you used and you are too scared to gamble on a lawsuit. You call the magazine to whom you sent it, explain the situation, and ask the editor to pull the article and replace it with another one on the same topic that you sit up all night to write. You keep quiet about the third article because it is in the public domain and because the magazine that originally published it is no longer in business. And you never again try to pass off anyone else's work as your own, even if it is in the public domain.

Q You are the music director for an ad agency. When your boss asks you to write a theme song to be sung in television and radio ads for a new client, the manufacturer of a line of herbal teas called Granny's Old-Fashioned Teas, you spend several days trying to come up with a melody that works. You want something that is easy to sing and memorable, but every melody you come up with is too complicated—at least according to your boss. Then one weekend, you are watching college football on TV—your alma mater, the University of Tennessee, is playing Auburn. It's a tough game for the Vols, but they are winning. You love the fact that every time your team scores, the UT band plays the school fight song, the bluegrass classic "Rocky Top." As you are singing "Rocky Top" along with the enormous crowd of UT fans at the game, it comes to you! The melody for "Rocky Top" is exactly the sort of simple but memorable melody you need for Granny's Old-Fashioned Teas. As soon as the game is over (the Vols won), you head for the office to do a little weekend work.

Monday morning, you present the results to your boss: the melody from "Rocky Top" with original lyrics written by you to promote Granny's Old-Fashioned Teas. You especially like the way the name

Granny's Old-Fashioned Teas matches the melody and emphasis at the end of "your" song. "Granny's Old-Fashioned Teas" scans exactly the same way as the last words in the "Rocky Top" lyrics: "Rocky Top, Tennessee!"

The Granny's marketing people love their new theme song, and you schedule production for the television and radio spots. The day before the first television spot is to be filmed, another UT graduate who works at your agency walks into your office. "I hear you're using 'Rocky Top' for the Granny's jingle. I have to hand it to you—I didn't know the Bryants ever let anyone change the lyrics to their song." You were on your way to lunch, but this comment stops you in your tracks.

"What do you mean? Who are the Bryants?" you ask.

"The Bryants are Boudleaux and Felice Bryant—they're the people who wrote 'Rocky Top.' They've gone to court more than once to defend that song against copyright infringement. I really thought that they never let anyone change the lyrics. You must be very persuasive. Did it have anything to do with the fact that you're a UT graduate? I mean—their granting permission for you to use their melody with new lyrics for commercials." You stutter a hesitant answer, tell your buddy that you've just discovered that you've got to work through lunch, and sit down at your computer, where you run a Google search for "Rocky Top." What you find out in the next ten minutes makes you forget all about lunch. What you're trying to find out, of course, is, "Is it infringement?"

A You go to a page on the university's Web site that lists UT fight songs and find the lyrics to "Rocky Top" displayed under the song title and a notice that says, "Copyright 1967 House of Bryant Publications." You don't even have to do the math to figure out that there's no way that the song you thought was a traditional (i.e., very old) public-domain bluegrass song is, in fact, still protected by copyright and that it will be for many years to come.

Within milliseconds of running another Google search, you have the contact information for House of Bryant. While your courage is up, you dial the phone number listed for the publisher. A woman with a pleasant Southern voice, a Mrs. Jenkins, tells you that she administers licenses for the songs owned by House of Bryant, but that the current owners of the company, the sons of Boudleaux and Felice Bryant, make it a policy never to allow the melodies of their songs to be used with lyrics different from those that their parents wrote originally. You are desperate. You ask, "But my agency is prepared to *pay* for the right to use new lyrics with your melody. And they are innocuous lyrics— they advertise herbal teas. I'd be happy to fax a copy of the new lyrics to you."

"You may fax the lyrics if you like, but I don't think that will convince the Bryants to give you the license you want," Mrs. Jenkins says.

"What about money? Won't money change their minds?" you ask.

"I don't think so. They've turned down pretty big offers in the past when someone wanted to change their lyrics. They think that changing the lyrics would erode the distinctiveness of their songs. Their parents felt the same way; they never allowed their lyrics to be changed," she says.

"I'm going to fax the new lyrics," you say, with a cheer you don't really feel, "and I'll get back to you about the money."

"I'll expect to receive the lyrics, and I'll present your request, but don't get your hopes up," Mrs. Jenkins says. "You have a good day, now," she adds. You march down to your boss's office to let him know the predicament you're in.

"But we've got the TV studio and a crew and talent booked for *tomorrow*," he says, "and a recording studio and talent for next week!"

"I know, I know," you say, miserably.

"Do we really have to get their permission before we produce these spots? Can't we just do what we want and get permission later?" he asks.

"We could try," you say, "but if they don't want to grant us permission to use the new lyrics with their melody, they don't have to. Then we'd be stuck with TV spots and radio ads that would be good only as evidence against us in a copyright infringement suit, which we would lose. In fact, House of Bryant doesn't have to let us use 'Rocky Top' at all, not for ads. I'm really sorry, boss," you say.

"Well, this is a fine mess," your boss says. "How much money do they want?"

"They say they won't let us change the lyrics to their song, that they *never* let anyone change any of their lyrics. But I want to make them an offer. How much can we pay?" you ask timidly.

"Offer them $25,000," he says. You rush back to your office and get Mrs. Jenkins on the phone. Unfortunately, although she says she will present your offer, she doesn't hold out much hope that the Bryant brothers will accept it and grant the permission you want. "Don't feel too bad," she says. "We've had to take several people to court who thought that 'Rocky Top' was a public-domain song. It's understandable that you might think that because it sounds like a traditional song. But it's not, and we always win in court," she adds. Despite her kind tone, you don't feel any better hearing this. And you feel even worse when, later that afternoon, she calls to tell you that the Bryants have turned down your offer to pay them $25,000 to use new lyrics with their melody in an ad. You spend the weekend coming up with another jingle for Granny's Old-Fashioned Teas. It's not as memorable as the one you "wrote" using the "Rocky Top" melody, but it works pretty well. You try to tell yourself that you saved your agency $25,000 in licensing fees, but you know that's not really what happened.

Q You develop a series of bumper stickers, posters, and T-shirts designed to promote awareness of the environment. You sell them through health-food stores, bookstores, and retailers of camping and hiking gear. Partly because the slogans on your bumper stickers and tees are witty and novel ("My other car is a bike"), sales are good from the onset of your venture. You have a hard time producing enough new items to meet the demand until you run across a mail-order catalog for similar items; you choose some of the slogans from the catalog products that you like best and use them for your own new products. They sell as well as your first, original products and you're pretty pleased with yourself until one of your retailers shows you two T-shirts and a bumper sticker manufactured by rival companies that bear slogans identical to some of your own.

You assure him that he won't get into trouble by selling your products even though they're imprinted with slogans other manufacturers are already using, but on your way home you begin to worry. You call the lawyer who handled the incorporation for your tiny business to ask whether you're in trouble. He turns you over to another lawyer in his firm—"Brian, our intellectual-property guy," he calls him—and Brian gives you a short course in copyright law. What you want to know is, "Is it infringement?"

A "The slogans and sayings you tell me you're using are all very short," Brian says. "There's no copyright protection available for short slogans and catchphrases. That means that you can use any such slogan or popular saying without permission from anyone."

"Even if I stole them from another marketer of novelty products?" you ask, hesitantly.

"Even if you stole them," Brian says. "Short phrases and slogans are deemed to be too short for copyright protection—they're almost the smallest units of cultural expression and because they're already stated in the briefest form that can convey the thought, they're treated like mathematical formulas or geographic coordinates or recipes."

"Some of the tees and bumper stickers I've seen have a copyright notice on them, so I stayed away from them," you say. "But if the slogans on them aren't protected by copyright, how do you explain the copyright notice?"

"Whether something is protected by copyright is determined by the copyright statute and the nature of the material. It either is or is not eligible for copyright protection and using a copyright notice doesn't change whether it's protected. If the products you've seen with copyright notice bear only short slogans or phrases, they're not protected by copyright despite the use of the copyright notice," Brian says. "But you want to stay strictly away from any slogan or phrase on any product that appears with an 'R-in-a-circle' [®] near it—that's not a copyright notice, but it's a notice that the slogan or phrase is a federally registered trademark. A trademark belongs to whoever uses it first and even slogans or phrases can become trademarks, regardless of the fact that copyright doesn't protect them. Following me so far?" he asks.

"I think so," you say. "I'm developing a poster around the Joyce Kilmer poem *Trees*. You know, 'I think that I shall never see a poem lovely as a tree'—that one. Can I do that?"

"It depends," Brian says. "Usually it's dangerous to use more than a line or two of any poem without permission because poems— and song lyrics—are, in their entirety, so short as to be likely to be infringed by the use of more than a line or two. That is, if the work as a whole is short, more than a line or two of it is likely to constitute substantial similarity, so using more than a very small portion of the work without permission is copyright infringement."

"I guess I won't be producing my *Trees* poster after all," you say.

"Maybe you can, after all," Brian answers. "I think *Trees* is an old poem. Find out when it was first published and call me back." You do call Brian after you dig out the poetry anthology that includes Kilmer's classic poem, which was published first in 1913. "You're good to go," Brian says. "That poem is now in the public domain and anyone can use it. But be careful—you can get in a lot of trouble using other people's work without permission unless you know for sure that what you're doing is legal."

PART II

Fair Use and How It Works

CHAPTER 5

Copyright Fair Use

AS IN ANY CIVIL OR CRIMINAL LITIGATION, the defendants in copyright infringement suits may offer various arguments to demonstrate that their actions either did not infringe the plaintiffs' work or, if they did, that there are good reasons why the court should not punish them. The arguments that a defendant makes in self-defense are called "defenses." Many defenses to charges of copyright infringement are technical in nature. Others are rarely used. The most important and the most commonly used of such defenses is that of "fair use." There are situations in which you may use parts of another person's copyrighted work without that person's permission and without infringing that person's copyright. The fair-use defense can render otherwise infringing actions non-infringing.

Fair Use Defined

Fair use is a kind of public policy exception to the usual standard for determining copyright infringement; that is, there is an infringing use of a copyrighted work but because of countervailing public interest, that use is permitted and is not called infringement. Any use that is deemed by the law to be "fair" typically creates some social, cultural, or political benefit that outweighs any resulting harm to the copyright owner. In one fair-use decision, the U.S. Supreme Court characterized fair use as a "breathing space within the confines of copyright."

The courts often view a fair-use defense with some suspicion—after all, it contravenes the instincts of most lawyers and judges to accept that there are situations in which it is legal and even socially useful for one person to use the property of another without the consent of the owner.

The courts consider a long list of factors in determining whether a use is "fair." The factors that courts must consider in determining whether a use of a copyrighted work is a fair use are enumerated in Section 107 of the U.S. copyright statute. It's worth quoting this short section in its entirety to set out exactly what the copyright statute has to say about fair use. Here it is:

§ 107. Limitations on exclusive rights: Fair use

Notwithstanding the provisions of sections 106 and 106A,[1] the fair use of a copyrighted work, including such use by reproduction in copies or phonorecords or by any other means specified by that section, for purposes such as criticism, comment, news reporting, teaching (including multiple copies for classroom use), scholarship, or research, is not an infringement of copyright. In determining whether the use made of a work in any particular case is a fair use the factors to be considered shall include:

1. The purpose and character of the use, including whether such use is of a commercial nature or is for nonprofit educational purposes [*Nonprofit educational, research, criticism, and news reporting uses are almost always fair; commercial uses, such as uses in advertising, are seldom fair uses.*]

2. The nature of the copyrighted work [*The permissible uses that may be made of informational works are considerably broader than permissible uses of creative works. However, the courts have yet to permit the fair-use defense to infringement in a case involving an unpublished work, where the private nature of the work is ordinarily protected.*]

3. The amount and substantiality of the portion used in relation to the copyrighted work as a whole [*This is the "substantial similarity" question again. It is quantitative and qualitative; that is, did you quote the twelve-page climactic scene of a mystery novel, thereby disclosing the identity of the killer, or did you quote only a three-paragraph section that describes the city where the detective works?*]

4. The effect of the use upon the potential market for or value of the copyrighted work [*This evaluation is often determinative in a court's decision whether the use constitutes infringement. It is undoubtedly the most important of the four factors to be weighed in determining fair use. If the market for the copyrighted work is significantly diminished because of the purported fair use, then it is not a fair use. Fewer readers will want to buy a book if its most sensational and newsworthy sections have been previously excerpted in a magazine. A related factor to be considered is the effect of the purported fair use on any of the rights in the copyright of the work said to be infringed. If, without permission, one person writes and sells a screenplay based on another person's copyrighted novel, the right to prepare and sell a screen adaptation of the novel may have been lost to the author of that novel.*]

---

[1] Section 106 gives copyright owners the exclusive rights of copyright; Section 106A gives visual artists certain "rights of attribution and integrity" in their works. The texts of those two sections are given in the Appendix section of this book.

The fact that a work is unpublished shall not itself bar a finding of fair use if such finding is made upon consideration of all the above factors.

The House Report that accompanied the 1976 Copyright Act is also informative because it illustrates the scope of the fair-use section of the statute with several examples of fair use:

[Q]uotation of excerpts in a review or criticism for purposes of illustration or comment; quotation of short passages in a scholarly or technical work, for illustration or clarification of the author's observations; use in a parody of some of the content of the work parodied; summary of an address or article, with brief quotations, in a news report; reproduction by a library of a portion of a work to replace part of a damaged copy; reproduction by a teacher or student of a small part of a work to illustrate a lesson; reproduction of a work in legislative or judicial proceedings or reports; incidental and fortuitous reproduction, in a newsreel or broadcast, of a work located in the scene of an event being reported.

Avoiding Claims of Infringement

Whenever you consider using someone else's work, you should take action to protect yourself from false claims of infringement. The best way to do this is to ensure that any use you make of another person's copyrighted work falls into one of the fair use exceptions to infringement. Creators and business people who deal in creative works can greatly diminish the likelihood of being sued for copyright infringement by using the simple techniques outlined below:

- **Keep your notes and the progressive drafts or sketches, and so forth, of your creative work to prove that you created it yourself.** Date each such document when you create it in the same pen or pencil used to write or draw the draft of your work. If you do not own the books, magazines, etc., that you referred to in the process of creating your work, make sure you keep a list of any such works to show where you got your information.
- **Parody of copyrighted works is not a permissible fair use unless the parody uses only so much of the parodied work as is necessary to "call to mind" the parodied work.** This is dangerous to attempt without very careful attention to the question of infringement. Anyone who must use more than a small segment or feature of a copyrighted work to make an effective parody of that work should consider approaching the owner of the copyright in the work for permission to use whatever portion of the work is necessary. In recent years, several court decisions have applied a doctrine of fair use called "transformative use" to parody uses. A transformative use is one that uses elements of a copyrighted work to transform the existing work; this is what happens in

a parody—some elements of the underlying work are used in addition to new, parodic elements created by the parodist.

- **If you are in any position or profession that involves the exploitation or creation of copyrighted works, be careful what you are exposed to**. This includes editors, publishers, movie producers or directors, music publishers, writers, artists, songwriters, screenwriters, and copywriters, among others. Promptly return manuscripts, scripts, songs, and so forth, submitted to you for possible use if you cannot use them. Keep a record of what and when and to whom such materials are returned. Consider refusing to examine any such material at all until it is registered for copyright, especially if it is unpublished, or without a release of liability from the creator.

  If you are a creator of copyrights, and especially if you are successful in your field, protect yourself from people who want to show you their newest work, especially if they are unknown to you. Disappointed and envious creators have been known to sue those who enjoy more success in the mistaken belief that part of that success originated with them—the envious unknowns.

- **Direct quotations should always be attributed**. Quotations of short passages of copyrighted works, such as the sort of quoting found in book reviews or news stories, is generally safe in any context where the First Amendment protection of free speech can be reasonably invoked, even if the piece that uses the quotation has a partially commercial purpose. You should also attribute closely paraphrased statements.

  It is very important to understand, however, that you cannot escape responsibility for copyright infringement simply by attributing the lifted portion of any work to its author; if the "borrowed" segment amounts to a substantial portion of the copyrighted work, attribution does not eradicate your sin. As indicated earlier, you should also avoid any use of even two- or three-paragraph direct quotations or close paraphrases if they embody the "meat" of the work from which they were taken or if use of them would diminish the salability of that work. And if you do paraphrase another writer's work, attribute the ideas you use to him.

  Do your homework; use as many sources as are available for your work. Remember the old saw that "stealing from one source is plagiarism, but stealing from several sources is research."

- **Working journalists and people affiliated with nonprofit institutions, such as schools and churches, have more latitude in using other people's copyrighted works than the average painter, writer, or composer**. A professor who duplicates a poem to use as a handout in an English class is probably not going to run afoul of the copyright owner of the poem. However, Kinko's encountered big trouble, in the form of a lawsuit for copyright infringement, when it disregarded this principle of the law of fair use. Without permission from the copyright holders, Kinko's was assembling from many sources "anthologies" consisting of writings taught in university courses and selling them to students. These makeshift anthologies hurt the market for the books that legitimately contained the copied writings. Kinko's, which lost the suit, has been remarkably attentive to the interests of copyright holders ever since.

• **Obtain permission to use any photo, letter, passage, illustration, etc., that is, either unpublished or, if previously published, possibly still protected by copyright.** Save the permissions you obtain in a file. Never exceed the permission granted and never use any material for which permission to use has been denied. (Several sample permission letters appear in appendix F of this book.)

And remember that using unpublished works without permission is especially dangerous, even if the use is minimal. A tension exists between the owners of such materials and biographers, historians, and other scholars who may want to quote from them. It is understandable that this restriction is disliked by anyone who needs to reproduce in a biography or journal article long passages from the unpublished letters or manuscripts of his or her subject. However, the law protects the privacy of those who do not wish to make their writings public and does not require them to pay any attention at all to even the most valid requests for permission to reproduce and publish such works. Presently, only the most narrow uses may be made of unpublished works without the consent of the owner of copyright in them, and disregarding restrictions placed on the use of unpublished materials is dangerous. Even close paraphrasing of such materials may be actionable.

Fair-Use Checklist

A useful tool for evaluating whether a use is a fair use or veers too close to infringement is the "Fair-Use Checklist" reproduced in the appendix A. Notice that the checklist leaves the decision as to whether a use is fair or infringing up to you. However, it can help you evaluate your use on a point-by-point basis using the only binding standard that exists—the four factors of the copyright statute (and their subcategories). There is no definite boundary between fair use and infringement, because no general rule defining infringement is possible—remember, the infringement evaluation must be made by weighing *particular* circumstances. Make a few photocopies of the Fair-Use Checklist and use it like a worksheet the next time you have a question about how much of someone else's work you can use without permission—or whether you can use it at all without tracking down the copyright owner and asking for a license.

Is It Fair Use?

1 Your cousin Bridget is an avid scrapbooker. She turns out beautiful and artistic scrapbooks for every family vacation and for each of her children's school years. You especially like her latest effort, a

family history scrapbook that contains old family photos as well as genealogical information about the branch of your family that you share. You peruse the book at a family gathering and are very impressed with her work. You like the Irish blessing that she used at the beginning of the book:

May the road rise to meet you,
May the wind be always at your back,
May the sun shine warm upon your face,
The rains fall soft upon your fields.
And until we meet again,
May God hold you in the palm of his hand.

You like the little verse so much so that you copy it into your pocket notebook. The very next week you are readying for the printer a brochure about the tours to Ireland offered by the travel agency you work for. You have assembled several great photos taken by the owner of the agency when he led last year's tour, and those photos, along with the copy about the tours the agency offers, nearly fill the space available in the brochure. But you need something else—a nice quotation of some sort for the front of the brochure that conveys the warmth of the Irish people. Then you remember the Irish blessing that you copied from your cousin's family history scrapbook. You dig it out of your purse and plug the blessing into the brochure.

You send the brochure to the printer and don't give the blessing another thought until your boss says that his wife, who is a lawyer, wondered whether his agency would get in trouble for using it for a brochure. You are forced to admit that you don't know the answer to his question, but you tell him you'll find out. Then you head to the library, where you hope you can find the answer you need.

To avoid wandering around aimlessly in the reference department of the library, you approach one of the reference librarians for help. "I need to find out about copyright infringement," you say. She helps you find a couple of books on copyright law and shows you the chapters on copyright infringement. What you read scares you. You find out that using in any way any substantial portion of someone else's work without permission is usually copyright infringement.

You read that there's something called "fair use" that is a sort of loophole to copyright infringement—that some uses of other people's work without permission are actually not copyright infringement because of the purposes of the uses. You figure that if you had used the Irish blessing in a church newsletter or on a school bulletin board for St. Patrick's Day, you would have nothing to worry about. But you also read that using someone else's work for any commercial purpose is especially likely to constitute infringement. And you realize that a brochure advertising tours offered by your employer—tours for which the travel agency most certainly charges and expects to make a profit—would be held by a court to be a commercial use in any evaluation of copyright infringement.

You are trying to figure out just how you will tell your employer that his travel agency's brochure may end up in court when the helpful librarian asks if there is anything else she can help you find. "I don't think there's anything else you can do for me," you say, "unless you have a magic wand that can turn copyright infringement into fair use."

"What, exactly, do you mean?" she asks. You tell her. She listens carefully to your tale of woe and then says, "Wait right here." You don't mind waiting because waiting will postpone your return to the office and your meeting with the boss. The librarian returns with a large volume called *Ireland and Its People*. She shows you a chapter on traditional Irish sayings, toasts, and blessings. You get a glimmer of hope.

"What does 'traditional' mean?" you ask.

"Usually, it means that the originator of a work is forgotten; the work has been around so long in the culture that no one knows when or by whom it was created. It may even have been created by many people over many years. See, here are several versions of your blessing. It seems that you haven't infringed anyone's copyright at all because this blessing is no longer protected by copyright. Maybe you shouldn't have used it in your brochure without first determining that it was safe to do so, but you got lucky this time. No one is going to sue you."

You hug the librarian and get her name so that you can send a letter to her supervisor telling him that she is a treasure. You rush out the door to return to your office. Your boss is very happy to have an answer to his wife's question and even happier that he's not going to be sued for something you did because you were pressed for time and failed to do your homework. You feel that the luck of the Irish has helped you through this dilemma, and you buy a copy of one of the books on copyright that you read at the library so that, next time, you won't have to depend on luck.

2 You develop a cologne from your own unique mixture of herbal essential oils that is such a hit with your family and friends that you decide to market it. You call your cologne and the soap and bath salts of the same fragrance "Love Potion No. 9." One of your first marketing efforts is setting up a Web site so that you can sell your products online. You hire a Web designer to create a really cool site and give him a copy of the lyrics to the famous old doo-wop hit recording "Love Potion No. 9" by the Searchers, which you copy from an online song lyrics site. You figure that you need to create a certain "mystique" for your cologne and that the

lyrics of the old song, describing a potion that makes a guy love everybody he encounters, will do it. You figure that women will buy the cologne, because the implication is that it will make them irresistible to men.

You advertise your site as widely as you can afford to and start getting orders for your products. Then, among some online orders, you get a message to call a guy who says he is the lawyer for the publishers of the song. You call, wondering what interest he has in your cologne. What you find out when you get him on the phone is that he is only interested in your cologne as a possible source of revenue to pay a federal court judgment for copyright infringement.

The lawyer you call says he represents the interests of Jerry Lieber Music and Mike Stoller Music; you learn that "Love Potion No. 9" was written by Jerry Lieber and Mike Stoller and that each writer owns half the copyright in the song, along with the copyrights in a long string of other famous late-twentieth-century hit songs. "But what has that got to do with me?" you ask.

"Just this," the Lieber-Stoller lawyer replies. "I will recommend to my clients that they bring a suit against you for copyright infringement if you do not immediately stop any use of their song."

"You must be joking," you say, since you are really surprised that a) two writers and their lawyer in California have even heard of you and your fledgling personal-care products business and b) that they have anything at all to complain about, since your business has nothing to do with music.

The lawyer sets you straight. "It's not my job to educate you to the particulars of federal law, but, in the interests of saving my clients the expense of filing a lawsuit, let me give you a short course in copyright infringement," he says. "Your Web site posts the entire lyric for my clients' song, "Love Potion No. 9." That, in itself, is probably sufficient to constitute copyright infringement, since you are using an undeniably 'substantial' portion of the entire work. Furthermore, you are using the song lyrics for a commercial purpose—to advertise and promote your products. That is also infringement. And, third, you have used the title of my clients' song to name your products. There is no copyright protection available for titles of any kind, but by your use of my clients' title you may be creating a false association between my clients and your products. That's trademark infringement or, at least, unfair competition," he says. "Do you have anything to say for yourself?"

"Not at the moment," you reply. "I need to talk to my lawyer."

"Have your lawyer call me with any questions. And either you or your lawyer need to get back to me by next Friday at noon; otherwise, I'm going to start drafting the complaint for the lawsuit," he adds in an ominous tone.

You call your own friendly lawyer as soon as you get off the phone with the ominous one. You don't like what your lawyer tells you, but he assures you that he can probably save you lots of money and trouble if you will authorize him to take immediate action to placate everybody in California.

"You have committed one of the most common sins of entrepreneurs," he says. "You leapt before you looked. In your eagerness to sell your products, you have ignored the rights of others. I know you have a business license, because I filed for it. And I know that you have made sure that your products and their labels meet FDA standards, because I also helped you attend to those requirements. But you didn't even ask me about copyright. I'm a little hurt—I took a course in copyright and trademark law in law school and I got a really good grade. I could have helped you avoid this problem."

"I'm so happy for you," you say. "But, counselor, cut to the chase. What do I have to do to keep myself out of court? And make it a short answer—I haven't made a nickel in profits yet."

"What do you have to do? Just this—everything the Lieber-Stoller lawyer asked. And you need to do it in a hurry and with great deference toward his clients. A little kowtowing in the right direction has saved lots of potential defendants from lawsuits."

"You mean he's right?" you ask. "But he's complaining about my infringing a song and I didn't use any music at all—not even the *written* melody. And I got the lyrics off the Internet—there are lots of lyrics sites out there. What about them? Doesn't it matter that those sites have posted the song lyrics?"

Your lawyer dismisses these arguments. "Using the lyrics of a song is plenty for infringement. Songs—and poems—are short, and using most or all of the words to either a song or a poem without permission is infringement. And it doesn't matter how many lyrics sites there are on the Internet. First of all, you can't get away with stealing something by pointing out that other people have done it before. And secondly, if those sites don't charge for the lyrics or otherwise make money off the lyrics, the copyright owners may have decided to ignore them. But that doesn't give you the right to use the lyrics in a commercial setting."

Your lawyer emphasizes that your use, for a commercial purpose, destroys any possibility that you could claim it was a "fair use." He says he's not so sure about the Lieber-Stoller lawyer's claim that naming your cologne with their song title constitutes trademark infringement, but he tells you that it is a very good rule to avoid annoying people richer than you, since they can better afford to sue you than you can afford to be sued. You say that you suppose all this means that you will have to stop using the Lieber-Stoller lyrics and re-name your product. He says that if you'll promise to accomplish this before Friday, he can call the California lawyer and get you off the hook. "I'll tell him that you are *not* a 'deep-pocket' defendant," he says.

"I'm more like an 'empty-pocket' defendant," you say. "Do it." You call your Webmaster and take down the Web site until you can redesign it and rename your product. Then you call your printer to stop the presses that are ready to roll on five thousand new Love Potion No. 9 labels. You try to feel good about having to completely redirect your marketing for your products and remind yourself that you were never happy about the sections of the song lyrics that say that Love Potion No. 9 "smelled like turpentine and looked like India ink." Then you consider renaming your products simply "Potion." But you make a note to call your lawyer first so that he can put his law-school course to work advising you.

3 You are the sales manager for an auto-parts distributor. One of the toughest tasks you face is educating your salespeople. One day you have a bright idea: You start a weekly program of mailing a packet of information to each of your seventy-five sales reps. You include the spec sheets on new parts that the manufacturers of those parts furnish to you, memos that you write regarding clients, and copies of important articles from auto-industry publications and books on sales techniques. You are very pleased with the effectiveness of your campaign to keep your reps up to date—sales have increased, and your clients seem to like and respect your salespeople.

Then one day your new assistant asks a question. You ask her to prepare twenty-five photocopies of an article from *Automotive Age* and burn twenty-five CDs of one of the first sections of the audio version of *The Dale Carnegie Leadership Mastery Course: How to Challenge Yourself and Others to Greatness*, and she wonders whether your directive is kosher. You try to brush off her concerns because you don't understand why she is worried—after all, your former assistant never raised any such questions. However, she is so persistent that you figure you'll investigate the issue just to shut her up. You call the company lawyer to ask him whether your assistant knows what she is talking about.

Your company lawyer is a very nice man named Nick. You have never seen him lose his cool, but you think he may be on the verge of it when you explain your question. At his insistence, you pause in your phone conversation to instruct your assistant to halt work on this week's packet of materials for your sales reps. Then, again at Nick's insistence, you take the originals of the materials you had planned to send out to him for his examination. He spends a few minutes examining the documents and then tells you that your efforts to educate your salespeople could get your company sued for copyright infringement.

"I don't understand," you say. "The company has a subscription to *Automotive Age* and I paid for the CDs of *The Dale Carnegie Leadership Mastery Course* with my company credit card, so we own it, too. I was planning on sending the sales reps one or two articles from every issue of *Automotive Age*, and sending one section of the Dale Carnegie course every week until the reps have heard all of it."

Mild-mannered Nick is suddenly adamant. "Not if I have anything to say about it, you won't!" he says. "Because if you continue with this plan, you will be jeopardizing the company. A subscriber to *Automotive Age* could make *one* copy of one article from one issue and put it in a file for reference purposes without problems; that would be a fair use of the publication. And you could also probably make a duplicate of a short section of one of the Carnegie course CDs for your own use after you had bought the set. But it's definitely not permissible to make twenty-five photocopies of the article and twenty-five duplicate CDs of part of the course and distribute them to the whole sales staff."

"But why?" you ask. "The *Automotive Age* subscription is expensive, and we paid $35 for the Carnegie course. Those guys are making money off us."

"Not enough," Nick says. "First of all, you are copying substantial portions of *Automotive Age* each week and will eventually copy the entire Carnegie course. That alone is copyright infringement. And in any context where you are making copies of any copyrighted work, you have to consider the effect that your copies will have on sales of that work. It's one of the most important factors in evaluating whether a use of a copyrighted work is a fair use. If the use replaces a sale of the copyrighted work, it's almost certainly not a fair use. You're making it unnecessary for your sales reps to subscribe to *Automotive Age* or buy their own copies of the Dale Carnegie course. That alone is also infringement. You lose all the way around on this one. And I don't think the company would be very happy with you if you got it sued—remember that your actions in the course of your job are attributable to the company. *Automotive Age* and the publishers of the Carnegie course would sue the company, not you." Nick doesn't let you leave his office until you promise that you will never again make copies of anything you didn't create from scratch without running it by him first. You return to the office, call *Automotive Age* to try to negotiate a group discount for subscriptions for all your sales reps, and order sets of the Dale Carnegie course for each of them as part of their Christmas bonus. Then you give your new assistant a raise.

4 You are a reporter for the morning newspaper in Springfield, Illinois, where you live. Your editor chooses you for a plum assignment in Chicago because you are a fan of live theater and you can stay free overnight with your sister. You are to cover the opening night of a play written by your city's only famous playwright, Mr. Montmorency. He hasn't been home in years, but he used to teach English at your high school and you hope he'll remember you and give you a personal interview. You write him a note and call your sister to let her know to expect you.

You interview Montmorency briefly after the play; he seems to have become much more grand since he became a successful playwright, but he is courteous to you and doesn't even mention that he gave you a very bad grade once for a lame term paper. Because you are grateful not to have been reminded of your adolescent ineptitude, you decide not to mention that Montmorency appears to have acquired an English accent since he left Springfield. However, you feel that your credibility as a journalist is at stake when you write your review of Montmorency's play, *The Yearning Heart*, and you decide that you must call it as you see it—that is, you must give your honest opinion of the play, which is that it stinks. You write and rewrite your review, trying to be objective and honest. To illustrate that Montmorency's dialogue has become stilted and florid and pompous since he wrote his first play—the one that allowed him to leave teaching and Springfield for the bright lights of New York and Chicago—you quote several short sections of dialogue from the notes you took the night of the play. Your editor reads the review and tells you that it takes a brave man to criticize a favorite son in print in his own hometown but that being able to occasionally say that the emperor has no clothes is a prerequisite to good journalism and that he is proud of you.

You are feeling pretty good about your first effort as a theater critic until about two weeks after your review is published, when your editor calls you into his office to tell you that the newspaper has been sued by Montmorency for copyright infringement. You listen to your editor as he tells you that you probably don't have anything to worry about. Then he asks you if you still have the notes you used to write your review—it seems that he wants to give them, your story, and a copy of the play to the newspaper's lawyer. He tells you that you and he have an appointment with that lawyer the next day. You smile bravely, dig out your notes and the copy of your story that you had laminated to give to your mom, and go back to work. But you can't concentrate on your piece about last night's city council meeting because you keep asking yourself whether you're going to lose your job over your review.

You have always admired the man who is the lawyer for your newspaper, but after you hear what he has to say, you like him even better. As you and your editor sit in his office, he tells you that the only reason that he can come up with to explain Montmorency's lawsuit is that Montmorency was so angry that his hometown paper panned his play that he shopped around until he found a lawyer incompetent or greedy enough to file a copyright infringement suit that is without any real foundation in the law.

"I've reviewed the portions of dialogue from Montmorency's play that you quoted in your story, I've compared them with the whole text of the play, and I've reviewed the law regarding fair use and copyright infringement, but I can't find any legitimate basis for Montmorency's accusation of infringement," he says. After you stop grinning, you ask him just how much of the dialogue from the play you would have had to quote in your review before your actions amounted to infringement.

"I'm not sure that I—or any lawyer—can answer that question. Each case of accused infringement is judged on the particular facts of that case, and there just is no 'bright-line' standard for infringement. I can tell you that you would have to have quoted far more of the play than you did for it to amount to infringement," he says. He adds that, as a drama critic, you should know that the law presumes that any reasonable amount of quoting of the text of a play in a review is a "fair" use—that is, that such quoting is a permissible use of the copyrighted play because of society's interest in knowing about new works of art and what informed people have to say about them.

Your editor grins at you. You are smiling, too, and feel far more important when you leave the lawyer's office than when you walked in. Within a month or two, your lawyer does what he said he would be able to do—he gets the judge of the federal court where the lawsuit was filed to rule in favor of your newspaper even before there is a trial. He calls it a "summary judgment" and tells you that such judgments are usually awarded where there is really no basis for a suit in the first place. And you really feel vindicated when you read in a Chicago newspaper that *The Yearning Heart* has closed after only a brief run due to poor ticket sales. But you are very careful from that point on about what and how much you quote in any story you write because you don't like the feeling of being a defendant, even for a little while.

5 You are a college economics professor with a special interest in the migration of poor Southerners to the industrial Midwest during the mid-twentieth century and the resulting economic effects on their home communities. You wrote your dissertation on this topic and have since bought every scholarly treatise you have encountered that touches on it. You are excited—and a little envious—when you hear that another academic with interests similar to yours, Professor Moira Kelly, has published *her* dissertation as a book called *Sharecroppers to Autoworkers: The Displacement of Poor Southerners to Detroit's Factories.* As soon as you receive the copy you ordered, you scan it to determine whether Kelly's book has anticipated your own, which will be called *Sending Money Home: Exiled Southern Workers in the Industrial Midwest.*

You are happy to discover that her book has a somewhat different focus than yours. However, you find that a series of three graphs in her book that compare blue-collar income in West Virginia and in Michigan during the 1940s, 1950s, and 1960s is applicable to your study of the topic. You copy the pertinent graphs for classroom use and begin displaying them via an overhead projector for lectures. When you are selected to present a paper at an academic conference, you doctor up your class-room lecture that includes Professor Kelly's graphs and plan to present it. In order to ensure that your audience will grasp and remember your paper, you convert it to a very nice PowerPoint presentation that includes all the visuals you will use along with an outline of your points and copy the presentation to a CD, which you duplicate. You prepare a hundred CDs—one for every member of the audience for your presentation.

Because it is expensive to produce the CDs, you ask the association that sponsors the conference to reimburse you for the expense you incurred in producing them; you are paid $500—$5 per CD. Your paper is a hit, and you feel as if you are really beginning to make your mark in the field of twentieth-century American economics. You get several e-mails from people who heard your presentation and received a copy of it on CD. They are uniformly complimentary; two even contain job offers. You get about twenty more e-mails from other people who heard about the presentation and want to buy their own CD copy of it.

Then you get an e-mail message from Professor Kelly. She is livid that you have used her graphs and is threatening to file a complaint with the academic association that sponsored the conference. She says in her message that she is shocked that a fellow academic is not more sensitive to the copyrights of other scholars. She asks you to explain your actions, telling you that she won't file her complaint until she hears what you have to say for yourself. You call the legal counsel for your university to ask whether you have violated Professor Kelly's rights.

The university lawyer says that it wasn't infringement—and then it was. "What you have done is to exceed fair use," she says. "It's not an uncommon event. People who use the copyrights of others in their own works often forget that not all the material in the finished product is theirs. Your using Professor Kelly's original graphs and to illustrate your classroom lectures was fair use—you made one copy of the graphs, displayed them to your students during your lectures. That is definitely fair use, especially since you actually purchased a copy of her book."

"Then I'm in the clear?" you ask, tentatively.

"No, you're not," she says, "because you didn't stop there. Using the graphs in your presentation at the academic conference was also fair use, because you used them in another classroom setting. You could even have gotten away with turning your presentation into a CD for your own use for the sake of convenience. *One* CD. But you overstepped the bounds of fair use when you had all those CD copies made of your presentation—including Professor Kelly's graphs, when you distributed them to the other conference attendees, and especially when you charged for them."

"But I paid a significant amount of money to reproduce the CDs—it's not fair that I should have to bear the cost of the CDs myself," you say.

"What isn't fair," she answers, "is that you took Professor Kelly's graphs—graphs she worked several years to research—and distributed them without her permission or that of her publisher, to the very people who are the audience for her book. Those graphs weren't the whole book, but they are separate works on their own and are important parts of her book. Did you ever consider the fact that now lots of the conference attendees will not buy her book because they already have, thanks to you, an important part of it? They may feel that they don't want to pay $35 for her book when they already have one of the most useful features of it—for free. Furthermore, because you furnished the graphs to them in CD form, it's a safe bet that many of them will send one or all three graphs around to their colleagues without paying anything to you or Professor Kelly. Are you getting the picture? Do you now realize why Professor Kelly is so upset?"

"What can I do?" you ask.

"If I were you," she replies, "I would write to every single conference attendee and explain your error—that you used Professor Kelly's graphs without permission and that although academic freedom depends on free use of materials in classroom settings, you were wrong to make copies of her graphs, distribute them, and charge for them. Ask them all to return their CD to you and to go out and buy her book. Then you can send another copy of your presentation to everyone, if you want, sans the Kelly graphs. That may be enough to forestall a lawsuit. And it may get you off the hook with the university ethics committee. And I'd sure like to be able to tell the legal counsel for Professor Kelly's college, who called me this morning, that you are doing everything you can to remedy your egregious error."

You hurry back to your office to respond to Professor Kelly's e-mail and write what you hope is not a groveling letter to everyone who got a copy of your ill-fated CD. And the next time you copy anything you didn't create yourself, you check first with the university counsel so that she won't have to save your bacon ever again.

6 You are managing the gubernatorial campaign for your old college roommate. You feel that he can't help but make a big difference if he is elected, because he's smart, hardworking, and really interested in the future of the state where you both live. You also think that almost anyone would be an improvement over the incumbent, a man who was elected primarily because his father used to be governor and who has done little during his term to improve state government or the economic climate in the state. You especially loathe his habit of being out of town whenever a crisis arises—so far, during the four years he has been in office, he has traveled to six foreign countries on so-called trade missions that you think are really just nice trips at state expense

for him and his wife, not to mention a total of six months in Aspen in his family's ski lodge and two months attending various conferences.

In planning your candidate's campaign, you come up with the idea of creating a television spot from a selection of news clips of the incumbent governor waving goodbye to the press as he boards the jets that took him to his many out-of-state destinations. You get the news footage you need from the television stations that originally aired it, select the clips you need, and synchronize the resulting film to the old Peter, Paul,and Mary recording of the John Denver song "I'm Leaving on a Jet Plane." The resulting ad is hilarious and effective. TV viewers see their governor, waving goodbye over and over, as they hear Peter, Paul, and Mary sing "I'm leaving on a jet plane. Don't know when I'll be back again. . . ." Your candidate's campaign is off to a great start.

Then you get a phone call from a lawyer who represents Cherry Lane Music, the publisher of the song. It seems his client is upset because you have used the song without permission. The lawyer keeps referring to something called a "sink license." When you tell him that you don't even know what a "sink license" is, he suggests that you make an appointment with a lawyer and says he is sending you a letter via FedEx that explains his complaints. You hang up and call the campaign's lawyer, who passes you off to another lawyer in his firm, a Ms. Johnson who is an intellectual-property lawyer. You ask her "What is a 'sink license?'" and then, more timidly, "Is it infringement?"

Ms. Johnson says that she has seen the campaign ad incorporating the Peter, Paul, and Mary recording of the John Denver song. She thinks it's hilarious, too, but she tells you that it won't be on the air long if you fail to placate the lawyer for the music publisher who owns the copyright in the song. She tells you that it's a "synch license," not a "sink license," and that the word "synch" is short for "synchronization," which means combining a performance of the song with film or video footage. "Song publishers grant these licenses all the time for use in commercials," she says. "They charge whatever the traffic will bear. There are some guidelines that they use, but it really gets down to how you want to use the song, for how long, and for what purpose. How popular the song is has a lot to do with how much you have to pay, too."

"So we're going to have to pay to keep using our TV spot?" you ask. "Great. How much, do you think?"

"More than if you had asked first," Ms. Johnson says. "And lots of music publishers don't like to let their songs be used for any commercial purpose—they think it hurts the value of the composition."

"But this *isn't* a commercial purpose," you protest. "It's political speech—you know, the First Amendment and everything. Doesn't that count for something?"

"Not with copyright," she says. "Copyright owners can deny the right to use their copyrighted works for any reason, whether the requested use is a good one or a bad one. They pretty much have a monopoly on the use of their works, for a while, anyway. No one can use them without permission."

"So will you call this guy back and negotiate the right to use the song for as little as possible?" you ask, trying not to whine as you do so.

"Sure," Ms. Johnson replies. "And I suppose I should call Peter, Paul, and Mary's record company, too. If you didn't call the music publisher about using the song, you probably also didn't call the record company about using the recording. Am I right?" You admit that she is and also admit that it never occurred to you that *in addition* you'd have to contact Peter, Paul, and Mary's lawyers for permission to use their recording so as to avoid infringing something called their "right of publicity."

"Let me get this straight," you say in an exasperated tone. "I have to get permission from the music publisher to use the song. I have to get permission from the record company to use the recording. And I have to get permission from Peter, Paul, and Mary to use their per-formance. And I have to *pay* everybody for those permissions. Is that what you're telling me?"

"Exactly," Ms. Johnson says. "I can plead your ignorance (which, you now realize, is vast), and I can plead your small budget, but we have to get these permissions *now*—we should have had them *before* the TV spot ever aired. I'll get right on it." You feel a little better, but not much. You figure that you're going to have to spend a big chunk of your advertising budget on the "Jet Plane" TV ad to avoid being sued for copyright infringement and infringement of Peter, Paul and Mary's right of publicity. But, you think, it will be money well spent, since being sued in the middle of a campaign is definitely bad publicity, so in a way your advertising budget will go for its intended purpose—promoting your candidate. Anyway, you hope your candidate will see it this way.

7 You are a rookie high school teacher who volunteers to teach an art-appreciation course as part of an extra-credit program. You minored in art history in college, so you search for material in your old textbooks and the many art books you have collected since graduation. You have only a small budget for your class, and you spend most of that on a set of "Sister Wendy" videos that you use to introduce your students to some of the more famous paintings in Western art. In order to show your students other examples of the various schools of painting, you haul a stack of your art books down to the local copy shop and make color photocopies of a bunch of significant paintings. Then you mount the color photocopies on poster board and carefully write the names of the painting and of the painter under each photocopy. You plan to pass the photocopied paintings around the room and to make a famous-paintings "art exhibit" on a bulletin board in your classroom that changes weekly.

One afternoon, as you are arranging some color photocopies of Impressionist paintings on your bulletin board, the teacher from down the hall stops in. She asks where you got the copies of the paintings; you tell her. Then she launches into a long tirade about how you are probably guilty of copyright infringement and that the school board could be held liable for your infringing actions because it employs you and that you had better destroy all the nice color photocopies of Cezanne, Matisse, Van Gogh, Monet, Degas, Morisot, and Cassatt paintings that you were tacking to your bulletin board before the principal sees them.

Even though you think she's just jealous because you were voted "Coolest Teacher" last year and none of the students like her, you thank her for her advice and tell her you'll look into it. You don't even mention the photocopies of the other paintings that you have stored in the closet. That night, you put in a call to your old college roommate, who is now a lawyer for a big firm in Chicago.

The first thing your roommate says, after listening closely to your tale of your art-appreciation course and the photocopied masterpieces and asking a few questions is, "Fair use. It's fair use and nobody is going to sue you." You ask her why, since you want to be able to quote her accurately the next time somebody tries to make you feel like a criminal for doing your job. "Well, the paintings you copied are probably in the public domain. If they were created before the turn of the twentieth century, those paintings can be copied by anyone at any time."

"What a relief," you say, prematurely.

"However," she adds, "more recent paintings may still be protected by copyright, and the photographs of those paintings in the art books you used to make your photocopies are certainly protected." You get nervous again. "But the real trump card in the whole chain of analysis is that you are a teacher," she says.

"How is that important?" you say. "It's never stopped me from getting even a parking ticket—surely it can't keep me from being sued for copyright infringement,"

"Actually, it can," she says. "You won't be sued for copyright infringement—at least not *successfully*—because all your activities with regard to the paintings you copied amount only to something called fair use. Because you prepared the photocopies of the paintings—and only *one* copy of each painting—for use *in the classroom* and because you don't plan to use the photocopied paintings for any commercial purposes, and because there will be zero effect on the market for the art books from which you copied the paintings and for the paintings themselves (all of which are in museums, of course), your behavior is not infringement. Instead, it is a permitted use of the paintings and of the photographs, even those that are still protected by copyright."

"And using the Sister Wendy videos in class?" you query.

"For the same reasons," she says, "I think that's a fair use, too, and I don't think you have to worry about it, either." You reflect that it's a good thing to find out that you're not in trouble with Sister Wendy. But you ask one more question that has confused you.

"Let's say it was infringement," you say. "Could somebody really sue the school board for something I did?" Your old roommate tells you that your employer can be sued for anything you do as part of your job that violates anyone's rights of any sort but that since you have not violated anyone's rights, you and the school board are safe from suit. Then she tells you that you should find a copy of something called the CONTU guidelines. You ask her to spell this name; she tells you it is C-O-N-T-U for "National Commission on New Technological Uses of Copyright Works." You run a Google search for "CONTU" and come up with several sites with copyright information, including some with copies of the CONTU guidelines. You read them all until your eyes hurt, especially the ones that address fair use of copyrighted works in the classroom. You realize that there could be a lot more liability involved in teaching than you thought and are glad you bookmarked some of the sites you found because you know that you'll need to check them in the future to figure out whether your classroom plans will infringe anyone's copyright. Then you continue as you had planned with your art-appreciation course. You are again voted "Coolest Teacher," which makes a certain fellow teacher envious, but you are able to bear the pressure because you know it's always lonely at the top.

CHAPTER 6

Fair Use in News Reporting

NEWS REPORTING IS ONE OF THE ACTIVITIES that can, in some situations, escape the tight grip of the copyright monopoly. This is probably because U.S. law has always valued and protected freedom of speech. As with the other "loopholes" that fair use of copyright offers those who use the copyrighted works of others, news reporting fair use does not give *carte blanche* to journalists to ignore the strictures of copyright. Rather, it is a starting point for determining whether a use is fair. That is, if your use involves news reporting, it *may* qualify as a fair use of a copyrighted work, depending on the circumstances. And it is helpful, in considering the analysis that must be made to determine fair use, to review what the copyright statute and the legislative history of the act have to say on the topic of news reporting.

The copyright statute lists four factors that courts must weigh in determining fair use; these factors are the starting point for any evaluation of fair use:

1. The purpose and character of the use, including whether such use is of a commercial nature or is for nonprofit educational purposes
2. The nature of the copyrighted work
3. The amount and substantiality of the portion used in relation to the copyrighted work as a whole
4. The effect of the use upon the potential market for or value of the copyrighted work

Although the copyright statute itself does not discuss the kinds of uses that may qualify as fair uses, several varieties of *news* uses that qualify as fair uses are specifically mentioned in the House Report that accompanied the 1976 Copyright Act. This is the pertinent language from the House Report:

> [Q]uotation of excerpts in a review or criticism for purposes of illustration or comment; quotation of short passages in a scholarly or technical work, for illustration or clarification of the author's observations; use in

a parody of some of the content of the work parodied; summary of an address or article, with brief quotations, in a news report; reproduction by a library of a portion of a work to replace part of a damaged copy; reproduction by a teacher or student of a small part of a work to illustrate a lesson; reproduction of a work in legislative or judicial proceedings or reports; incidental and fortuitous reproduction, in a newsreel or broadcast, of a work located in the scene of an event being reported.

Perhaps the best way to understand the sort of journalistic fair use permitted by copyright law is to consider several examples of the fair-use evaluation "in action." Here they are:

Is It Fair Use?

1 Your ambition is to land a job in TV news. To that end, you monitor a police scanner whenever you can in hopes of rushing to the scene of a bank robbery in progress or a big fire and scoring some video footage that one of the local stations will buy from you and run on the eleven o'clock news. The second half of the scenario is that no one but you is there to document the big news event, which is reported by the national news organizations, who want to buy your videotape of the event for some giant amount of money *and* hire you, thus catapulting you into a much higher tax bracket and a network job within days of your scoop. That's the dream, anyway.

One evening while you are on your way home from your day job at the furniture store, you hear on your scanner about a news story in progress and drive to a small, old movie theater that is now used only for screenings by the local film society. You find a police car in front of the theater and head into the auditorium with your camera because that seems to be where all the excitement is and because nobody stops you and tells you that you can't. You arrive just in time to see two tuxedo-clad men yelling and slugging each other and, unfortunately, a policeman who is trying to calm them down. The policeman's partner arrests both men, to the dismay of the audience for the movie that is still being projected during the fistfight despite the fact that most of the house lights are turned up. You get footage of the fight and the arrest along with a few comments ("Disgraceful!" "A disappointing display!") from well-dressed audience members as they exit the auditorium.

On your way to rush the videotape right over to Channel 9, you hear from one of the kids behind the lobby refreshment counter that the combatants are the film-society president, who is also a local councilman elected on a law-and-order platform, and the filmmaker for the movie that was being screened, who is a teacher at the local high school. You figure that Channel 9 will want to cover the story of a slugfest among the swells at a movie premiere. It seems that the law-and-order council-man felt obliged to apologize to the audience in advance of the screening of the teacher's film, which contained more nudity than the councilman approved of. The two men then had a heated discussion in the rear of the theater, which became the fistfight.

Channel 9 runs five minutes of your footage with a voice-over commentary from a reporter who, like the councilman, warns viewers in advance that there is what he calls "objectionable" content in the film, which is visible in the background of most of your videotape. You're starting to think that you may actually have what it takes to be a TV newshound when Channel 9 calls to tell you that you and they have been sued by the filmmaker-teacher, who objects to the fact that some of his short movie was aired on the local news without his permission. You think your career as a newsman is over before it begins until you call your old journalism professor to ask him for the name of a lawyer. Your professor says he does know a lawyer but that you don't need one. "What do you mean, I don't need a lawyer?" you say. "I've been sued for copyright infringement! In federal court! I'll never work in this town again!"

"Calm down, son," your professor says. "What you have done is not copyright infringement, and I expect that the lawsuit will be dismissed on summary judgment by the judge, if the lawyer for the TV station knows his stuff. This is a case of 'fortuitous reproduction.' "

"It's not very 'fortunate' for me," you say glumly.

"Not 'fortunate'—'fortuitous,' " your professor replies. "I guess you skipped English as often as you skipped my broadcast-law course. What you have done is reproduce by accident—or *incidentally*—a portion of the teacher's film in the course of filming a legitimate news story. Such incidental reproductions are a kind of fair use—a use of a copyrighted work that is not infringement because of the circum-stances surrounding the use. The public has a right to know what is going on—the citizens in that little city where you live have the right to know that a local council member and a local high school teacher have so little control that they behave like ill-mannered children in public. That means that your footage of the fistfight and the audience's reac-tion to it are news and that although the teacher's movie is visible in the background of your footage, your 'use' of that movie is a fair use. This is where the First Amendment meets copyright law—the First Amendment will always win if you cover a truly newsworthy event and little of the copyrighted work is reproduced or broadcast."

"Gee, thanks, Professor," you say. "I feel a lot better now. Guess I should have showed up more often for your class."

"Guess so," the professor says. "Tell the lawyer for the TV station that I am available as an expert witness—for a fee—if they need a briefing on broadcast law. And keep chasing ambulances—maybe Channel 9 will buy some more video from you."

Your professor proves to be right. The filmmaker's suit is dismissed on summary judgment, which you find out means that the judge agrees with the defendant that there is no real basis for the suit in the first place. You dig out your old broadcast-law textbook and buy a new, fancier, police scanner.

2   You are a rookie reporter for your city's daily newspaper. Because you are the lowest reporter on the totem pole, you are often given assignments no one else in the newsroom wants. One of these is covering various civic and professional organization lunch and dinner meetings; usually the speakers at these meetings are stunningly boring. However, you perk up during the monthly dinner meeting of the Springfield Registered Dieticians Alliance when the speaker, a college nutrition professor named Dr. Maybelle Johanson, starts recounting to her colleagues the results of her recent research.

It seems that Dr. Johanson and her staff got a large grant from the American Grocery Retailers Association to evaluate the nutrients—including calories, fat, sugar, and salt—in the dishes sold by ten popular American fast-food chains. After three years, Dr. Johanson and her researchers have completed their task and she is speaking at the meeting to give the members of the Dieticians Alliance the shocking news about many of the fast foods consumed by Americans. Her speech focuses on several of the most nutritionally harmful fast foods; when she recounts the number of calories and the amount of fat, sugar, and salt to be found in the entrees sold at several of the more popular fast-food restaurants in Springfield, the audience gasps at just how un-nutritious these dishes are.

You jot down many of the calorie counts and most of the bad news about the fat, sugar, and salt in what used to be some of your favorite fast-food meals. You leave the dinner meeting as soon as Dr. Johanson finishes her speech and don't stick around for the end of the program or the sale of autographed copies of Dr. Johanson's new book, *Fast-Food, Early Death*, because you have only a little over an hour to write up a short report about the meeting before the deadline for the next day's paper.

The next day, your story gets unusually good placement for a report on the meeting of a professional organization. The Metro editor made it the lead story in that section and used for the headline of the story the name of Dr. Johanson's book, *Fast-Food, Early Death*. And you are delighted to see that he used every bit of your story, including all the calorie counts you noted during the speech. On the whole, you are very pleased with yourself because you feel that your story reports on a topic that should be of interest to every reader of your newspaper and because the editor saw fit to use all of it in such a prominent position.

Your pleasure in the story is diminished considerably about an hour after the paper comes out, when you get a call from Dr. Johanson herself. You are anticipating that she will commend you for your accuracy in reporting her speech. Instead, you get an earful of abuse.

"How dare you quote the calorie counts and nutritional content of the fast-food dishes I mentioned in my speech!" she says. "I have a new book that contains all the food counts produced by my research. The research for that book was expensive and hard to accomplish, and I should be the one who profits from reporting what my research produced—not you! None of the readers of your newspaper will feel that they have to buy the book—you already gave them some of the most valuable information in it—for free! And you're not even a member of the Alliance! You shouldn't have been allowed to attend the dinner."

After Dr. Johanson stops yelling, you tell her that you'll let your editor know of her displeasure and that you'll call her back, because you are truly puzzled. You don't know exactly what you did to prompt such a reaction from such an educated woman, but you feel that if she's so mad, you must have done something pretty awful. Then you gather your courage and sit down with the Metro editor to let him know that Dr. Johanson is angry and is threatening to sue. For the first time since you came to work for the newspaper, you're glad that your editor is a gruff, tough old newspaper hand. He isn't spooked by the angry phone call. After questioning you carefully about the circumstances surrounding your story and examining your notes, your mean old editor grins at you!

"The Doc is just angry because she thinks we scooped her," he says. "She's probably so protective of her new book and of the royalties she thinks it's going to produce that she overreacted. She may be a brilliant researcher, but she doesn't know beans about journalism. Or the law."

"What do you mean?" you ask, warily. "Do you actually mean I didn't do anything wrong?"

"That's exactly what I mean, little lady," your editor says. "You work for a newspaper. We are in the news business. You were invited by the Springfield Registered Dieticians Alliance to attend their dinner meeting and to report on the proceedings. You did that. I can see by your notebook that you took extensive notes, and the Doc made no accusations of inaccuracy in your reporting, so you must have reported what she said accurately."

"But what about her book? She said that my story would hurt her sales," you respond.

"Well, that may or may not be so, but it's immaterial in any case," your editor says. "You have the right to accurately report her speech, to quote some of her comments, and to summarize the rest of it. That is called 'fair use' under copyright law. It's also the way news works in a free society. If she didn't want the content of her speech reported, she shouldn't have put that content into her speech. And I really doubt that what you wrote will have any effect at all on her book sales other than to promote them."

"Will you call her and tell her all this?" you ask. "I don't want her to yell at me again."

"No, I won't," your editor says. "That's your job. But if she is still yelling by the time you tell her what I said, tell her to see her lawyer. She'll learn that she has nothing to yell about" You call Dr. Johanson, who doesn't yell because she has been receiving calls for three hours from people who read about her speech in the newspaper and want to know where to buy her book. You try to sound as if you know what you're talking about when you tell her what your editor said and you do a pretty good job, but you plan to find out more about fair use before you cover another after-dinner speech.

3 You are an accountant by trade, but you also write a gardening column for the local daily newspaper. One week, your editor asks you to review a new gardening book, *Growing Roses in Maryland*, written and published by Timothy Allen, a local lawyer who is an enthusiastic rose grower. You find to your chagrin that Allen's book is filled with misinformation and bad advice, but you feel that you owe it to the readers of your column to point out his mistakes. You spend some time researching those of Allen's instructions and techniques that you feel would be ineffective or harmful if followed by readers of his book and when you write your review of it, you enumerate the most egregious of his errors, quoting the erroneous passages and then rebutting them.

Your long review of *Growing Roses in Maryland* is printed on the first page of the weekend Home and Garden section of the newspaper, under the headline "Growing Roses in Maryland? Don't Buy This Book." You feel that your review is fair and that it does a real service to fans of your column by warning them away from faulty advice.

Timothy Allen does not agree. He calls your office and leaves a message to tell you that he's planning to sue you for libel and copyright infringement. You're terrified when you read the message—after all, he *is* a lawyer. That evening you call your son, who is a third-year law student. He says he'll research your situation and get back to you. What you want to know is whether Allen can really sue you—and win—for what you wrote about his gardening book. Your son calls you back on Sunday afternoon.

"I've got your answers, Mom," he says. "I don't think you have anything to worry about." He tells you that he thinks your review of

Allen's book, no matter how negative, will not subject you to a claim for copyright infringement or libel—at least not a successful claim, anyway. "As a book reviewer, you have the right and duty to state your honest opinion of the book you are reviewing," he says.

"But I'm really only an accountant," you protest.

"Not when you're writing a book review," your son replies. "Reviewing a book in a newspaper makes you a book reviewer and invokes the protections of the First Amendment, which gives you the right to publish your opinion of Allen's book. Opinions are not actionable as libel, so that part of his threat won't hold water. And quoting sections of his book in your review is 'fair use,' not copyright infringement; the copyright statute specifically allows—wait, I have the statutory language here somewhere—'quotation of excerpts in a review or criticism for purposes of illustration or comment.' So he can't sue you for copyright infringement, either."

"But he's a lawyer," you say. "Why would he threaten to sue me when he knows he would lose if he did?"

"Maybe he doesn't know he has no grounds for suit," your son says. "Maybe he does know, but he's just a bully. Either way, I don't think you're in any trouble." Your son proves to be right.

When you tell your editor that Allen threatened to sue you, your editor says, "Yeah. He called here with the same message. Our lawyer called him back and told him he was out of his league—that he has no grounds for suit. That shut him up. I hope you weren't worried."

"Not really," you say. "And if you've got any other gardening books to review, let me know."

CHAPTER 7

Fair Use in Creative Works

IT'S SOMETIMES HARD TO DETERMINE whether uses of copyrighted works in creative works are permissible as fair uses, because creative people are often, well, *creative* in the ways they use the works of others. Again, the only real guidance we have in evaluating fair use in creative works is what the copyright statute and the legislative history of the act have to say about situations in which the doctrine of fair use applies.

The four factors mentioned in the copyright statue that courts must evaluate when determining fair use are:

1. The purpose and character of the use, including whether such use is of a commercial nature or is for nonprofit educational purposes
2. The nature of the copyrighted work
3. The amount and substantiality of the portion used in relation to the copyrighted work as a whole
4. The effect of the use upon the potential market for or value of the copyrighted work

The House Report that accompanied the 1976 Copyright Act mentions several examples of uses of copyrighted works that qualify as fair uses. This list is not exhaustive—that is, the examples of permitted uses are not the only uses that could conceivably qualify as fair uses—but it does demonstrate the extent and character of uses that Congress intended to allow:

> [Q]uotation of excerpts in a review or criticism for purposes of illustration or comment; quotation of short passages in a scholarly or technical work, for illustration or clarification of the author's observations; use in a parody of some of the content of the work parodied; summary of an address or article, with brief quotations, in a news report; reproduction by a library of a portion of a work to replace part of a damaged copy; reproduction by

a teacher or student of a small part of a work to illustrate a lesson; reproduction of a work in legislative or judicial proceedings or reports; incidental and fortuitous reproduction, in a newsreel or broadcast, of a work located in the scene of an event being reported.

The best way to understand what uses of copyrighted works copyright law permits creative people to make is to consider several examples of the fair-use evaluation involving creative works. Here they are:

IS IT FAIR USE?

1 You are the lead guitarist for a rock band. Your band has saved some of its profits from playing the frat-party circuit and books studio time to record an album. You don't have a record deal, but you figure that you can sell your CD after gigs and on the Internet through CD Baby. You and the other guys in the band spend several long nights in the studio before your album is finished, but you like the product and think your fans will like it, too. You are especially proud of your original arrangement of the old Jimmy Buffett standard "Margaritaville" and feel that the band's recording of your arrangement of this song is the centerpiece of the album.

The finished CD is a hit. You sell twenty copies the first night you announce from the stage that it's available for sale and within two weeks you have sold almost fifty CDs through CD Baby. You feel pretty good about the album—and the money you're making from it—until you run into a musician from a rival band at your next club date. His name is Bongo and he thinks he knows everything. Bongo tells you that he has heard your new CD, that he thinks it's "pretty good for a party band," and that he's glad you came out with your CD before he and his band release theirs so that you'll be able to sell a few copies before all your fans start flocking to their shows.

You withstand Bongo's boasting by ignoring it until he says something that catches your attention. He asks, "So, all the songs on your CD are original except for "Margaritaville"—how much do you have to pay Jimmy Buffett when you sell a CD?" You brush him off by telling him you can't talk any longer because you're due onstage again shortly, but his question leaves you wondering whether he could be right. Maybe you do owe Jimmy Buffett money every time you sell one of your CDs. But, then, again, you and the band recorded your arrangement of "Margaritaville" and it's significantly different from his original version.

You make an appointment with a music lawyer to find out what the situation is. The lawyer, a really cool guy named Eric who's not much older than you, listens to your story, asks a few questions, and says, "Well, I think you owe Jimmy Buffett some money."

"But why?" you ask. "I worked for several days on my arrangement of 'Margaritaville'—it's really different, and longer, than his version. Don't I get some sort of credit for my work, for my arrangement?"

Eric listens and says, "Maybe. Whether an arranger of a copyrighted song gets credit for his work depends on two things—whether the arrangement is significant enough to amount to a new version of the underlying song and whether the arranger has permission to create a new version of the song. If the arrangement is just a particular method of playing the song and doesn't include any significant changes in the underlying music, it's not protectable by copyright—it's just a way of playing the song as the song is written. And if the arrangement *is* more than just a particular method of playing the song and *does* include significant changes in the underlying music, it's a derivative work based on the original song and it is thus protectable by copyright. However, in order to create a derivative work from a copyrighted work you have to have the permission of the owner of the copyright. Have you spoken to Mr. Buffett or to anybody at Coral Reefer Music to get permission to create this arrangement—this derivative work—from his song?"

"Uh, that would be a no," you say. "I didn't know I needed anybody's permission to write an arrangement."

"You don't," Eric says, "unless the arrangement amounts to a new version of the song."

"I don't think I understand," you say.

"Let's review," he says. "You don't own an arrangement unless it amounts to a new version of the song, and because you can't create a new version of the song without permission from the copyright owner, you don't even own your arrangement *then*, since no copyright owner is going to give you permission to create a new version of a song without also requiring that you sign over ownership of that new version to the copyright owner—in this case, to Coral Reefer Music."

"Sounds like I can't win for losing," you say.

"Well, think of it this way," Eric says, "you can write new versions of public-domain songs all day long without anyone's permission. And you will own any new version of a public-domain song that you write."

"Like that's got anything to do with pop music!" you say.

"That's where Elvis got one of his hits," he says. " 'Love Me Tender' is just a reworking of a popular Civil War-era ballad called 'Aura Lee.' "

"No kidding?" you say.

"It's true," Eric says. "And more than one songwriter has used the melody from a piece of classical music as the basis of a new song. If you know a few famous classical melodies, you can recognize them in new versions throughout every era of pop music."

"So how much do we owe Jimmy Buffett?" you ask.

"Taking into account your sales to date," Eric replies, "not much. I'll call Coral Reefer and let them know we'll be sending a small check soon. And if you don't mind, I'm going to keep this CD. I've heard about you guys and I'd like to pitch you to a buddy of mine who owns a small record company distributed by a much bigger one." You are glad to find out you're not going to copyright jail and glad that Eric knows somebody at a record company. And you grin when you imagine how envious Bongo will be if you and your band get a record deal.

2   You are a painter whose beautiful landscapes sell very well as limited-edition art prints. You like your job, but it keeps you busy and you don't have time to sketch interesting vistas on the spot anymore but must rely on photographs and your own imagination. Most of the photos you use are your own, and many of the scenes you paint are imaginary or include picturesque elements from several different photos. Your newest painting is a depiction of a real scene, however. It's a beautiful red barn surrounded by a field of sunflowers. You didn't find this lovely scene yourself—not in real life, that is—but spotted it on a calendar as the cover photograph. You don't recognize the name of the photographer, but you do recognize a good eye for perspective when you see it. You use the photograph of the red barn in the sunflower field as a reference when you create your painting. In fact, your painting and the reference photograph would be identical except for the facts that your painting is considerably larger than the calendar photo and that you added a pair of barn swallows flying through the hall of the red barn and three cows standing beside it. The publisher of the limited-edition prints of your paintings is delighted with your newest creation and predicts that prints of *Red Barn and Sunflowers* will sell very well.

But right after the prints go on sale in his new spring catalog, he calls to tell you that he received an angry phone call from the calendar photographer, who is accusing you of copyright infringement. When you call the photographer, you point out that you used his photograph only as a reference, that you added the birds and the cows to the image, and that, in any event, you could have spotted the actual red barn yourself and made sketches or taken your own photo. He doesn't buy your arguments and tells you that you'd better call a lawyer because he's getting ready to sue you. You hang up and call your lawyer. What you want her to tell you is that your use of the calendar photo is a fair use of that photo and that you're not guilty of copyright infringement. Unfortunately, being a skilled lawyer, she can't do that.

"You're in a jam," she says. "The photographer is right. The use you made of his photo is not a fair use. It's infringement."

"I don't understand," you say. "Using a photo as a reference for a painting is infringement? That barn is there for anyone to see—for anyone to paint! And I *added* some elements to my painting. Why isn't it fair use?"

She says, in a calm voice that makes you nervous, "Using a photo as a reference—to figure out what the human body looks like in a particular position, for instance, or to paint a tree accurately—is all right; copying the whole photograph is not—it's infringement, not fair use. And let's just consider the four factors for determining fair use that are listed in the copyright statute. The first factor is 'the purpose and character of the use, including whether the use is a commercial use.' Your use of his photo is definitely commercial—you sell prints of your paintings," she says. "And the second factor, 'the nature of the copyrighted work,' is no help to you, either, since your limited-edition prints are similar to the use he makes of his photo—both of you are selling the image. Are you with me so far?"

"I suppose," you say, grudgingly.

"O.K., the third factor is 'the amount and substantiality of the portion used in relation to the copyrighted work as a whole'—as I understand it, you used essentially the whole photograph as a—what did you call it?—'reference' when you painted *Red Barn and Sunflowers*, right? So that can't help get you off the hook. And the fourth factor, 'the effect of the use upon the potential market for or value of the copyrighted work,' is just as damning—the photographer said your prints would kill sales of copies of his photo, didn't he?"

"Yes," you say, "he did. So what you're telling me is that the additions I made to the image and my skill as a painter and the fact that I could have stood on the same hill he did and painted the same exact scene—you're telling me that none of that makes any difference at all?"

"Sorry," she says, "but you *copied* a copyrighted photograph. Your additions and your skills as a painter don't change that fact. We'd better settle with him. And you need to get out more. You wouldn't have this problem if you had worked from your own sketches of the barn."

"Send me your bill," you say as you hang up. Then you remember that there's a covered bridge near your brother's home and that you haven't seen him for nearly a year.

3 You have collected interesting quotations for years. You find them in magazine articles, on television shows, in books, and in movies. You also have amassed a large collection of books of quotations, and when you have the time you read them and mark the quotations you think are particularly memorable. One day when you are organizing your quotations files, you realize that you have a large number of quotations about cats. This isn't surprising, since you are a cat lover and because many articulate people over the centuries have been as crazy for cats as you are. You realize that you have collected more than enough cat quotations to fill a little book. You type your cat quotations into your computer and take the resulting collection to a copy shop, where they turn your pages into a nice little spiral-bound book.

You give copies of your homemade book to your cat-loving friends as birthday presents. They are all delighted with your compilation of cat quotations. In fact, one of your fellow cat lovers shows your little book to her sister, who is the owner of a small book publishing company. This woman calls to offer you a contract to publish your book of cat quotations. You are ecstatic until your neighbor, who is a dog person, bursts your bubble. "I'm sure that's a very interesting collection of quotations," she says, "for people who don't own a dog. But how did you ever get permission from all these people to use what they said in your book? Like this quote by, uh, some guy named Montaigne: 'When I play with my cat, who knows if I am not a pastime to her more than she is to me?' How'd you get *his* permission—especially with only one name?"

You show your neighbor and her big, ugly dog out of your house and start worrying. Then you call your brother, who teaches law at the state university. "I think I'm in trouble, Mark," you say.

"Just what did you do, sis?" he says. You describe your project and recount your conversation with your neighbor.

"I signed the publishing contract already because I thought I had finished the book," you tell him. "But if I have to contact everybody in the book whose quotations I used, I can't possibly deliver my manuscript when I said I would. Do you think they'll sue me?"

"Do I think *who* will sue you?" he answers. "The publisher, or the people whose quotations you used?"

"I meant the publisher," you say. "I'm afraid that they'll sue me for non-delivery or something. But wait—you mean the people I quoted can sue me, too! I can't believe my little book is going to result in *two* lawsuits and I haven't made a nickel from it yet!"

"Hold on, sis," your brother says in a soothing voice. "I don't think anyone is going to sue you." Then he asks some questions; he wants to know how many quotations you used in your book, how long the quotations are, how many sources you consulted to gather them, and how many of the quotations you used came from each source. Then he gives you good news.

"There is no copyright in short quotations like the ones you have used in your book. Short quotations like the ones usually used in books of quotations are simply too short to qualify for copyright protection. That means that you can copy them from almost any source so long as you don't use too many from any one source; that's because a compiler—like you—does have rights in the compilation *as a whole*," he says. "Because you don't need permission from any of the speakers or from any magazine or book publisher or author to use the short quotations you've gathered, you don't have to worry about not meeting your publisher's deadline. But you should have thought of all this before you signed a publishing agreement, and you should be very careful never to use long quotations without permission or to take more than a very small percentage of the content from any published work."

"Got to go, bro," you say. "I've got to take my cat for a walk. And maybe visit my neighbor—I want to break the news that Montaigne is dead and that I didn't need his permission anyway."

4 You are a first-year law student who works as a freelance writer to earn part of your living expenses. Freelancing doesn't pay very well, but it's interesting and it lets you fit your work around the demands of your classes. And you're hopeful that as you build a portfolio of work, your freelancing income will increase. This means that you're excited when a friend of a friend asks you to write a biographical sketch about B.B. King to be used in a small booklet that will accompany the newly mastered release on CD of some of King's most significant recordings. The pay is good and you're anxious to do a good job. You do some Internet research and spend some time at the local library and end up with a pile of copies of published articles about King. You write your essay over one long weekend, using information and quotations from the articles you have gathered. You're planning to e-mail the article to the re-issue record company until your friend Fred reads it. His questions make you uncomfortable.

"You mean you interviewed B.B. King?" Fred asks. "How did you manage to land an interview with him? And where did you get all this information about where he was born and his childhood and the early days of his career and his success as a musician? You must have had to talk to a lot of other people, too, to get all that! I'm impressed!"

"Actually," you say. "I didn't talk to anybody. But those quotes from King are all accurate. I got them from interviews he has given over the years. And all that other stuff—the quotations from other people and all that information about his life—all that came from other articles about him that I collected before I wrote my piece."

"Huh," Fred says. "Aren't you worried that somebody will sue? Isn't what you did like downloading music through a file-swapping service? Or like plagiarism, or something?"

You assure Fred that you didn't do anything wrong, but the next day you look up the intellectual-property law professor whose class in copyright law you'll take next year. You show him a printout of your essay on B.B. King and the fat file folder that contains the photo-copies of all your source material. Then you ask him what changes you need to make before you send off your article to avoid being guilty of infringement. He makes you point out where you got each quotation in your story and each statement of fact. Then he reads your essay, stroking his little goatee all the while. You're prepared to hear him tell you that there's no way to fix your article—that you need to begin all over again, research every fact yourself, and spend hours on the phone trying to interview the people you quote in your article, including King. Just thinking about the work involved makes your head hurt. But then Professor Robinson gives his judgment.

"I don't think you have anything to worry about," he says. "It seems to me that every use you have made of other people's materi-als is a fair use. I can't see that anyone has any legitimate reason to complain about your essay."

You resist the urge to kiss Professor Robinson. "How can that be?" you ask. "I got every single fact in that article from the stories of other writers. And I didn't talk to a single person who is quoted—I got all those quotes from other writers, too. It didn't feel wrong when I did it, but Fred Karpinsky—you know, he's in your copyright class this year—Fred made me feel like a crook."

"Ah, yes, Mr. Karpinsky," Professor Robinson says. "He must have been reading ahead in the textbook again. And he must have misinterpreted what he read, as usual. He may have meant well, but Mr. Karpinsky is no Melville Nimmer."

"Who?" you ask.

"The famous writer of a standard treatise on copyright law," Professor Robinson says. "Nimmer really *understood* copyright law—in fact, you could say that Melville Nimmer was no Fred Karpinsky. So to speak."

"It appears not," you say. "I'm very interested in what Nimmer would have said about my article, if he would have let me off the hook."

"Well, perhaps I can tell you what Nimmer would have said," Professor Robinson says. "First, there is no copyright in facts. That means that none of the historical information you used in your article is protectable by copyright, so there is no sin in taking that information from other articles."

"What about the quotations?" you ask again.

"Well, it is true that the person who conducts an interview will own the copyright in the interview, even though the meat of the interview is in the quotations from the subject of the interview," Professor Robinson adds. "That is, the interviewer, because he or she asks the questions and records both the questions asked and the answers of the interview subject, owns the copyright in the interview. But facts of all sorts are granted less protection than creative works and these quotations are like facts—they are information conveyed by conversation of people who knew and worked with B.B. King. And there is such a thing as fair use of copyrighted works. Using short sections of an interview—short quotations as you have used here—is a fair use of an interview, even if it was conducted by someone else. All your quotations are less than three sentences long, and you appear to have used small parts of ten or twelve published articles, rather than taking the quotations from only one or two articles. That means that the portion taken from any one, copyrighted article is small, and that means it is a fair use."

"Gee, that's great!" you say. "So, basically, you're saying that I never have to do any original research for any article."

"Not so quick, Ms. Trent," the professor says. "You're on the safe side of copyright law in this instance, but it's a dangerous thing to go around using the work of other people too freely in your own creations. Any quotation that is long enough to be treated as a 'block quote' deserves some scrutiny to determine whether it is such a substantial part of the work from which it was taken that using it constitutes copyright infringement. If you had used longer quotations or had taken the quotations from a smaller number of published articles, you could very well be in big trouble, depending on whose rights you violated. Remember, I said that interviews are protected by copyright."

"But not facts," you say.

"Not facts," he agrees. "However, you should know and remember that even factual works are protected by copyright as a whole—it's just that each individual piece of information is unprotectable. Again, had you taken all your facts from one or two published articles, you could be in trouble, depending on the circumstances. Be careful about taking a significant amount from any copyrighted source, no matter what the nature of the material you take."

"So, Prof," you say, "can I publish this as is, or not?"

"You may," Professor Robinson says, "but I give you my blessing only if you promise to be more careful in the future and to read this law review article about fair use of copyright. It's one of my better efforts."

"Gee, thanks," you say. "I think I'll give it to Fred after I've read it."

CHAPTER 8

Fair Use in Education

THE USE BY EDUCATORS, WITHOUT PERMISSION, of copyrighted material is one of the sorts of uses that can be a fair use, according to the copyright statute, which specifically mentions "nonprofit educational purposes" as one of the purposes for which the rules of copyright infringement are suspended—a little—in the right situations. However, too many people think that if there is any way at all to characterize their use as educational, they may do whatever they want with a copyrighted work. This is a dangerous position and it leads teachers of all sorts all over the United States to mistake infringing uses for fair uses of copyrighted material. A review of the pertinent language in the copyright statute and the legislative history of the act make it clear that other factors must be considered and that fair use of a work for educational purposes has limitations.

The four statutory factors that courts must consider in determining fair use are:

1. The purpose and character of the use, including whether such use is of a commercial nature or is for nonprofit educational purposes
2. The nature of the copyrighted work
3. The amount and substantiality of the portion used in relation to the copyrighted work as a whole
4. The effect of the use upon the potential market for or value of the copyrighted work

The House Report that accompanied the 1976 Copyright Act mentions uses of copyrighted works that qualify as fair uses:

[Q]uotation of excerpts in a review or criticism for purposes of illustration or comment; quotation of short passages in a scholarly or technical work, for illustration or clarification of the author's observations; use in a parody of some of the content of the work parodied; summary of an address or article, with brief quotations, in a news report; reproduction by a library of a portion of a work to replace part of a damaged copy; reproduction by a teacher or student of a small part of a work to illustrate a lesson; reproduction of a work in legislative or judicial proceedings or reports; incidental and fortuitous reproduction, in a newsreel or broadcast, of a work located in the scene of an event being reported.

But there is much more pertinent language in the same House Report to guide educators. The House Report also includes a lengthy but informative section that specifically discusses classroom reproduction of books and periodicals. Incorporated into this discussion are "Guidelines for Classroom Copying in Not-For-Profit Educational Institutions with Respect to Books and Periodicals," which were agreed upon by representatives of the Ad Hoc Committee of Educational Institutions and Organizations on Copyright Law Revision and of the Authors League of America, Inc., and the Association of American Publishers, Inc. These guidelines were written for the purpose of insertion into the House Committee Report. Also included in the House Report are a similar set of guidelines, written to guide educators who teach and study music, agreed upon by representatives of the Music Publishers' Association of the United States, Inc., the National Music Publishers' Association, Inc., the Music Teachers National Association, the Music Educators National Conference, the National Association of Schools of Music, and the Ad Hoc Committee on Copyright Law Revision. (The Copyright Office publishes a thorough booklet called *Reproduction of Copyrighted Works by Educators and Librarians* that discusses the House Report at length, as well as other important parts of the legislative history of the present copyright statute that deal with the question of fair use of copyright by educators and librarians. This booklet, called Circular 21, is available from the Copyright Office free of charge and can be printed off or read on the Copyright Office Web site.)

Both the books-and-periodicals guidelines and those for music are prefaced by this statement, which is an important indicator as to the scope of authority intended for both sets of guidelines:

The purpose of the following guidelines is to state the minimum and not the maximum standards of educational fair use under Section 107 [the fair-use section] of H.R. 2223 [the House version of the bill eventually adopted as the U.S. Copyright Statute]. The parties agree that the conditions determining the extent of permissible copying for educational purposes may change in the future; that certain types of copying permitted under these guidelines may not be permissible in the future; and conversely that in the future other types of copying not permitted under these guidelines may be permissible under revised guidelines.

Moreover, the following statement of guidelines is not intended to limit the types of copying permitted under the standards of fair use under judicial decision and which are stated in Section 107 of the Copyright

Revision Bill [the four statutory factors reproduced above]. There may be instances in which copying which does not fall within the guidelines stated below may nonetheless be permitted under the criteria of fair use.

These guidelines, as we have seen, are not definitive. However, they are probably a more reliable guide than several other sets of guidelines created and promulgated by various groups and consortiums in an effort to clarify exactly what is and is not fair use. This includes the CONTU guidelines mentioned in chapter 5, even though using them is far preferable to proceeding under the blind assumption that any use in education is fair use. The question of fair use in education is just as complicated as the question of fair use in other settings. However, the House Report guidelines, which accompanied the House version of the (eventual) new copyright statute are, as are other sections of the House Report, very instructive on the question of what sort of uses legislators and representatives of concerned organizations felt were fair and proper. The texts of the two sets of guidelines follow:

Guidelines for Educational Uses of Books and Periodicals
I. *Single Copying for Teachers*
    A single copy may be made of any of the following by or for a teacher at his or her individual request for his or her scholarly research or use in teaching and preparation to teach a class:
    A. A chapter from a book
    B. An article from a periodical or newspaper
    C. A short story, short essay or short poem, whether or not from a collective work
    D. A chart, graph, diagram, drawing, cartoon or picture from a book, periodical, or newspaper
II. *Multiple Copies for Classroom Use*
    Multiple copies (not to exceed in any event more than one copy per pupil in a course) may be made by or for the teacher giving the course for classroom use or discussion, *provided that*:
    A. The copying meets the tests of brevity and spontaneity as defined below; *and,*
    B. Meets the cumulative effect test as defined below; *and,*
    C. Each copy includes a notice of copyright.
    Definitions
        Brevity
        (i) Poetry: (a) A complete poem if less than 250 words and if printed on not more than two pages or, (b) from a longer poem, an excerpt of not more than 250 words.
        (ii) Prose: (a) either a complete article, story or essay of less than 2,500 words, or (b) an excerpt from any prose work of not more than 1,000 words or 10% of the work, whichever is less, but in any event a minimum of 500 words. (Each of

the numerical limits stated in "i" and "ii" above may be expanded to permit the completion of an unfinished line of a poem or of an unfinished prose paragraph.)

(iii) Illustration: One chart, graph, diagram, drawing, cartoon or picture per book or per periodical issue.

(iv) "Special" works: Certain works in poetry, prose or in "poetic prose" which often combine language with illustrations and which are intended sometimes for children and at other times for a more general audience fall short of 2,500 words in their entirety. Paragraph "ii" above notwithstanding, such "special works" may not be reproduced in their entirety; however, an excerpt comprising not more than two of the published pages of such special work and containing not more than 10% of the words found in the text thereof, may be reproduced.

Spontaneity

(i) The copying is at the instance and inspiration of the individual teacher, and

(ii) The inspiration and decision to use the work and the moment of its use for maximum teaching effectiveness are so close in time that it would be unreasonable to expect a timely reply to a request for permission.

Cumulative Effect

(i) The copying of the material is for only one course in the school in which the copies are made.

(ii) Not more than one short poem, article, story, essay or two excerpts may be copied from the same author, nor more than three from the same collective work or periodical volume during one class term.

(iii) There shall not be more than nine instances of such multiple copying for one course during one class term. (The limitations stated in "ii" and "iii" above shall not apply to current news periodicals and newspapers and current news sections of other periodicals.)

III. *Prohibitions as to I and II Above*

Notwithstanding any of the above, the following shall be prohibited:

A. Copying shall not be used to create or to replace or substitute for anthologies, compilations or collective works. Such replacement or substitution may occur whether copies of various works or excerpts therefrom are accumulated or reproduced and used separately.

B. There shall be no copying of or from works intended to be "consumable" in the course of study or of teaching. These include workbooks, exercises, standardized tests and test booklets and answer sheets and like consumable material.

C. Copying shall not:
   (i) substitute for the purchase of books, publishers' reprints or periodicals;
   (ii) be directed by higher authority;
   (iii) be repeated with respect to the same item by the same teacher from term to term.
   (iv) No charge shall be made to the student beyond the actual cost of the photocopying.

Similarly, the guidelines for the use of music cannot settle all questions of fair use of music by educators, but they do suggest the kinds and extent of uses that are deemed to be fair and proper by the music industry groups and legislators who wrote them. These are the music guidelines:

Guidelines for Educational Uses of Music

A. *Permissible Uses*
   1. Emergency copying to replace purchased copies which for any reason are not available for an imminent performance provided purchased replacement copies shall be substituted in due course.
   2. For academic purposes other than performance, single or multiple copies of excerpts of works may be made, provided that the excerpts do not comprise a part of the whole which would constitute a performable unit such as a section, movement or aria, but in no case more than 10 percent of the whole work. The number of copies shall not exceed one copy per pupil.
   3. Printed copies which have been purchased may be edited or simplified provided that the fundamental character of the work is not distorted or the lyrics, if any, altered or lyrics added if none exist.
   4. A single copy of recordings of performances by students may be made for evaluation or rehearsal purposes and may be retained by the educational institution or individual teacher.
   5. A single copy of a sound recording (such as a tape, disc or cassette) of copyrighted music may be made from sound recordings owned by an educational institution or an individual teacher for the purposes of constructing aural exercises or examinations and may be retained by the educational institution or individual teacher. (This pertains only to the copyright of the music itself and not to any copyright which may exist in the sound recording.)
B. *Prohibitions*
   1. Copying to create or replace or substitute for anthologies, compilations or collective works.
   2. Copying of or from works intended to be "consumable" in the course of study or of teaching such as workbooks, exercises, standardized tests and answer sheets and like material.

3. Copying for the purpose of performance, except as in A(1) above.
4. Copying for the purpose of substituting for the purchase of music, except as in A(1) and A(2) above.
5. Copying without inclusion of the copyright notice which appears on the printed copy.

Anyone who is smart enough to be a teacher—of anything—can probably figure out from these guidelines whether copying is permitted in a given situation and the amount of copying that is deemed permissible. However, a few examples of the educational fair use question can help clarify just what is and what is not permitted. Here are several:

IS IT FAIR USE?

1 Because you want to help your students save money, you don't ask them to buy the $12 paperback edition of the Samuel Beckett play *Happy Days* at the campus bookstore but instead make twenty photocopies of the play and distribute them to your Modern Drama class—after all, you plan to spend only a few days on the play before moving on to another play. Your office mate, who is, like you, just a newly hired associate professor, is vocal in his disapproval of your actions when he notices the stack of photocopied and stapled copies of the play on your desk. You tell him that because you made the copies for classroom use by students at a nonprofit university, you are simply taking advantage of the "fair-use" doctrine, which holds that some otherwise infringing uses of copyrighted works are permissible if made for certain purposes—such as classroom instruction. Your office mate refuses to believe that educational uses always qualify as fair use.

You dismiss his concerns until the day after you have distributed the copies of the Beckett play to your students. You get a note telling you that the university counsel wants to talk to you. Puzzled as to why the university lawyer wants to see you, you walk directly over to his office. He asks you a few questions about your Modern Drama class and the Beckett play and your photocopies of it, and then he tells you that you need to ask your students to turn in the photocopies, that you should then bring them all to him, and that he will personally supervise you while you use his office shredder to destroy them. You are indignant. "Why do I have to retrieve those photocopies?" you ask. "And why do they have to be shredded? Haven't you ever heard of fair use?"

The university lawyer's reply is curt. "I've heard of fair use, just as you have. The difference is that I understand it," he says. "Fair use is a doctrine of copyright law that permits some uses of copyrighted works on the grounds that those uses are made in the pursuit of some goal that we as a society want to encourage. Education is one of the goals that can excuse the use, without permission, of copyrighted works. But *not every* use of a copyrighted work for educational purposes is a *fair* use. Your making twenty copies of the entire Beckett play is an example of a use that is *not* a fair use. First of all, you have made too many copies of too much of the play—had you made three copies of two pages of it, to pass around to your students in class or to project with an overhead projector, you would have been all right. Secondly, you have affected the market for the published play—I'd say you have deprived the publisher of the American paperback edition of *Happy Days* of twenty sales. Beckett's play was first published in 1961, and Beckett didn't die until 1989. That means that *Happy Days* is still protected by copyright and will be for several more decades. You can't legally do what you did with his play until you're very old. Third, you charged for the photocopied plays—five dollars per student, I'm told—and I know you didn't have to pay for the photocopying because you had the English department secretary make them on the department photocopier. You can't substitute and sell your own bootleg copies of the play for the one the publisher sells—it's piracy and you're lucky I'm letting you off without writing a letter to your department chairman. Any questions?"

You don't have any, and you trudge back to his office the following day, after picking up all twenty of your illicit photocopies, which you then shred one by one. You are embarrassed by the whole situation, but you never again forget that even educators can infringe copyrights.

2 You are a third-grade teacher and you are having problems teaching your class the multiplication tables. You think that your students need more practice with their multiplication, but you don't like the exercises given in their math textbook. Then you buy a great math workbook online from a teacher-supply company; this workbook is filled with one-page multiplication exercises that are graduated from easy to difficult. You start with the first one by making a photocopy of the exercise for each of your pupils. The kids finish it off quickly, so you copy the second exercise for the next day. They also work the problems in the second exercise quickly. It seems that having problems they can work is increasing their confidence, so you proceed through the workbook, giving them copies of another worksheet every day.

You are happy with your plan until your principal sees you making copies one afternoon and asks what you are copying. You eagerly explain your plan and emphasize how well it seems to be working. "Maybe for your students," your principal answers, "but not for the school board. You can't do what you're doing without subjecting the county school system to the possibility of a claim for copyright infringement."

"Why?" you ask. "I bought the workbook, fair and square."

"Yes," your principal says, "but the . . . what? . . . $11.95 you paid for it didn't give you the right to make twenty copies of each exercise in it. Before the end of the term you will have, in essence, created a copy of this workbook for each of your twenty students."

"But I thought classroom use of copyrighted materials was permissible," you say. "Isn't it called 'fair use'?"

"An educational use can be a fair use of a copyrighted work, but the mere fact that you use a work in a classroom doesn't turn *any* use into a fair use," she answers. "You are reproducing what is known as a 'consumable' copyrighted work. That is specifically prohibited in the guidelines for classroom use of books that were agreed upon by various author and publisher groups before the current copyright act was passed."

"But how am I supposed to teach my kids the multiplication tables?" you ask. "The exercises in their textbook aren't nearly as good as these exercises."

"I suggest that you find another way," your principal says. "Because I am confiscating this workbook. Good day, Ms. Adams."

"Good day, Mrs. Jordan," you say. Then you get a brainstorm. You can't copy the workbook to use in class, but no one says you can't come up with your own worksheets. You spend part of the weekend designing worksheets similar to those in the workbook. You don't copy the workbook—your principal took it with her, along with the copies you were making—but you use the same system of focusing on one small section of the multiplication tables your kids are studying in each worksheet. It doesn't take long to come up with each worksheet, and you are able to create a week's worth over the weekend. You take a set to Mrs. Jordan on Monday.

"I solved my problem," you say. "I created my own worksheets. You'll see that I printed them off my home computer and then duplicated them in the copy room. I thought you'd like to see the first five of my worksheets."

"Very good, Ms. Adams," Mrs. Jordan says. "I like a teacher who can overcome an obstacle so creatively. I think I'll put a note in your personnel file about this." You are so happy to have gained Mrs. Jordan's approval after her lecture to you about copyright that you ask her for a copy of the guidelines she mentioned and are very careful to avoid any further copying of workbooks. You also save the exercises you write for the day when you may publish your own math workbook.

3 In order to make an attractive copy of each of the articles you have assembled for your *Twenty-First Century Biology* anthology, you pay a student to type the short articles into your office computer. The articles for your anthology are from a weekly publication called *Science News*, so you are careful to see that there is an attribution and citation at the end of each of the articles you include. Each term, you update your collection of *Science News* articles, replacing outdated reports with newer pieces. Then you have the revised and updated collection of printouts photocopied and spiral-bound at a local copy shop. You sell your *Twenty-First Century Biology* anthologies to your students at your cost. You feel that your anthology keeps your students excited about biology as a discipline and informed about new discoveries in the field.

Then one semester a troublemaker signs up for your class. His name is Rob, and he questions you right away about the newest edition of your anthology. It seems that Rob's dad is a science writer and that he once worked as a *Science News* editor. Rob asks you whom you talk to at *Science News* when you call to get permission to reprint their stories. You manage to avoid answering his question, but you decide to seek out the advice of the university law librarian, a friend of yours who also happens to be a lawyer.

When he hears your story, he is horrified. "You can't do that!" he says. "You could get the university sued!"

"What do you mean?" you ask. "I *subscribe* to *Science News*, and every one of the articles I use is properly attributed. And I seldom take more than one story from any single issue of the magazine. Anyway, I figure that I'm doing *Science News* a favor—probably lots of my students will go on to subscribe to it."

"You are too smart to be so dumb," your friend the librarian says. "This is *not* fair use. What you are doing is copyright infringement. You can't escape blame for copyright infringement by attribution of the articles—that's just naming the publication you stole from. And one article from each issue of *Science News* is more than enough to constitute infringement—I've seen that publication, and it's never more than about eight pages long. And I don't think *Science News* will feel that you're doing them any favors—copying their stories for your so-called anthology and requiring your students to buy it is stealing from them. They may feel that some of those students would have bought a subscription to their publication by now if you hadn't made it unnecessary."

"What can I do?" you ask.

"First of all, retrieve every copy of your so-called anthology from your students," he says. "And destroy the computer files that contain copies of *Science News* articles. And *never do this again* without permission in advance from *Science News*. Ask the librarian to subscribe to *Science News* for the library and from now on, send your students there to read any pieces you consider critical. You could also submit your personal copy of the magazine or *one* photocopy of the article to the library's 'course reserve' department, where students can access heavily used or hard-to-find material for classes. Check with the library for details on their policy. Or encourage your students to get their own subscriptions to *Science News*.

You do what he says, but mainly because he told you that he'd report you to the university counsel's office if you didn't—"for your own good," he says. Then you sign up to audit a course in copyright law at the law school so you won't make such a dumb mistake again.

4 You are the music director for a high school choral group and you are looking for something different for the choral group to perform for the annual school talent show. You decide that you will compose new lyrics for a familiar song—to "personalize" a set of existing lyrics for your choir. You debate between several songs as the basis for your "new" song, but finally choose "My Favorite Things" from *The Sound of Music*. You start rewriting the familiar lyrics by Oscar Hammerstein:

Raindrops on roses and whiskers on kittens,
Bright copper kettles and warm woolen mittens,
Brown paper packages tied up with strings
These are a few of my favorite things.

Instead of "Raindrops on roses and whiskers on kittens," your lyrics refer to "Field goals by Johnson and slam dunks by Harper," mentioning the school's current football and basketball stars. In a little over an hour, you have written new lyrics for the whole melody, lyrics that mention people and events related to your school. You rehearse the new version of "My Favorite Things" with your choral group until they can perform it flawlessly.

On the night of the talent show, the "new" song, due partly to your choral group's enthusiastic performance of it, steals the show. During the week after the show, you bask in your success until you run into a music professor from the local university in the hardware store. He congratulates you on your choral group's performance and asks you how you managed to get permission from the publishers of the musical to change the lyrics to the song.

"I've tried writing people like that before for permissions to modify either the melodies or the lyrics to their compositions," he says. "The only response I ever got was from a songwriter who denied me permission to alter her song and told me that if I did it anyway and the altered song was performed publicly, she'd sue me," he says. "All I can say is that you're a better man than I am—or at least a better negotiator."

You smile nervously while he relates his story and wave goodbye as he takes the nails he bought and leaves the store. Then you leave yourself, forgetting entirely the errand that brought you to the hardware store in the first place. You want to get home to call your cousin, who is a lawyer in a big firm in California. You want to find out if you should start looking for a defense lawyer now or should wait until you receive your copy of the lawsuit that you feel sure must be on its way. Your cousin sets you straight.

"So you changed the lyrics. A little bit? Or all of them?" he asks.

"All of them. But we kept the melody," you say. "Am I in trouble?"

"Probably not," he says, "since it sounds as if this was a one-time performance. Am I right?"

"Yes" you say. "I'm the music director for the choral group and if I say that the song with the changed lyrics will never be performed again, it won't. But the music professor I mentioned seemed to indicate that you can't change lyrics without permission. I didn't even *ask* for permission. In fact, I didn't realize I *should* ask. Are you telling me I didn't do anything wrong?"

"No, that's not what I'm saying," your cousin says. "You *did* do something wrong—in fact, by writing new lyrics to the Rodgers and Hammerstein song, you infringed the copyright in that song. You can't change the lyrics to a song without permission to do so unless the song is in the public domain. "My Favorite Things" is from a Broadway musical from the late 1950s, as I recall. The movie version of *The Sound of Music* premiered in the mid-1960s. I don't remember exactly when Rodgers or Hammerstein died, but their song is and will be protected by copyright for several decades to come."

"So how come I'm not in trouble?" you ask.

"Because I don't think the publishers of the play and the songs in it are ever going to hear about your rewrite. And if they did, they'd probably just write you a stern letter telling you that you'd better never perform your 'rewritten' song again. Don't get me wrong; I'm not condoning your mistake. I'm just saying that as a practical matter, I don't think there'll be any consequences to your having performed the song with new lyrics just that one time."

"Could I ask one more question, cousin?" you ask.

"Sure," he replies.

"Do you think they would have let me use the new lyrics if I had thought to ask for permission?" you ask.

"Maybe," your cousin says. "But maybe not. Nothing can compel a copyright owner to give you permission to do anything with the copyrighted work that fair use doesn't allow. Copyright owners don't even have to answer letters or phone calls asking for permissions to use their works."

"I suppose I was wrong when I thought anything connected with education got a free ride as far as copyright goes," you say.

"You were wrong," your cousin answers. "You can get in trouble just like anyone else. The law gives teachers some elbow room with the use of copyrighted works, but rewriting the lyrics to a copyrighted song and performing it in public for an event for which admission was charged is way out of bounds."

He yawns. "You know, cousin, it's early in the morning here. Could I go back to sleep now?"

You let your cousin go back to sleep and then you hasten to your computer and erase the file that contains the new lyrics to the Rodgers and Hammerstein song. You figure you dodged a bullet this time. And you decide that if you ever get the urge to write lyrics again, you'll either write the music to go with them or use a public-domain song.

Appendix E contains an excerpt from the U.S. copyright statute, *Exemptions from Infringement for Certain Performances by Nonprofits of Copyrighted Works*, specifically written to exempt certain uses of copyrighted works by nonprofit educational institutions from being treated as infringements. This section of the statute outlines several such exemptions in fairly specific language. Few of these exemptions concern the sort of uses that occur daily in the lives of educators, but most are likely to be pertinent at least occasionally. Read the appendix material to familiarize yourself with the kinds of education exemptions that exist and remember to consult it when you have a question about fair use. After all, the only "get out of jail free" card better than fair use is an exemption from infringement that is written into the statute.

Appendix D contains *Exemptions from Infringement for Certain Uses by Libraries and Archives of Copyrighted Works*. Like the section of the statute that exempts some uses by nonprofit educational institutions, this section outlines uses that are permitted by libraries—uses that don't even require the fair-use evaluation, because they are exemptions from copyright infringement rather than fair uses. Be careful to determine that any use that seems to be an exemption really does qualify. If you work in either a nonprofit educational institution or a library, you should familiarize yourself with the exemptions Congress allowed for use of copyrighted works in those settings.

CHAPTER 9

Fair Use and the Internet

The Internet is a true frontier, one of the few left to us in the twenty-first century. As with all frontiers, its enormous potential is coupled with significant risk. For copyright owners, the primary danger presented by the Internet is the possibility that their works will be copied without authorization and disseminated without payment. For copyright users, the danger is infringing the copyrights of others—perhaps unintentionally—in the free-and-easy spirit that has characterized many users of the Internet since its inception.

Again it is helpful, in considering the analysis that must be made to determine fair use on the Internet, to review what the copyright statute and its legislative history have to say about situations in which the doctrine of fair use applies. The four statutory factors that courts must consider in determining fair use are:

1. The purpose and character of the use, including whether such use is of a commercial nature or is for nonprofit educational purposes
2. The nature of the copyrighted work
3. The amount and substantiality of the portion used in relation to the copyrighted work as a whole
4. The effect of the use upon the potential market for or value of the copyrighted work

The House Report that accompanied the 1976 Copyright Act mentions uses of copyrighted works that qualify as fair uses:

> [Q]uotation of excerpts in a review or criticism for purposes of illustration or comment; quotation of short passages in a scholarly or technical work, for illustration or clarification of the author's observations; use in a parody of some of the content of the work parodied; summary of an address or article, with brief quotations, in a news report; reproduction by a library of a portion of a work to replace part of a damaged

copy; reproduction by a teacher or student of a small part of a work to illustrate a lesson; reproduction of a work in legislative or judicial proceedings or reports; incidental and fortuitous reproduction, in a newsreel or broadcast, of a work located in the scene of an event being reported.

Perhaps the best way to better understand what Internet uses of copyrighted works are permitted by copyright law is to consider several examples of the fair-use evaluation "in action."

IS IT FAIR USE?

1 Your buddy Hal is earning enough every month from his blog to pay his rent and you think that if he can make money from *his* opinions that you can, too. You decide to launch your own blog. Unlike Hal's rants, your blog is a *humorous* commentary on daily life. Word gets around about your blog and you soon have enough hits on your site every day to sell some advertising. Life is good.

Then, a few months after you launch your blog, you feel that you're running dry and that your posts are beginning to sound repetitive. You need more material. You re-use some of the humor columns you wrote for your college newspaper. You reprint your letters home from summer camp. You describe the antics of your comical cat. You mine books of quotations for humorous quips. But the ravenous blog demands more content on a daily basis. One night you are reading a new book by one of your favorite comedians, George Carlin. You realize that you've been too narrow in your vision for your blog in thinking that you had to come up with everything you post yourself.

The next day, you post a really funny section of Carlin's book, a meditation about getting older. Your readers love it, so you decide that you'll post a short section of Carlin every week. When you have exhausted the material in Carlin's book, you turn to one by P.J. O'Rourke, who has a lot of funny things to say about politics in the modern era. When Adam, your brother the law student, writes to congratulate you on netting enough from advertisers to be able to pay Mr. Carlin and Mr. O'Rourke and their publishers for the material you use, you're puzzled.

You call Hal, who tells you that neither he nor any of the other bloggers he knows pay for any of the content they use that is written by other people and that he's never been challenged by anyone. In fact, Hal says, he feels that blogs and the Internet exist to allow the free exchange of ideas and that having to actually *pay* for material would greatly impede his expression of his own—and others'—ideas. When you try this argument on your brother the law student, he laughs. "Sounds like you've been talking to Hal again," Adam says. "And it sounds like Hal's arguments are no more valid than they were in high school."

"What?" you retort. "You don't believe in the free exchange of ideas?"

"Let me 'splain it to you, bro," Adam says. "What you are doing in posting sections of George Carlin's and P.J. O'Rourke's books is copyright infringement. Copyright law actually exists to promote what the Founding Fathers called 'science and the useful arts'—to encourage creative people to create. It does this by giving them the right to control their own creations."

"If copyright law is supposed to promote creativity, how come it's stopping *me* from writing my blog?" you ask.

"It isn't. Because of the First Amendment, you can write just about whatever you want, all day long every day, and print it or broadcast it or post it on the Web. What you can't do is hijack somebody else's work without his or her permission."

"But I'm only using short sections of Carlin's stuff and O'Rourke's," you protest. "Those guys make a lot of money—I'm not hurting them!" Your brother doesn't buy this either.

"You *are* using only short sections of their books," he says. "But over the last six weeks you've posted almost the entire text of Carlin's book. I checked it against my copy of his book. That is definitely not fair use."

"What's fair use?" you ask.

"You really need to know what it is," your brother says. "Fair use is when people can use the copyrighted works of others without permission. But it's because of the nature of the use—like an educational use, a very minimal use, or a news use—that the law doesn't call it copyright infringement."

"And you think that what I've done with Carlin's book isn't fair use?" you ask.

"It's definitely not," your brother says, "for several reasons. You've used too much of Carlin's text—all together, almost the whole book. You're hurting his book sales because your readers can read practically his whole book for free. But the worst thing you've done is to use his material commercially—by using it to make money from your advertisers."

"So I'm basically out of business," you say.

"Not necessarily," he says. "You should take all the material that you didn't write off your site and never do anything like this again. And you should send a check for about a thousand dollars to George Carlin's publisher."

"What about P.J. O'Rourke?" you ask.

"You haven't used much of his book yet. Why don't you just reform and hope he never finds out about you?" Adam says.

"What about the fact that Hal says that none of the bloggers he knows ever pays to use other people's material. Doesn't that have some sort of effect—you know, like it's not common practice in the industry to pay?" you ask.

"All that proves is that the people whose copyrights are being used without their permission haven't made it to the courthouse yet," Adam says. "Get it straight—even if it isn't customary for bloggers to pay to use other people's material, their behavior is still wrong, still actionable in court, and most importantly, it doesn't set any sort of precedent that can be used to excuse what you did."

"Well, what about the humorous quotations?" you whine. "Do I have to take them down, too?"

"No, bro, you don't," Adam says. "Strangely enough, using very short quotations from many writers and from multiple books of quotations is fair use. Just don't post one whole section of anybody's book again, not even a book of quotations."

You make note of your brother's advice and follow it. You also read the material on fair use that he sends you. And you stop taking phone calls from Hal, who got you into this mess in the first place.

2 Since college, you've been an enthusiastic Internet file swapper. You figure that you have collected most of the significant recordings in pop music since at least 1970 and you feel certain that in a few months you'll have everything you want from the 1960s, because you've found a couple of new sources for classic rock. You're especially proud of your ability to sequence the recordings to make listening to your compilation CDs more fun. So many of your friends have asked for copies of your party CD—a brilliant compilation of fifty dance tunes that you named *Dancin' Fool*—that you have a hard time keeping up with the demand.

Your co-worker Jeremy, whose sister is a recording artist, doesn't approve of your collecting pirated recordings; he refused to accept a copy of your dance compilation and made you take it out of his office. You think he's just a killjoy and pay no attention to his arguments that you are stealing profits from the very recording artists that you admire and are committing copyright infringement whenever you download an unauthorized copy of one of their records. You continue working to complete your collection of historic pop music until something happens that makes you reconsider your position . . . you get sued.

The Recording Industry Association of America, in one of its regular attempts to eliminate file-swapping, picks you as a defendant. That's scary enough, but you're really freaked by the fact that the RIAA serves the papers initiating its suit against you at your office and includes your employer as a defendant. You figure there must be some mistake, since you aren't a record pirate—you're just a mild-mannered account exec for a software company. You decide the best thing to do is to consult a lawyer. You're on your way out the door when you get a message that Mr. Levine, your boss, and Mr. Harmon, the company's in-house lawyer, "will see you *now*, in the small conference room."

Mr. Levine and Mr. Harmon don't look happy when you enter the conference room. You try a little levity. "So how's it going, Mr. Levine?" you say.

"Not well, Conrad," your boss says. "Would you like to explain this?" He tosses a copy of the RIAA complaint on the conference table; you know what it is because it's identical to the one you just received.

"Well, boss, I think that must be a misunderstanding," you say. "I'm not a record pirate! That lawsuit accuses me of copyright infringement! And I have no idea why they included the company as a defendant—that must be a mistake, too."

"I don't think there's been a mistake," Mr. Harmon says. "This complaint is very specific. It says that you made unauthorized copies of this list of recordings—look at Attachment A. That *is* record piracy." Then he shuts up and just glares at you.

"But I can explain," you say.

"You can?" says Mr. Levine.

"Yes. I, uh, I think there's some mistake," you say. "I just downloaded those songs for my own use—you see, I'm sort of the life of the party among my friends. They depend on me to furnish the music for all our parties. They think I have real talent—that nobody can compile party music like I can. Why, last Saturday at a party at my girlfriend's apartment, the only music we played were CDs I made. There's this one dance CD that I compiled . . ."

"Young man, be quiet," Mr. Levine says.

"What?" you say. "Uh, yes, sir. I was just trying to explain how. . . . Yes, sir, I'll be quiet."

Mr. Harmon speaks again. "This complaint says that you made your unauthorized copies in your office by using a computer owned by this corporation—is that true?" he asks.

"Uh, well, you see, my computer at home isn't as powerful as the one in my office, so . . ." you say.

"Just answer the question, Conrad," Mr. Harmon says.

"Yes. I did use the computer in my office to download those songs," you admit.

"Attachment A lists about two hundred recordings that you are supposed to have downloaded. Is that number correct?" he asks.

"Uh, yes. I guess so. Or maybe a few more," you answer. Mr. Harmon closes his file, stands, nods at your boss, and leaves. After a few moments, you venture a question.

"Mr. Levine? Sir? Why did Mr. Harmon leave? Does that mean the meeting is over? Should I go back to work?" you ask.

"Yes, Conrad, the meeting is over. But you shouldn't go back to work. Ever." Mr. Levine says. "Security will be here in a moment to escort you out. They'll bring the personal items from your office. You're fired." A big guy in a security guard's uniform comes into the conference room, hands you your coat and a cardboard carton with a few items off your desk, and says, "Follow me." You don't see any of your newest song CDs in the cardboard carton, but you don't think this is the time to ask about them.

Later, your friend Steve, who is a lawyer, tells you that you made two big mistakes: downloading so many unauthorized copies of copyrighted recordings that you looked like a good target for one of the RIAA's lawsuits and doing it at the office on company equipment. He says that *even a little* "file sharing" is still copyright infringement, but that probably no one would have sued you over copies of two or three recordings. And he says that even though your use of your office computer to make your bootleg copies was unauthorized, it was enough to get your employer named as a defendant in the RIAA suit and that the company will probably find that the simplest way to get out of the suit is to pay a small settlement.

You ask him if firing you was part of your company's effort to prove to the RIAA that they disavow your actions. Steve says, "Yeah. And I don't suppose they were too happy to find you spending office hours making party CDs, either." Then he says that you, unemployed though you are, will also have to pay the RIAA a settlement of several thousand dollars. That or go to trial, which would cost more.

You write him a check for almost all the money in your savings account so that he can make a reasonable settlement offer to the RIAA and, as soon as you get home, round up all your party CDs, which don't seem like so much fun now. You dump them in a trash bag and toss them in the garbage. You hope you didn't miss any. Then you start searching the want ads for a new job.

3 In order to keep yourself busy after your retirement, you start a small furniture repair and refinishing business. You have been a woodworker for years, but the furniture pieces your clients bring you present such an array of problems that you have to study many of them before you can begin work. You find that the Internet is even more helpful as a source for "how-to" information than your small library of books on furniture finishes and woodworking.

You are careful to print and save the Internet pieces that you find particularly useful, and before too long you have a sizable collection of articles on furniture repair and refinishing. When you are approached by the local school board to teach an adult-education night class called "New Life for Old Furniture," you quickly agree. The pay's not great—you get to keep the tuition that your students pay after the school board recoups its administrative costs—but you're excited about teaching what you know and meeting other woodworking enthusiasts. Your course proves to be a popular one—twenty students sign up for the first semester and thirty for the second semester. And you're making more money from the course than you had anticipated—$600 the first semester and $1,000 the second semester.

You also make some money, about $300, on the "textbooks" you require each student to buy from you—after all, it takes a little effort to have the local copy shop duplicate and bind your collection of woodworking and repair-and-refinishing articles, and it took you *months* to collect the materials themselves. You sock away the tuition and the profits off your "textbook" to pay for the vacation that you plan to take with your wife after the end of the semester—the money you've earned from your night classes will let you go farther and stay longer this year.

Then you get a visit from a local lawyer who tells you that he has been asked by the publisher of the magazine *Restore and Repair* to investigate a case of copyright infringement. He questions you about your class, and you show him your cobbled-together and photocopied "textbook." After he asks his questions, he hands you a legal document, which he identifies as an advance copy of the lawsuit he plans to file in federal court unless you can convince his clients—before the end of the week—that you have ceased infringing their copyrights. Then he leaves.

You call your own lawyer, John Palmer, right away and tell him what's up. When you meet him in his office, he examines your "textbook," asks some questions, and tells you that you need to do whatever you can to stop the lawsuit, because it will cost you much, much more than the "vacation fund" you've earned from your night class if it goes to court.

"But how can that be?" you ask. "All I did was copy a few articles off the Internet!"

"Actually," Palmer says, "you copied fifty-three articles, by my count. And of that number, sixteen were published originally by *Restore and Repair*."

"But they didn't make me pay anything to read those articles online," you protest feebly. "And there was nothing on the *Restore and Repair* site that said I couldn't print the articles."

"Actually," Palmer says, "by posting those articles online without asking for payment or prohibiting your printing them, the magazine gave you, arguably, what is called an 'implied license' to both read them and print them. However, such an implied license did *not* give you any right to make multiple copies of the articles or to sell them in a collection."

"What about the fact that I used the articles as part of my adult education class?" you ask.

"Use in a classroom or in connection with a class doesn't always transform a use into a *fair* use," he says. "It depends on the circumstances. You make money off your classes and a profit off this 'textbook'—that's a commercial use, which almost always puts an end to any argument of 'fair use.' And you made many more copies of the articles than were strictly necessary to teach your students. Had you simply passed around individual articles or referred your students to the *Restore and Repair* Web site, you wouldn't have a problem. They probably feel that you have, by compiling and selling this 'textbook,' siphoned off potential visitors to their Web site, potential subscribers to their magazine, and potential buyers of the books on furniture repair and restoration that they publish."

You make one last argument: "But they don't publish a book that covers the same ground that my collection of articles covers. Doesn't that count for anything?"

"No," Palmer answers, "it really doesn't. You can't escape a charge of copyright infringement by saying that you can make better use of the material you stole than its owner does."

"OK," you say with a sigh, "I'm convinced—sort of. Where do we go from here?"

"How much did you make off your class and the sales of your 'textbook?'" Mr. Palmer asks.

"Altogether, about $1,900," you answer.

"Then that's what I'll offer the *Restore and Repair* lawyer. They probably don't really want to have to go to court, and if we offer them all the money you've made off their material, they'll probably refrain from filing the suit," Palmer says.

"But some of that money is due to my ability to teach and to what I know about furniture repair and restoration!" you protest.

"That's true," Palmer says, "but because part of it is due to your ability to find a copy shop that's not too particular about what they photocopy, we'd better see if they will accept *all* your profits as a fair settlement. And you'll be lucky if they do—my fees are going to bring the cost of this misadventure to about $2,500."

"Do it," you say. "I've got to go home and shoot my computer."

CHAPTER 10

Fair Use in Commerce

The mere fact that a copyrighted work is used without permission in a commercial context is a big—and often effective—argument against fair use. This is not to say that no commercial uses of copyrighted works qualify as fair uses, but the "commercial use" factor in the fair-use evaluation is perhaps the weightiest argument that can be made against fair use. The first and fourth of the statutory factors that courts use to evaluate a purported fair use refer to commerce—whether the purported fair use is commercial and the effect that the purported fair use will have on the commercial value of the copyrighted work used. But no examples of commercial uses as fair uses are listed in the House Report that accompanied the 1976 Copyright Act, perhaps because commercial uses so seldom are fair uses.

The four factors enumerated in the copyright statute that courts must evaluate in determining fair use are:

1. The purpose and character of the use, including whether such use is of a commercial nature or is for nonprofit educational purposes
2. The nature of the copyrighted work
3. The amount and substantiality of the portion used in relation to the copyrighted work as a whole
4. The effect of the use upon the potential market for or value of the copyrighted work.

This is the pertinent language from the House Report:

[Q]uotation of excerpts in a review or criticism for purposes of illustration or comment; quotation of short passages in a scholarly or technical work, for illustration or clarification of the author's observations; use in a parody of some of the content of the work parodied; summary of an address or article, with brief quotations, in a news report; reproduction by a library of a portion of a work to replace part of a damaged copy; reproduction by a teacher or student of a small part of a work to illustrate a lesson; reproduction of a work in legislative or judicial proceedings or reports; incidental and fortuitous reproduction, in a newsreel or broadcast, of a work located in the scene of an event being reported.

Commercial fair use is rare and very narrow, as these examples of fair-use evaluation in commercial settings demonstrate.

IS IT FAIR USE?

1 You are the art director for an ad agency hired to produce an annual report for the Mega Corporation, one of the agency's biggest clients. Since the corporation is healthy and growing and has recently garnered a lot of very good press, you want to convey this to stockholders in the design for the annual report. There's not much chance to do this in the annual report itself, since the report must meet SEC specifications and is filled with accounting information and other boring content.

You decide, however, that the cover of the report offers a great opportunity to trumpet just what a great corporation Mega is. You review the recent press coverage for Mega Corporation and select one article from the *Wall Street Journal* as especially useful for your purposes. In the cover design for Mega Corporation's annual report, you use a three-by-two-inch photo of a small segment of the *Wall Street Journal* article that contains a twenty-five-word quotation naming Mega Corporation as an innovator in its field. The Mega Corporation people love the design, and you are preparing to send the cover to press when you get nervous that maybe you need someone's permission to use the short *Wall Street Journal* story segment.

You call the lawyer your ad agency uses to ask him whether your use of the quotation is going to get you—and your client—in trouble. He asks a few questions and has you fax over a copy of your cover design. Then he gives you his blessings for the cover design.

"I don't think anyone will or properly can complain about your use of this very short *Wall Street Journal* quotation," he says. "Your use of the quotation is a fair use of that publication's copyrighted story in two ways: it is a properly attributed short quote used in a First Amendment context, since the annual report is the corporation's way of informing its stockholders about the corporation, and you used only a very small portion of the *Journal* story."

"Gee," you say, "if this is all right, maybe we should just reprint the whole story. It's very flattering to the Mega Corporation and particularly to the new Mega CEO—the Mega management team would really love our agency if we spread the word that, in the eyes of the *Wall Street Journal*, they're doing a great job."

"Not so fast," your lawyer says. "Fair use determinations can change pretty quickly when you change the facts. In fact, you have just described an actionable scenario—reprinting the whole story, without permission, for distribution to stockholders would *definitely* be copyright infringement unless you—or Mega—bought the right to do so from the *Wall Street Journal*."

"Oh. What's 'an actionable scenario?'" you ask.

"They can sue you—and win," your lawyer answers.

"I see," you say. "Well, I had another idea that I suppose I ought to check out while I've got you on the phone. What about an ad campaign based around the *Wall Street Journal* story? You know, something like 'The *Wall Street Journal* can pick a winner—Mega Corporation!' Wouldn't that be a great ad?"

"Maybe," your lawyer says, "but it might also be a lawsuit unless the *Wall Street Journal* agreed, in advance, to allow it. Otherwise, you'd be treading pretty close to a kind of trademark infringement by suggesting that the *Wall Street Journal* endorsed Mega Corporation."

"But they did endorse Mega Corporation!" you say.

"Perhaps," your lawyer counters. "But not for all purposes. They almost certainly would not like to see their good name used in an ad campaign to say or imply things they didn't mean. Don't even suggest a campaign like the one you describe unless you run it by me first—and give me time to call the *Wall Street Journal*—almost certainly to get their refusal to allow such a campaign. Remember, it doesn't much matter if you escape a suit for copyright infringement if you land in federal court anyway charged with trademark infringement."

You are glad to hear that you can use the annual report cover design as planned, but chastened to realize that you know so little about what constitutes copyright—and trademark—infringement. You put your lawyer's number on speed dial for your desk phone and vow to consult him often. You figure paying his hourly fee for a few consultations beats even ten minutes of a lawsuit.

2 You develop a board game for kids that is designed to help them learn and remember the basics of biology. One of the features of the game is the "What do you know?" square on the game board. When a player lands on this square, he or she must answer a biology question correctly or be penalized five squares. You make up most of the questions (after all, you are a middle-school biology teacher) but for the definitions of many terms you rely on several biology textbooks and dictionaries. You copy the definitions of the terms verbatim for your quiz cards. For example, when a quiz card question asks, "What is a small, slender, often brightly colored salamander of the European genus *Triturus* or the North American genera *Notophthalmus* and *Taricha*, living chiefly on land but becoming aquatic during the breeding season?" the player must answer "A newt" or be penalized.

Although you can't get any big toy manufacturer interested in producing and marketing your board game, a small educational-toy marketer, Big Brain Toys, is interested. You fly to Minneapolis to meet with the development department of Big Brain Toys, hauling the prototype of your board game along so that you can demonstrate how wonderful it is. Your game is a success with the people in the meeting; in fact, you can't get them to stop playing it and they seem to like being able to stump each other with your quiz cards.

You are feeling pretty good about your game, and to show the Big Brain executives that you are a dedicated professional, you say, "I can guarantee that the facts in the definitions are 100 percent accurate. They all came from dictionaries and textbooks."

"Oh, was it hard to get permission to use them?" one of them asks.

You're stumped for an answer and admit that you hadn't really considered the question of permissions. You ask the Big Brain vice president who is chairing the meeting, "Do I *need* permissions to use the definitions on my quiz cards?" He tells you that he doesn't know because he has never been confronted with the question before.

"Well, isn't that something your people would handle after you buy my game?" you ask. He is a little chilly when he tells you that "his people" make and sell toys—that he doesn't have any employees who have the time to do your homework for you. He also tells you that *if* he decides to buy your game, you would be asked to sign an agreement holding Big Brain Toys harmless in the case of any copyright or trademark infringement dispute or suit. That means, he says, that if there were a suit, you would be responsible for paying any damages awarded in court as well as attorney fees.

You say, with a weak chuckle, "I suppose I'd better figure this out before you spend any more time considering my board game, huh?" He agrees. As soon as you get home, you call your lawyer. He doesn't know whether you need to obtain permission to use the definitions that appear on your quiz cards, but he refers you to a lawyer who does, one who specializes in intellectual-property law. You go to see her as soon as you can get an appointment.

This woman, Ms. Brown, listens to your story and asks a few questions. "You say you used about fifty definitions in all on your quiz cards?" she says. "And you copied them from about ten different textbooks and dictionaries? Would you say that you copied more than four or five definitions from any one book? No? Then what you have done

is to make what is called a 'fair use' of the content of those books."
You, of course, are relieved to hear this because it doesn't sound as
if it will result in a lawsuit, and you want to find out everything you can
about "fair use," since it has apparently saved you a lot of trouble. You
ask Ms. Brown to explain just why your use of definitions of biology
terms that were written by someone else is *not* going to get you in
trouble.

"It's simple," she says. "Fair use of copyrighted works is when
you use so little of a work that it's not an infringement or when the
circumstances surrounding your use are such that society allows a
little trespassing on copyright owners' monopoly. Like a use by a nonprofit corporation or by a teacher for educational purposes."

"I see," you say. "Well, I certainly haven't made any money off this
board game, so I guess I'm a nonprofit, and the game is educational,
so I qualify on that count, too, right?"

"Wrong," she says. "What you are doing is making a *commercial*
use of the definitions you copied from your books. Commercial uses
usually don't qualify as fair uses. But in this case, you took so little from
copyrighted books that your use is *de minimis*—not enough to present
a problem to the copyright owners. It's also a good thing that you "borrowed" from several books—if you had simply copied all your definitions
from one dictionary, you might have a problem because you would have
taken from one copyrighted work a much larger percentage of the
whole work."

"And," she adds, "it has nothing to do with whether you've made
any money—you're not a charity or a school or any kind of legitimate
nonprofit organization. Nor does the fact that your board game is
designed to teach transform your commercial use of the material you
copied into an educational use—educational uses must be much closer
to an actual classroom in an actual school in order to qualify as fair
uses. Got it?"

You nod because you think you do. Anyway, you are so happy to
find out that you aren't a copyright infringer—and to be able to say so
to the Big Brain folks—that you decide to call Ms. Brown any time you
have a similar question before some "big brain" in Minneapolis tells you
that you should have done your homework.

3 You are a blues enthusiast and decide to put your business-school
training to work helping a local blues musician who spent the last
three decades working as a bus driver. Phineas Ward is a talented
and respected singer and musician, but he found early in his career
that he couldn't support his young family with his music. Now that his
children are grown and he has retired from the bus company, he has
decided to return to his real career—music. You can't believe such

a gifted man has been driving buses right in your own city for most of your life, and you think you can get him a recording contract and some better paying club dates if you can only create a little interest in his music.

You round up all the recordings you can find from his early days as a performer and assemble them into a CD that you play for club owners who you want to book him. You also distribute the CD to some blues-format radio stations and programs. You are very proud of yourself because, in the case of each recording, you sought permission from the record company that owns it to use the recording for your promotional CD.

When your efforts on behalf of Mr. Ward begin to succeed, you make more copies of the CD and begin to sell them at his club dates. Mr. Ward is happy, you are happy, the clubs are happy. Then your nephew the law student questions you about the CD and tells you that you are a copyright infringer. "You're wrong, Mikey," you say. "I spent weeks contacting the record companies that originally released those recordings, getting permission to use them on a promo CD. It was hard work finding them all—and some of them had been sold and re-sold to other companies! But your old uncle didn't get an MBA for nothing—I covered all the bases. There's nothing to worry about, Mikey."

"It's Michael, not 'Mikey,' " your nephew says. "And don't break your arm patting yourself on the back. Maybe you did get permission to use the recordings on a promotional CD—and I have to admit that I'm impressed that you thought to do that—but has it occurred to you that you are now *exceeding* that permission?"

"Uh, what do you mean, Mikey? Uh, Michael?" you say.

"Just this," Mikey—uh, Michael—says. "You're now *selling* your 'promotional' CD. Nobody gave you the right to do that. Using the recordings to promote an artist is one thing—record companies are usually happy to allow you to promote their acts and to cooperate in helping you do so. But selling the CD robs them of sales of their own albums."

"I don't think so," you protest. "Almost all the albums I used to assemble the CD are out of print. The recordings I used are not available."

"Did it occur to you that the record companies may decide to reissue some of Mr. Ward's recordings, now that you've created such a buzz around him?" Michael asks. "And, in any event, you did not secure the right to sell copies of the recordings—that's copyright infringement, plain and simple. I wouldn't be surprised if you were sued."

You are forced to admit that your smart-aleck nephew makes sense and ask him how to remedy the situation. "Stop selling this CD immediately. Give it away to radio stations and club owners, but stop selling it. And go back into the studio and produce new recordings of the same songs so that you can assemble—and sell—your own CD. That's perfectly legal. You'll have to pay royalties to the songwriters and you'll have to pay the musicians and backup singers the correct rates for a commercially released CD, but I can help you handle all that. I graduate next week and I should have passed the bar by the time Mr. Ward's new CD is released."

"Thanks," you say. "I don't suppose you'd accept a case of promotional CDs as payment for your work, would you?"

4 As the first part of your plan to escape from your boring day job as an accountant, you start a small, part-time book-publishing company in your garage. You plan to publish only a few titles a year and want to concentrate on books that don't have to be updated and that people will collect. Those criteria, and your life-long passion for baseball, dictate that you will publish books about all things baseball—the teams, the players, the coaches, the stats—anything and everything about baseball. You figure that if a book interests *you*, it will interest other diehard fans and their $25 will end up in your pocket. You decide that the first book you publish will be a volume about the top fifty baseball stars of the twentieth century. You plan to publish a photo of each player, a short biography of each, and a page of his career statistics. You also decide to write the book yourself, since you don't know anyone more enthusiastic about baseball than yourself and, also, you don't have any money to pay another writer.

You work on your book at night and on weekends except during tax season. Within six months, you have finished it. Then you collect photos of all fifty baseball stars—some from other books, some from baseball cards, some from publicity photos distributed by the teams—and you scan them into your computer to use as full-page illustrations of the players in your book. You put the entire book on a disk and take it to a local short-run printer. Then you head home to spend the rest of the weekend planning your marketing program for the book, because the printer says it will be printed and delivered in ten days.

You're feeling as if you might really have started a viable enterprise when you read an article in the Publishers Marketing Association newsletter that discusses the dangers of using photos without permission. The article details several steps that small publishers should take to avoid claims of copyright infringement; your stomach sinks when you realize that you didn't take any of these steps before sending your book—with fifty photos—off to the printer. In fact, you realize, you didn't even consider the issue of copyright in the photos you used. You can hardly wait until Monday morning, because you realize you need to make some phone calls to clear up the dilemma you've created for yourself.

As soon as you have your Monday-morning coffee, you call your office to tell them you're taking a sick day (you *are* feeling sort of green), call the printer to tell him to halt work on your book until further notice, and call a lawyer you know to ask just how much your blunder is likely to cost you. He asks you to gather the source material for the photos you scanned and meet with him that afternoon. You're waiting in his reception area when he gets back from lunch.

"So, tell me again what sort of mess you've gotten yourself into," the lawyer, Mr. Elliott, says. You tell the sad story all over again, this time with visual aids. Mr. Elliott looks at each photo during your account of your problem and, after asking a few questions, divides the fifty photos into three piles.

"What's that? Triage?" you ask.

"In a manner of speaking," Mr. Elliott says. "This pile presents definite problems because the photos were taken from books published and copyrighted by someone else. It doesn't much matter who at this point, because none of the publishers are *you*. The copyrights in these photos almost certainly belong to someone else and you need permission to re-publish them in your own book."

"And the second pile?" you ask.

"The second pile contains photos of early twentieth-century baseball players," he says. "I can't tell without knowing more about when each photo was taken, but many or all of these photos may be old enough that they are now in the public domain. That means the photographers who took them—or, at this point, perhaps their heirs—have no legal rights in them anymore; those rights having expired. It may have been OK to use these photos."

"I'm afraid to ask about the ones in the third pile," you say.

"This is the 'maybe' pile," Mr. Elliott says. "These are publicity photos taken by photographers hired by the baseball teams. The photos were then distributed to news outlets. Usually, the teams themselves will have acquired the copyright in such photos—the copyrights are almost certainly no longer owned by the individual photographers. By their actions in distributing them to news organizations, the teams have created what could be termed an 'implied license' to publish the photos, since the whole idea of distributing the photos was to get them published in newspapers and magazines. That implied license would include books such as yours and you're probably not going to encounter any trouble from the teams for publicizing their players."

"Does that mean I can call the printer and tell him to start the presses again?" you ask.

"Not just yet," Mr. Elliott says. "You need to investigate the status of almost all these photos first—my grouping them into 'no,' 'yes,' and 'maybe' piles is based only on guesswork. But those are the three categories of photos we're dealing with. You just have to figure out whether each photo is in the correct pile. Here's a printout of a copyright-duration chart and here's a Copyright Office pamphlet on determining the copyright status of a work. Read those, do some investigation by calling the team offices or the photographers for the photos, redivide the photos based on what you learn, and bring them all back to me as soon as you can. And make sure that you get correct information for credit lines from each photographer—people really get angry when they don't get credit for their work."

You do what you're told. The investigation takes three weeks of lunch-hour calls and e-mails, but you nail down the status of all but two photos. Mr. Elliott tells you that you can use those two if you reserve enough money to pay modest fees to the copyright owners in the photos if they contact you. Then, after he reviews your notes, he gives you the go-ahead to print the book. You add credit lines to each photo, tell the printer resume printing, pick up the finished books (with your name on the spine as author!) in two weeks, and haul them to a baseball-fan convention, where you sell all but ten copies.

And you ask Mr. Elliott if he will handle the legal work for your blooming new venture.

PART III

Permissions and Licenses

CHAPTER 11

Understanding Permissions

IT IS OFTEN VERY DIFFICULT FOR would-be copyright users to understand is that copyright owners control almost absolutely both how and whether their works are used by others.

There are only a few exceptions to this rule; the most important such exceptions in the United States are called compulsory licenses. For instance, if your song has been recorded previously with your permission and the recording was distributed in the form of phonorecords to the public within the United States, anyone can issue another recording of the song, subject only to the obligations imposed by law to notify you in advance of releasing the new phonorecord, to pay you royalties at a prescribed rate, and to furnish you with monthly royalty statements. This provision of the copyright statute is referred to as the "compulsory [mechanical] license" provision. (There are three other, less important and more obscure, uses specified in the U.S. copyright statute for which compulsory licensing is prescribed.)

Other exceptions to the rule of absolute control by the copyright owner are those uses that are "fair" uses of the copyrighted work. We already know the name for any use that is made without specific permission and that is neither governed by the compulsory license provisions of the copyright statute nor a legitimate fair use of the copyrighted work—any such use is called copyright infringement. In fact, it's safe to say that many infringements result from a would-be user's inability to understand the word "no"—or the reluctance, for whatever reason, to ask for permission to use the copyrighted work in the first place. The ability to ask correctly for permission to use a copyrighted work is an art—in some situations, it may approach diplomacy. That's because the more you need to obtain permission to use a work, the more you may need to call on everything you know about copyright and everything you know about diplomacy in order to make your request properly and to enhance your chances of getting the permission you need.

It's important to understand that, other than in a very few instances involving musical compositions, there are no fixed fees prescribed by the copyright statute or the Copyright Office or otherwise for the right to use copyrighted works. This lack of universal standards for what is charged for permissions means that each request for a permission leads to a negotiation with almost no parameters—in some cases, the only standard for what a copyright owner can charge for a copyright license is what the traffic will bear.

It's also important to understand before seeking permission to use a copyrighted work that a copyright owner's agenda may not include accommodating yours. If you request the right to use a copyrighted work in the same format as that the copyright owner markets, you are likely to be denied permission to use the work. And even if the work is not presently being used in the form in which you want to use it, the copyright owner may have plans for a similar use or a more profitable license may have been offered by someone else. These are reasons not to assume that you will be given the right to use the work in the way you request—but the only way to find out what you *will* be permitted to do is to ask.

Permissions to use copyrighted works are called permissions or licenses. "Permission" often denotes that the right to use a work has been granted without the payment of a fee, whereas a "license" often denotes that some money has changed hands. Although this is the way these terms are sometimes used, the words themselves mean the same thing and in this book the terms are used interchangeably. There are two sorts of licenses—exclusive licenses and nonexclusive licenses. An exclusive license is a permission to use a copyrighted work that has been granted to one person with the limitation that no other similar license to use the work will be granted to anyone else; exclusivity of use usually costs more. A nonexclusive license is a permission to use a copyrighted work that has been granted to one person *without* the limitation that no other similar license to use the work will be granted to anyone else. The person granting the license is called the "licensor"; the person to whom the license is granted is called the "licensee."

An important factor in negotiations for any license is what portion of the copyrighted work is to be licensed. Many proposed uses of a work require permission to use the entire work; in the case of other proposed uses, permission to use only a part of the work is sufficient. And how long the work is to be used is another factor that can determine whether the copyright owner will or will not license the work for the proposed use and, if payment is to be made for the license, what the license fee will be. A third factor in negotiations is territory—over what geographic area will the licensed work be used or in what segment of the market for that work. A work may be licensed for "the entire United States" or for "the world" or for "the state of Oklahoma." It may be licensed for use as part of an anthology of literature or for the soundtrack for a television commercial or as an article in an encyclopedia. Any combination of geographic area and market segment may be specified—as the soundtrack for a television commercial for the entire United States or for the state of Oklahoma.

Nonexclusive licenses of copyright do not have to be written to be effective. You can say, "I'll let you use my photograph of a sunset as the background for your public-service television ad, Jamal, and I won't even charge you for the use." This would give your friend the right to use the photograph in the way you specify. However, Jamal may want to remember that nonexclusive licenses of copyright granted in this way (i.e., verbally) are also terminable at will—that means that he is at your mercy as to how long you will allow him to use your photo, because you can terminate the permission at any time. It's far better to get a written document outlining the terms of any license, even a nonexclusive one, in order to be sure that everyone involved understands just what has been agreed. Unlike nonexclusive licenses, exclusive licenses of copyright have to be in writing to be effective.

The Copyright Clock

The first determination you must make in seeking permission to use a copyrighted work is whether the work is still protected by copyright. This seems almost too obvious to mention, but skipping an examination of the copyright status of the work you want to use can end up costing you whatever time you spend seeking a permission you don't need. Always devote your first efforts to figuring out whether the work is protected by copyright or has fallen into the public domain.

This exercise can do more than keep you from spending time requesting permission to use a public-domain work. It may be that you will be able to trump a copyright owner who is reluctant to grant permission to use a work by simply biding your time—if you find that copyright protection for the work is running out and will expire soon, perhaps you can simply wait until copyright protection expires and save yourself the effort of asking for permission to use the work. Read the Copyright Office circular *How to Investigate the Copyright Status of a Work* (reprinted in appendix B of this book) for information on determining the copyright status of a work. This publication includes information that will be invaluable in any effort to determine whether a work you want to use is still protected by copyright. And remember that all Copyright Office publications are very reliable—in fact, when it comes to copyright information, if the Copyright Office has spoken on the topic, that information is the *most* reliable available, because Copyright Office publications come, in a manner of speaking, direct from the horse's mouth.

What Do You Need?

The second determination you must make in seeking permission to use a copyrighted work is exactly *what* rights you need. Do you want to reprint the entire scientific paper, or would being able to reproduce the chart on page eleven suffice? Do you want to use the photograph as the cover of your book, or is it better as an illustration in one of the chapters? Do you plan to mount a full production of the play and charge admission to those who see it, or are you planning only to recite one of the monologues in a one-night, free-admission talent contest?

Attention to this question can even eliminate the need for a permission alto-gether—perhaps the portion of the copyrighted work that you really need to use is so small as to qualify your proposed use as a fair use of the work. For example, maybe you need to quote only two sentences from the *New York Times* review that praises your first documentary in the prospectus that you're writing to raise money for the second one. Using the entire review would be superfluous and would require that you obtain the right to reprint it, but you don't need permission to quote only a very brief section of the review.

Narrowing your request to obtain only the rights you actually *need* can also save you money. Using an entire musical composition as the soundtrack for your short animated film will cost you more than using only a few bars as incidental music in one scene. It may even be useful to come up with two possible approaches to using a work—what is the minimum you need and what is the maximum you could use? If the copyright owner agrees to grant permission for the minimal use of his or her work, ask what it would cost to make the maximum use of it. Or, conversely, if permission to make maximum use of the work is too expensive or is denied, find out whether it's possible to get permission to use the work minimally.

Whom Do You Ask?

Your skill as a researcher can be an important factor in whether getting permis-sion to use a copyrighted work is a relatively straightforward task or a months-long wild goose chase, because before you can ask for permission you must find where and to whom to send your request. It may be all but impossible to trace the copyright owner for an unpublished work, but a published work will almost certainly bear some information about the publisher and/or the copy-right owner. Somewhere on the physical object that embodies a published work, there will be publication information that can lead you to the copyright owner or the owner of the exclusive right to publish the copyrighted work, which are different statuses from the viewpoint of the copyright owner, but are functionally the same from the viewpoint of a would-be user of the work, like you.

With a poem, play, book, or any other published literary work, write or call the "permissions department" of the publisher of the work to request permission to use it. Depending upon the nature of the use for which you request permission, they will grant or deny your request or forward your letter to the author of the work for his or her consideration.

Copyrights in popular songs and other contemporary musical compositions are usually owned by music publishers. If you call one of the performing rights soci-eties that collect royalties for broadcast uses of musical compositions (BMI, ASCAP, and SESAC) with the title of the composition and the name of the songwriter or composer, you can determine the name of the publisher of the composition, from whom you should request permission to use it. (Contact information for BMI, ASCAP, and SESAC are given at the University of Texas at Austin's "Getting Permissions" Web site, the address for which is given below.) Record companies own the recordings of songs that are released on CDs and cassettes; write the record company if you want permission to use the *recording* of the song, as opposed to the song itself, *in addition to* the publisher, who can grant permission to use the *song*.

For works of the visual arts such as paintings or sculptures, you should contact the artist directly or, in the case of a deceased artist, the artist's estate. Galleries and museums may be good sources for such address information. However, don't assume that because a painting is owned by a museum or an individual collector the copyright in the painting or sculpture is also owned by the museum or collector. Although the owner of a painting or sculpture is, of course, allowed to display it, ownership of a work of art does not automatically bestow on its owner the right to exercise any of the other exclusive rights of copyright. Requests to use photographs of the art should be addressed to the photographer or his or her licensing agency.

Finding the owners of copyrights in other sorts of works may be more difficult. If you can't find the information you need about the owner of a copyright, you may be able to get it online. If you know the title of the work or the name of the author, start with the Copyright Office. Go to *www.copyright.gov/records* to search the registration and ownership records for books, music, films, sound recordings, maps, software, photos, art, multimedia works, periodicals, magazines, journals, and newspapers recorded since 1978. The Copyright Office allows members of the public to search its records, but this requires that you go to Washington or hire a copyright search service to search for you. A better method of determining the ownership of a copyright may be to hire the Copyright Office to search its records for you; at $75 an hour, having the Copyright Office search for you isn't cheap, but the results of such a search may be more reliable than a do-it-yourself effort. The Copyright Office publication *How to Investigate the Copyright Status of a Work*, reprinted in its entirety in appendix B, and Circular 23, *The Copyright Card Catalog and the Online Files of the Copyright Office*, which is available online or can be mailed to you without charge from the Copyright Office. Both publications will give you more information about searching the records of the Copyright Office.

Another excellent source of information is the "Getting Permissions" source list maintained by the University of Texas at Austin (*www.utsystem.edu/ogc/ intellectualproperty/permissn.htm*). This site offers links to a variety of organizations that can grant permission to use all sorts of copyrighted works or, if they can't grant permission, can give you the information you need to find the right person or company to ask for permission. Many online sites give information about copyright clearance; like the UT-Austin site, many of them are operated by universities, perhaps because universities are concerned, justly, about the liability inherent in the unauthorized use of copyrights by their faculty, staff, and students.

The age of the work can be important in determining whom to ask for permission to use it, because the owner of an older work may be hard to find, even if you have a name and address. Lots of things can happen during the term of copyright in a work—publishers may be bought by other publishers, authors may sell copyrights or die and leave them to their heirs, contracts that give someone the right to use a work may expire, and so forth. If you have a copy of the work you want to use that indicates a publisher or copyright owner, you may be in a better position than someone who has no leads whatsoever, but you can't assume that the copyright owner or publisher named on the copy of an older work still controls the copyright in it. View such information as a starting place and in any situation where there may be a later edition or version of a published work, try to find the later edition so your information about the copyright owner will be as recent as possible.

The prominence or obscurity of the owner of copyright in a work can determine how difficult it will be for you to get permission to use the work. You won't have the same trouble locating a copyright owner who is a big company or prominent person. But that same prominence may make it harder to get permission to use the copyrighted work—a work owned and exploited by a successful publisher or a well-known author may be more valuable than an obscure work and thus less likely to be licensed for use by someone else.

CHAPTER 12

Getting Permissions

Permissions, also called licenses, do not have to take any particular form. In fact, *nonexclusive* licenses, which make up the majority of permissions, don't even have to be in writing to be effective. However, you should not depend on anyone's ability to recall the terms of a verbal license.

This means that you should request any permission in writing. Fortunately, permissions are simple enough documents that you may be able to secure any permission you need yourself. The simplest form for requesting a permission is a letter that includes a space for the counter-signature of the person who is in a position to grant your request to use the copyrighted work. (A signature at the bottom of a letter to indicate someone's assent to the contents of the letter is called a "counter-signature.") If all the terms of the proposed permission are stated unambiguously in the body of the letter, the signature of the person to whom the letter is addressed will transform the letter into a binding agreement. (Appendix F of this book includes several sample permission letters with footnotes explaining important points that may be used as models for your own letters.)

Nothing compels anyone to grant your request for permission to use a work. Some materials such as unpublished letters and manuscripts may contain confidential or embarrassing information, at least in the view of the person who wrote them or whose relative wrote them. This means that permission request letters should be polite and deferential. Furthermore, although many such requests are granted without payment, it may be that offering even a small amount in return for the requested permission will increase your chances of being accepted. After all, if the material you want to use is important to your project, it is probably valuable enough to pay for.

Permissions Letters

Even if you are able to reach the owner of the copyright you want to use by phone or e-mail, it is necessary to follow up this initial contact with a letter. You may be able to write this letter yourself, without the help of a lawyer; you can certainly gather all the information you need and negotiate the terms of your license. Whether you write the letter or hire a lawyer to do it, your request letter should include a clear statement of the details of the license you wish to acquire. The important points to cover in any request of this sort are listed below:

1.   Describe **the work you want to use**: Give enough information that the work and the portion of it you want to use can be identified with certainty. If you can attach a photocopy or other sort of identification to the permission request letter, do so. Instead of, or in addition to, attaching a copy, you should include in your letter descriptions of the following:

   a. **The full, correct title of the work**. Examples include: "*The Florence King Reader*"; "*The Billie Holiday Collection: The Golden Greats*"; "*Pilgrim at Tinker's Creek*"; "*The Way of Zen*"; "*W.H. Auden Selected Poems New Edition*"; "*The Wives of Henry VIII*"; "*The Dead and the Living*"; "*The Effect of Prenatal Maternal Nutrition on a Select Population of Newborns*"; "the 1991 French film *Baxter*"

   b. **The edition of the work**. Descriptors can include, "the hardback edition"; "the third edition"; "the revised edition"; or "the paperback edition." Do the best you can here; some works, such as Web sites or unpublished works, have no edition description. Some works, such as Web sites or unpublished works, have no edition description. Substitute the best description available, such as "the collection of poems privately published by the author in 1976, a copy of which was deposited in the Special Collections of the University of North Carolina Library by the author's estate"; "the unpublished diary of your grandmother, a photocopy of which was given to my professor, Dr. Clare Bratten, by your father in early 1999 when Dr. Bratten was researching her master's thesis"; "currently posted on your Web site, at *www.tennesseespelunkers.org*"

   c. **The publisher of the work**. Examples include: "published by St. Martin's Press"; "published by the fraternity's home office in Duluth"; "published by Xlibris at the expense of the author"; "Backstreet Films"; "unpublished, so far as I can tell by the manuscript copy of the play I found in my attic"; "unpublished except for the short excerpts published in the local newspaper soon after the letters were received by Mr. Boyd's mother during the war"

   d. **The date of copyright**. Examples include: "which shows a copyright date of 1995"; "which shows copyright dates of 1985, 1989, and 1994"; "which bears a copyright notice in the name of the author that does not include a year date"; "which is unpublished and therefore bears no copyright notice or year of first publication"

   e. **The owner of copyright**. Examples include: "the book reflects that the owner of copyright is Florence King"; "the author of the collection and owner of copyright in the poems in it is the poet, Sharon Olds"; "the album insert indicates that the collection is copyrighted by Déjà Vu and that the disc was manufactured in Austria by Koch DigitalDisc"; "Ms. Chapman's album is copyrighted by Elektra/Asylum Records for the United States and by WEA International, Inc., for the world outside of the United States"; "the recording of Beethoven's Fifth Symphony that I want to use was recorded in 1998 by the London Symphony Orchestra; the copyright in that recording is owned by the Orchestra"

2. Describe **how you want to use the work**: Some uses of some works will be inherently limited, such as the production of one mural of a painting, as in the example found later in this chapter. In any request for permission to use a copyrighted work, you should indicate, in as much detail as possible, the manner of your proposed use of the copyrighted work. This will entail descriptions of the following:

   a. **The exact portion of the work that you want to use**. For example, "the entire essay titled 'Big Daddy' from Ms. King's fourth book *Southern Ladies and Gentlemen . . .*" In the case of another sort of work, use whatever identifiers are available to precisely indicate the portion of the work that you want permission to use, such as "the drawings on pages 11, 17, and 49 of the aforementioned book"; "the third cut on this album, the recording of 'On the Sunny Side of the Street' "; "the entire poem *In Memory of W.B. Yeats*"; "chapter 6, titled 'The King and His Lady,' of the book *Part Two: Anne Boleyn*"; "the final three minutes and thirty seconds of the film"; "the 'Glossary of Looms' and 'Glossary of Weaving Terms' from pages 179 and 180." Remember, if you are in doubt about including any information that could help identify the work you want to use precisely, include it—too much information is far preferable to too little. In cases where it is practical, attach to your letter a two-dimensional visual copy of the work, such as a photocopy of the drawing, photograph, essay, poem, play, letter, diary entry, paper, or a printout of the Web page.

   b. **The method you want to use to reproduce the work**. Examples include: "to be printed in the forthcoming anthology of essays I am editing"; "to be used as illustrations for the association's Web site listing historic Native American sites in this state"; "to be engraved on a memorial plaque that will be placed inside the library's front entrance"; "to be used as part of the soundtrack for the short film I am producing"; "to be used as a clip in the instructional video I am producing"; "to be printed in a souvenir booklet that will be given, free of charge, to those who attend the awards dinner"; "to be used as an example of the free-verse form in the textbook on poetic forms that I am editing with another professor"

   c. **The number of copies you expect to make**. Examples include: "I have a contract for the publication of my biography of Ulysses S. Grant with the University of Georgia Press; my editor tells me that the initial press run for my book will be 2,500 copies but that there may be more copies printed in future years"; "Since I am preparing my instructional video for use only in the annual night course I teach through the adult-education program of the local school board, I expect to make no more than three or four copies of the video that would embody your photographs"; "I want to use the diary of your great-aunt as the basis for a chapter in my book on early women aviators, which will be published in hardcover by William Morrow, a division of HarperCollins; the initial press run will be 100,000 copies"; "I anticipate making only seventy-five copies of your poem, one for each member of the association, and would not make any additional copies without your permission"; "I want to create a medley of mid-twentieth-century pop recordings and would use the recording you own as part of this medley, which would serve as part of the musical accompaniment to my stage play and will be performed by a local little-theater group here for six nights only"

d. **Whether and how the copies will be distributed and/or sold**. Examples include: "My textbook on American literature will be sold for use in college-level classes and will be used primarily in the United States"; "I intend to enter my short film in several independent-film competitions, where it may be exhibited"; "The records of the plantation owned by your ancestors would be used as the basis for one section of my Ph.D. dissertation, which I would like to publish as a book; although I do not presently have a contract for any such publication and I am not sure that I will be able to obtain one, since there was a university-press book on a similar topic published last year"; "The recording that I seek permission to use would become part of a promotional CD to be given without charge to attendees of the 2005 American Bar Association convention to encourage them to attend my company's sales presentation. While the promotional CD would not be sold, it would be distributed as part of my company's effort to boost sales of its online database product"; "Your photo would be printed on the front of 450 T-shirts that would be sold to benefit the Davidson County Humane Association."

All these details concerning the copyrighted work and how and for what purpose you want to use it should be specified at the beginning of your request letter, perhaps in one paragraph. These points need to be addressed first because the person you are requesting permission from needs to know what you are asking to do. If you request the right to use a photograph to make five hundred posters to be sold for the benefit of a local animal shelter, the owner of the copyright in the photograph may be more inclined to grant your request than if you want to use the photo to produce five hundred posters supporting a controversial political candidate. This may be so even if you don't propose to pay to use the photo and even though the animal-shelter poster would create income and the political poster would not.

Tell the copyright owner what you want to do before you begin discussing the terms of the permission to do it. The terms of the permission, or license, should follow this initial description of the copyrighted work and how and for what purpose you propose to use it.

3. Request **the type of license** you want to acquire: Unless it is important to your project that no one else is allowed to use the copyrighted work, ask for a *nonexclusive* license to use it. A nonexclusive license will be more readily granted than an exclusive license, even an exclusive license for a short period. Furthermore, nonexclusive licenses are often granted free of charge (especially where the portion of the copyrighted work used is small or the use made of it is for nonprofit, charitable, or educational purposes), but exclusive licenses almost never are. If what you really need is to *own* the copyrighted work, you should hire a lawyer to advise you and to draw up the document that transfers ownership of the copyright. However, most uses of copyrights do not require ownership; a license that is drafted to permit the anticipated use would be completely sufficient in almost all cases.

4. Specify **the scope of the license**. How do you want to use the copyrighted work? Do you want to reproduce it in a CD? On a Web site? In a book, a magazine article, or an encyclopedia article? On a poster or a T-shirt? As the soundtrack for a slideshow presentation? In a video? In an ad or on product packaging? Be as specific as possible in your statement of the proposed use of the work.

   If you want to be able to edit or adapt the copyrighted work for your project, say so, because you will not have this right unless it is specifically granted by the copyright owner *in addition to* the right to use the copyrighted work. If you plan to adapt or edit the copyrighted work or prepare a derivative work from it, will the copyright owner have any right to approve the resulting product? If so, say so and say whether the license to use the copyrighted work is conditioned on the copyright owner's approval of the final product.

5. Specify **the territory of the license**. Is the license granted for the world, the continental United States, France, Sweden, the state of California, the Orlando television market, the county where your political candidate is running for council member, what? Again, be specific. State the territory you want as narrowly as will allow you to do what you want with the copyrighted work, but beware of confining yourself with boundaries that aren't really sufficient.

6. Specify **the term of the license**. How long do you need to use the copyrighted work? Forever, as in the case of an essay to be included in a book that may be reprinted numerous times? Or for a briefer time, such as through the end of a particular advertising campaign? (Remember, in negotiating the term of the license you want, to take into account the number of years more that the copyrighted work will be protected by copyright.) And do you want the ability to renew the license? If so, you should include language that allows you to renew for an additional period of the same length as the initial term of the

license upon your payment of a stated amount of money to the copyright owner. This amount may be the same fee you paid for the initial term of the license, or it may be less or more.

7. Specify **the payment you propose or have agreed to make** in return for the license. How much is the right to use the work worth to you? Is your project built around it? Will it be only an incidental part of the finished project? Decide what you can afford before you make the first contact with the copyright owner and negotiate with that figure in mind. And don't forget that many licenses to use copyrighted works are granted by the owners of the copyrights without any compensating payment. This is almost never true for the use of a commercially successful work, but it is common for scholarly uses of works that have little or no commercial value and for uses that are made for nonprofit purposes, such as those made for charity or the good of society.

If no fee is to be paid, state this fact in your letter. If there is to be a fee, specify it and include the payment schedule. This can be "one-half payment due on receipt of the counter-signed permission letter and one-half due on completion of the project"; or "the entire fee on receipt of the counter-signed permission letter"; or "five equal payments, due on the first day of each month after receipt of the counter-signed permission letter"; etc. It is usually more expensive to pay in a lump sum, whenever that lump sum is due, than to pay royalties, but paying royalties involves a lot more work tracking copies incorporating the copyrighted work, and sales, and returns, etc., and usually involves an obligation to render an accounting to anyone who is due royalty payments, as well as allowing access to financial records that concern sales.

8. Specify **the credits language that the copyright owner requires**. Negotiate language to attribute the copyrighted work that you use to the creator and/or owner of the work. This language should be specified or at least approved by the copyright owner when you negotiate the license. Look at credit lines from similar uses of similar works to get an idea as to what is customary. For example, a photo that was taken by Arnold Shutterbug but is licensed by Primo Photos may carry the following credit line: "Arnold Shutterbug/Primo Photos."

You should also include the copyright notice if you are using an entire work. For example, the copyright notice for the photo mentioned above could be combined with the credit line: "Copyright 2005 Arnold Shutterbug/Primo Photos." An author or copyright owner may require copyright notice when only a portion of a work is used, although notice is often omitted in such cases.

9. Specify that the person who will counter-sign your letter has **the authority to grant the license you need**. In spite of your research, you need a written guarantee that the copyright owner does own the copyright in the work and has the right to grant the permission you want or that an agent of the owner has the authority to grant that permission. Sometimes the authors of works assign

the copyrights in them to others and no longer have the right to dispose of any rights in the copyrights in those works. Language similar to this should suffice: "I, Mary Sue Smith, general manager of Primo Photos, state that Primo Photos is the agent for Arnold Shutterbug and that I have the authority to grant the permission made herein to use the photo described herein."

You can also leave a blank space after or under the space for the signature of the person who will counter-sign the letter; this blank space should have a caption under it that says "Title." Usually, asking someone to counter-sign a letter that asks for confirmation of his or her authority will eliminate people who really don't have the right to do what you need them to do. Of course, a dishonest person could decide to "grant" you a permission that he or she had no right to give and pocket the payment you offer; the best protection against a situation like this is to thoroughly research the ownership history of the licensed copyright and to ask enough questions of the person who appears to own it or have the right to license it to eliminate any doubt.

10. Specify **the reasons why the license agreement may be terminated**. Don't include this paragraph (a termination provision) in your permission letter unless the copyright owner asks for one. The copyright owner will probably not ask for a termination provision unless you have agreed to pay royalties or to make payments for use of the copyrighted work over a significant period of time. If you must include a termination provision, state that the license to use the copyrighted work may be terminated by the copyright owner if you fail to make any required payment within sixty days of the date it is due. You should make any such payment much more promptly, but give yourself a little room in case you need it.

Permissions Checklist

Use the following checklist as a tool for composing your own permission letter. Refer to the sample answers above if you need help describing what you need and what you plan to do. Photocopy this checklist and use it as a worksheet for your own permission letters. Just fill in the blanks and then hook the information together in a letter in the order you have written it. As long as you say what you mean and adequately describe what you want, no special legal jargon is needed. Aim for a completely unambiguous letter that covers all the bases. Or take this worksheet to your lawyer, if you think you need help drafting a letter. Here it is— a map for getting the permissions you need:

1. Describe **the work you want to use**. Give enough information that the work and the portion of it you want to use can be identified with certainty. This will entail descriptions of the following:

   The full, correct title of the work: _____

The edition of the work: _____

The publisher of the work: _____

The date of copyright: _____

The owner of copyright: _____

2. Describe **how you want to use the work**: Indicate your proposed use of the copyrighted work in as much detail as possible. This will entail descriptions of the following:

    The exact portion of the work that you want to use: _____

    The method by which you want to reproduce the work that you want to use:
    _____

    The number of copies you expect to make using the licensed work:
    _____

    Whether and how the copies of the licensed work will be distributed and/or sold:_____

3. Specify **the type of license** you want to acquire, whether exclusive or nonexclusive.

4. Specify **the scope of the license**: _____

5. Specify **the territory of the license**: _____

6. Specify **the term of the license**: _____

7. Specify **the payment you propose or have agreed to make** in return for the-license: _____

8. Specify **the credits language that the copyright owner requires:**
    _____

9. Specify that the person who will counter-sign your letter has **the authority to grant the license you need**: _____

10. Specify **the reasons why the license agreement may be terminated:**
    _____

Final Steps

Send two copies of your finished letter—along with a self-addressed, stamped envelope—to the copyright owner, one to be signed and returned to you and the other to be signed and kept by the copyright owner. If possible, attach to both copies of the finished letter a photocopy of the portion of the copyrighted work that you want to use. Specify a date by which you want to receive the counter-signed permission letter even if time isn't an issue—people tend to neglect chores that have no deadline. But give the copyright owner at least two or three weeks to return the counter-signed letter; the copyright owner may want to consult a lawyer or otherwise investigate the advisability of granting the permission you request. If you have agreed to pay for the license, send that payment immediately after you receive the counter-signed permission letter so that you and the copyright owner will both know with certainty that you have an agreement.

Caveats

As with any agreement, unless you are absolutely confident that you understand what is going on with your permission letter, consult a lawyer. This doesn't have to cost a fortune. You can save yourself hundreds of dollars in legal fees if you research the identity of the copyright owner yourself and negotiate with the owner regarding the terms of your license agreement. If you take your (detailed) notes to a lawyer skilled in copyright law and describe to him or her, maybe in a memo, exactly what has happened so far in your quest for the permission you need, you should be able to emerge from your lawyer's office with a short agreement that you can then send to the copyright owner for execution.

Use your common sense in whether to prepare your license yourself—the more important your project, the more money involved, and the longer the term of the license, the more you need a lawyer's advice, even if you handle negotiations with the owner of the copyrighted work yourself. And if the copyright owner sends you an agreement to sign or refers you to a lawyer, call your own—even an honest, principled lawyer is looking out for his or her own client, not for you.

It is worth noting that none of the information in this chapter will do you any good at all if you forget that you *need* a permission. It happens more than it should that, in the course of researching a project, someone fails to make good notes about the source of a photo, piece of music, or poem. Sometimes that photo or music or poem ends up, without even attribution, in the finished project. Faulty record-keeping can hinder you even if you do remember that you need permission to use a copyrighted work—knowing you need permission to use a work when you no longer have information about the source or owner of the work can result in your having to backtrack through all your research to find that information.

In most cases, you can determine whether you need a permission and, if you do, secure it yourself. Remember, although copyright owners have no obligation to allow you to use their works, many are happy to do so and even if your request for a permission is denied or is too expensive, it is often possible to tailor your project to eliminate the need for a permission by reducing your use of the copyrighted work to a fair use. And it's perfectly legal to do so—after all, what you're doing is carefully skirting the boundary of infringement, which is another way of saying that you're just staying on the right side of copyright law. The sooner you learn how to do this, the sooner you can complete your projects—all with the minimum of fuss, expense, and risk.

You should also remember that even if you have gone to the trouble of obtaining permission to use a copyrighted work, *it is still copyright infringement if you exceed the permission you have been granted.* This means that you need to predict your use, in all its dimensions (term of the license, territory of the license, purpose of the use, etc.), as accurately as possible and also that you should be vigilant that the use you actually make of the copyrighted work does not stray over the boundaries of the written permission you secured. Be sure to comply with any condition that requires you to return original copies of the work to their owner or to destroy any excess copies that you make of the owner's work.

Remember that obtaining permissions takes time. Don't wait until the last minute to request the licenses you need for your project. In fact, writing permission letters should be the first or at least a very early step in any project that would use one or more copyrighted works. If you do your research and write your letters early, you will have established contact with the people you need to convince to grant your requests or will learn that you can't find those people or that they won't grant the permissions you need. In any event, you will be better positioned to adjust your project to the realities of the situation, such as that permission to use a work is unequivocally denied or that the copyright in a work has been sold and you must write yet another person for permission to use it. Early attention to permissions will help you avoid ending up, at the eleventh hour, without permission to use a work that comprises a big part of your nearly finished project.

One word of warning about requesting permissions: Never decide to use a copyrighted work after you have been denied permission to do so. Your transgression will be no greater than it would have been if you had never requested such permission, but your action in defiance of the denial of permission to use the work is likely to anger the owner of the copyright. Anger is an important ingredient in lawsuits. Furthermore, your earlier request for permission to use the work may be used against you in court as evidence that the claimed infringement was not an innocent blunder.

A far better course if you are denied permission to use a work that is critical to your own project is to write again to the person who can grant that permission. In this second letter, if you think that doing so would help your case, recount your credentials as a scholar, journalist, artist, critic, or the like. Describe your project in detail and emphasize the value of the copyright you want to use to the project as a whole. Finally, acknowledge the reservations of the copyright owner, but politely ask him or her to reconsider your request. You may even ask your publisher, if you have one, or someone who is noted in your field, to write a similar letter. This sort of second assault may not produce the permission you want, but it can't hurt; the worst that can happen is that the copyright owner will say no again or won't reply to your second letter. All that means is that you're still where you were. However, as mentioned above, it also means that you should re-structure your project, substituting another work for the one you wanted to use. Or, if your project is really dependent on the work you have been denied permission to use, you may have to abandon it. An unfinished project, no matter how brilliantly conceived, is preferable to a lawsuit for copyright infringement any day.

SEEKING PERMISSIONS

1. You are preparing an article for publication in the magazine of a regional wildlife conservation organization. You find support for your arguments in a new biology textbook; in fact, chapter 5 of that book contains a graph that illustrates your point that wild deer are returning to the countryside and present an increasing problem to suburbanites. You want to use the graph to illustrate your article, and you plan to quote the textbook author throughout the first half of your piece. You write the textbook company asking for permission to use all of chapter 5 of the book. Someone in the textbook permissions department calls you to say that you can use the chapter in your article for a fee of $500. You argue that you will be paid only $200 for your article, but the permissions person refuses to budge.

   You call the magazine editor to say that you won't be able to write your article after all. He says that he has planned to use your article as the cover story for the next issue and refuses to let you off the hook. Instead, he asks you to come by his office to explain your dilemma with visual aids—the textbook and your nearly finished article. You go because you like the guy, but you think the situation seems hopeless. In the meeting, however, you find that there's hope.

   "Just as I suspected," your editor says. "You really don't need permission to use chapter 5 of the textbook, because you don't really need to use the *whole* chapter. Look at this section. You have quoted three paragraphs from the textbook verbatim, when you could just as easily have made your point by stating your own conclusions, based on the interviews you conducted, and then saying that Professor John Malcolm of the University of Iowa agrees: 'Accommodation has to be made for these increased populations of deer,' Malcolm writes in his new treatise *Return to the Wild*. 'Otherwise, they will continue to die and to present a hazard to drivers as their survival needs conflict with the interests of suburban homeowners.' You don't *need* permission to say that Malcolm agrees with you, or to quote those two sentences from his textbook."

As your editor examines your other quotations from the Malcolm book, he is also able to show you that you can instead make the assertions they contain in your own voice, based on your own research, and use very short quotations to confirm your findings. "I don't think you need permission from the textbook publisher to use any of this," he says. "Fair use allows you to read the Malcolm book, to say in your own words what it says—without paraphrasing too much of the chapter, of course— and then to back up your conclusions with very small quotations of what Malcolm wrote. You can accomplish what you want by quoting only about ten sentences from the whole chapter. Such a small use of a whole book—or even of just this fifty-page chapter—doesn't require permission."

"But the chart—what about the chart?" you say. "I need it. I can't do the research that went into this chart. And it makes my article much more convincing."

"Maybe you do need the chart," your editor says. "But that's *all* you need. Let's call the permissions person right now and ask whether he'll let us use *the chart* for free if we print information about how to order Malcolm's book."

"I never thought of that," you say. You and the editor place the call to the permissions person for Malcolm's publisher. She says that you can reprint the chart you need for only $100 and that she will, indeed, waive that fee if you will also give your readers information on buying the textbook. Your article appears, the magazine receives a nice letter from Professor Malcolm himself, praising the piece you wrote, and you get assignments for two more articles from your editor, who ups your per-article fee to $250. You vow to learn all you can about fair use, because it helped you pay your rent this month.

(A sample permission letter based on the circumstances of this example can be found in appendix F of this book.)

2 You inherit from your aunt an oil painting of a seashore scene at sunset. It becomes one of your favorite possessions, and you move it from apartment to apartment over the years, always giving it a place of honor. Then you decide to open a small restaurant called Terrence's by the Sea, in the seaside town depicted in your painting. You'd love to have the painting enlarged photographically and turned into a mural for the longest wall of your restaurant, but you know you need permission to make a copy of it, and you have no idea who the artist is or where to find him or her. The painting is signed only with a small signature in red paint that reads, "Morgan."

You have just about abandoned your idea to use the painting for a mural; then you decide to do a little research at the local library. The librarian recognizes the style of the painting when you show her a snapshot of it. She tells you that the painter is one Morgan Harrell, a woman who spent every summer in your seaside town for decades. She also gives you the number of Ms. Harrell's grandson, who tells you that she presently resides in an assisted-living facility but that she is perfectly able to make her own decisions. You write to Ms. Harrell, enclosing the snapshot of your painting. You tell her how you acquired the painting, that you treasure it, and that you want to copy it so that it can be used as a mural in your restaurant. You also offer her a fee of $500 for the privilege of using her painting as your mural.

Ms. Harrell writes back promptly. She has counter-signed the permission letter you sent after making an addition to the letter at the bottom of one page; she asks only that the title of the painting, *Sunset at Shell Beach*, and her name and the year she created the painting be displayed on a small plaque on the mural wall. You are happy to grant her request, especially since you didn't have this information about your painting, so you write your initials near her handwritten addition to the permission letter and send the check for $500 by return mail to Ms. Harrell.

Your mural is a success and becomes a drawing card for your restaurant. It also leads to a news story in the local newspaper about Ms. Harrell, your painting, and your mural. You are happy that you persisted in finding the artist who painted your painting and in asking her for the permission you needed and decide that you will never again assume that something is impossible just because it seems to be difficult at the beginning.

(A sample permission letter based on the circumstances of this example can be found in appendix F.)

3 While you are researching a book on the history of the twentieth-century growth of the town where you live, you run across three volumes of an old journal in the local history archives of the city library. It was kept sporadically for more than thirty years—from 1942 until 1973 by Matilda Simpson, a farm wife who lived just outside of town. In addition to documenting the events of her personal life and that of her husband and children, she noted many important local events, such as the electrification of the outlying areas of the town and the visits of two presidential candidates. By reading and referring to her handwritten journal, you are able to figure out several dates for local events of which you had previously been uncertain.

You make a photocopy of large sections of the Simpson journal and re-conceive your book to focus on it. Instead of discussing the history of the town generally, you start from the journal and discuss the life of the Simpson family in light of developments and events there. This makes a big difference in your book—suddenly, the chapters just seem to fall into place and the sections of Matilda Simpson's journal, which appear throughout your book, lend human interest to what may have otherwise been a somewhat dry historical account. You are able to persuade the local historical society to publish your book as soon as its members read your manuscript, because they really like the way you have configured the book and told the story of your town. But the day the publication of the book is announced in the local newspaper, you receive a call from a woman you don't know, a Margaret Atkins. From the sound of the voice-mail message she leaves, she is angry. She is accusing you of plagiarism and copyright infringement and is threatening to sue you.

You learn that the president and most of the members of the historical society have received similar calls. You are too scared to call Mrs. Atkins back before you attend the emergency meeting called by the historical society board, because although you don't think you have done anything wrong, you realize that you don't know enough about the law to be sure. The lawyer that the historical society board consults after your meeting tells you that the society cannot publish your book in its present form without permission from Mrs. Atkins, who, it turns out, is the sole living descendant of Matilda Simpson, who was her grandmother. You don't understand why Mrs. Atkins presents an impediment to publication of your book, and you ask exactly what she could do to you, and the historical society, if you publish it without her permission.

"She says that she will sue you for copyright infringement and for invasion of privacy," the lawyer says.

"How can she?" you ask. "I found the Simpson journal in the *public library*. It was there for anyone to see!"

"Perhaps," the lawyer says, "but it is an unpublished manuscript copy of a work that is now owned by Mrs. Atkins—the heir of the writer. Because it has never been published, it is protected by copyright until seventy years after the death of the author, Matilda Simpson. She died in 1985, which means that the copyright in her journal will not expire until the end of 2055."

"But I'm an historian," you say. "I need access to historical documents or I can't pursue my profession!"

"Perhaps," the lawyer says. "But Mrs. Atkins *has* allowed access to her grandmother's journal by placing it in the library. What she did *not* do by that action is to allow the journal—or any part of it—to be published. And it *is* an unpublished work, because copies of it have never been distributed or offered for sale. That means it is granted a high degree of protection from use by anyone who wants to publish any part of it without Mrs. Atkins' permission. Courts typically construe the 'fair use' of unpublished works very narrowly."

"But I didn't use all of it," you protest. "Just certain sections."

"Perhaps," the lawyer says. "But you have used far more than is allowed by fair use when a work is unpublished. Even *paraphrasing* sections of an unpublished work may be held to be copyright infringement."

"But nobody has a copyright on *history*, and the journal is an historical account," you say.

"Perhaps," the lawyer says. "It is true that no one owns historical facts. But what you have used—what this journal is—is a particular *expression* of one woman's view of history. That *is* protectable."

"What about this invasion-of-privacy thing?" you ask. "The people Matilda Simpson wrote about are all dead! You can't invade the privacy of a dead person."

"Perhaps," the lawyer says. "It is true that you cannot libel or invade the privacy of a dead person. But one person mentioned extensively in the journal is not dead. Mrs. Atkins is the 'Margie' her grandmother mentions throughout the journal, and she says that she prefers not to have the events of her childhood published in your book."

"Level with me. Can she stop me from publishing my book?" you ask.

"Perhaps," the lawyer says. "She can certainly sue for invasion of privacy, in addition to claiming copyright infringement. And she would almost certainly win on both counts."

"What do you suggest?" you ask. "Should I just throw myself on the mercy of Mrs. Atkins and try to persuade her to grant permission for the historical society to publish my book in its present form? Would that work?"

"Perhaps," the lawyer says. "If I were you, that's exactly what I would do."

You drive to see Mrs. Atkins that afternoon. You are as pleasant as you can be, emphasize the value of her grandmother's journal to your project and to the history of the town, and show her that no embarrassing events from her childhood are contained in your manuscript. She likes you. She agrees to sign a document giving her permission to publish the manuscript in the form you wrote it. The historical society lawyer tells you that he will be glad to advise you on future projects, that his fees are reasonable, and that you should call him the next time you need legal advice.

"Perhaps," you say.

[A sample permission letter based on the circumstances of this example can be found in appendix F of this book.]

4 You are chairman of the parents' committee for your daughter's high school debate team. The committee is trying to find a way to raise enough money to finance a trip for the debate team members and two parent-chaperons to a national debate convention, and they expect you to come up with some good ideas. You hit on the idea of offering suitable-for-framing versions of famous American speeches for sale and download copies of Patrick Henry's "Give me liberty or give me death!" speech, George Washington's farewell address, Abraham Lincoln's Gettysburg address, and Martin Luther King, Jr.'s "I have a dream" speech. The committee likes your idea and so do the members of the debate team. You get the texts for the four speeches off the Internet, print them out in an "antique" typeface, have them printed on "parchment," and sell the set of four for $20.

A week before the application deadline for the debate convention, you have made enough off sales of your "Famous American Speeches" reprints to pay for everyone to go. Then you get a letter from the people in Atlanta who license the use of Martin Luther King, Jr.'s famous speech on behalf of his estate. It seems that they are disturbed that you have been selling unauthorized copies of the speech; they politely but firmly ask that you stop any further sales and turn over to them all proceeds attributable to sales of Dr. King's speech as well as all unsold copies of the speech. You are amazed by the letter because you can't believe that anyone could object to your efforts to raise funds for your daughter's debate team, but you fax the letter to the lawyer for the county school board and ask for her evaluation of it.

She calls you back almost immediately. "You should have stuck with public-domain speeches," she says. "Nobody can complain about your selling the Patrick Henry speech, the George Washington speech, or the Abraham Lincoln speech, because all those speeches are old enough to have fallen into the public domain long ago. That's not true of the Martin Luther King, Jr. speech. That speech was made in 1963; copyright protection for it will last for some time yet."

"Even so," you say, "I thought that using something for education was sort of a free pass. What about that?"

"You're talking about fair use that *is* fair use because the use is an educational use. But you didn't use the King speech for education," the school board lawyer says. "You used it to make money. You did plan to use the money to pay for a trip for a debate team composed of high school students, but that's not the same as an educational use. An educational use would have been something like making a few photocopies of the speech so the debate team members could deliver it to practice their skills as orators. That would have been fair use; selling copies of the speech, even to raise money for a school-connected activity, is not."

Then the lawyer tells you that she'll call the King estate for you and explain the situation. "I'm sure that they won't pursue this any further when they find out what you're doing," she says. She calls back in an hour with good news. "The King estate agreed to let you keep the money you've made from selling Dr. King's speech. The guy I talked to liked the idea of the profits going to a debate team. But we have to promise that you'll never do anything like this again without their permission," she says. You readily agree.

"What made them change their mind?" you ask.

"Well, most copyright owners really dislike the idea of someone using their copyrighted works without their permission. Often, they will grant licenses to use the works for only a small payment—or for free—if they just feel that they have some control over who is using the works and how. The King estate wants to be sure that Dr. King's speech is used only in dignified ways and for purposes it supports. And like all copyright owners, they want to make sure that your use doesn't conflict with any other permissions to use the speech that they've already granted to other people—maybe for significant amounts of money. They were happy to be associated with a high school debate team—but they didn't know who was selling the speech or under what circumstances before I called. Asking permission is the best way to avoid any trouble."

"I'll remember," you say. "Do you think I should write a letter thanking the people in Atlanta?"

"Couldn't hurt," she says. "I was going to suggest that you write describing your use of the speech, acknowledge that they have granted permission for you to use it and sell it as you have been doing, and state that you will make no further use of the speech without their permission."

"Done," you say. And you do it that afternoon.

(A sample permission letter based on the circumstances of this example can be found in appendix F.)

CHAPTER 13

The Right of Privacy, the Right of Publicity, and Releases

People who think they have problems with copyright often, in fact, have concerns that involve the privacy and publicity rights of others. This chapter is included for those people who find that what they really need is a release for the use of a person's name or photograph, rather than permission to use a copyrighted work. Remember, too, that using a work can require both a release from the person(s) portrayed in the story or photo as well as a permission to use the copyrighted story or photo.

The Rights of Privacy and Publicity

The right of privacy and the right of publicity are related rights under United States law allowing individuals some control over the uses made in the media of their identities and of the facts concerning their lives, as well as the manner in which they are portrayed. Generally, private individuals possess and enforce the right of privacy, and celebrities possess and enforce the right of publicity, although private citizens can also sue for infringement of their right of publicity, and celebrities may sue for invasion of privacy. Although there are several important differences between the right of privacy and the right of publicity, the two rights are somewhat like fraternal twins—that is, they are not identical but they look a lot alike. We will consider these rights in this chapter, so that you will learn to recognize each and to tell them apart and so that you will never have to face down either evil twin in a courtroom.

Defining the Right of Privacy

The right of privacy is the right everyone in this country has to live free from four kinds of invasion of privacy:

1. **False-light invasion of privacy**: being placed in a "false light" in the public eye
2. **Intrusion invasion of privacy**: intrusion into some private area of life
3. **Disclosure invasion of privacy**: public disclosure of private facts
4. **Misappropriation invasion of privacy**: the commercial use of name or image *without permission*

The best way to understand these four kinds of privacy invasion is to consider each.

False-Light Invasion of Privacy

False-light invasion of privacy is very much like defamation. With false-light invasion of privacy, however, the harm that the plaintiff claims is not that his or her reputation has been harmed, but that he or she has been portrayed falsely to the public and his or her dignity has been injured, with resulting mental suffering. Many statements that defame someone also constitute false-light invasion of privacy, but defamation and false-light invasion of privacy are not always found in pairs. The following example illustrates false-light invasion of privacy:

> You use a photo from your files in a documentary film about singles bars showing well-dressed young professional men and women gathered around a bar, laughing and talking, with the caption, "Where Singles Swing." One of the men pictured sues for invasion of privacy, claiming that your use of his photo in a film about singles bars places him, a married man, in a false light and has embarrassed him among his friends, causing him to lose sleep and avoid answering his phone. Your lawyer advises you to settle the suit, since your use of the man's photo did place him in a false light, injured his dignity, and caused him mental distress.
>
> Your lawyer also tells you that you are lucky that the plaintiff did not also sue you for defamation, since, arguably, you have also defamed him by implying that his adherence to his marriage vows, an area of his morality, is less than wholehearted.

Intrusion Invasion of Privacy

Intrusion invasion of privacy involves some unreasonable intrusion upon the solitude and seclusion of someone or into her or his private affairs. Intrusion invasion of privacy lawsuits often involve some physical invasion analogous to trespassing, such as an entry into someone's home by journalists who employ false pretenses in order to get a story. Intrusion claims also quite often involve other sorts of unwelcome nosiness and pushiness, such as electronic eavesdropping, opening other people's mail, or photographs taken with a telephoto lens.

Jacqueline Kennedy Onassis' well-known suit against the paparazzi photographer Ron Galella was an intrusion invasion of privacy suit and was brought because he followed her and her children around constantly, leaping from behind bushes and chasing them in cars, in order to take photographs of them. Just as false-light invasion of privacy is related to and expands upon defamation law, intrusion invasion of privacy is related to and fills in some gaps left by the law of trespass.

As we have seen, intrusion invasion of privacy often involves an unauthorized entry onto someone's premises, which is trespass. The difference between trespass and intrusion invasion of privacy is that the harm for which a plaintiff sues in an intrusion invasion suit is not so much the physical trespass itself (which may be the subject of another part of the lawsuit), as the mental distress that results from the intrusion. The following example illustrates intrusion invasion of privacy.

In writing a newspaper story about a new "retirement village," you publish a photograph of an old man sitting inside the front window of a shabby little house. He stares sadly out the window. Your story emphasizes the advantages of living, in old age, among others in a community environment and implies that the old man is alone, lonely, and neglected.

He sues, claiming that the photograph of him was taken without his knowledge by a photographer who must have been standing on the sidewalk in front of his house, shooting through the window. At trial, the photographer is forced to admit that those were precisely the circumstances surrounding the photograph. The court finds the newspaper you work for guilty of intrusion invasion of privacy and of false-light invasion of privacy, since, despite appearances, the plaintiff is well cared for by his daughter, who lives with him.

Disclosure Invasion of Privacy

Disclosure invasion of privacy involves some public disclosure of embarrassing private facts about the plaintiff. It is the sort of invasion of privacy that most people think of when they hear "invasion of privacy." The elements of this sort of invasion of privacy are that the information disclosed must be of such a sort that its disclosure would be embarrassing, objectionable, and offensive to a person of ordinary sensibilities, and the information must not have been public prior to the complained-of disclosure.

Disclosure invasion of privacy differs from defamation in one very important way: To constitute defamation, the information published about the plaintiff must be untrue. There is no such requirement that the information involved in a disclosure invasion of privacy suit be false; in fact, it is the heart of a disclosure invasion of privacy suit that the information is true, but private.

In a way, defamation and disclosure invasion of privacy are each the converse of the other. In other words, if you publish untrue information about someone and that information damages the reputation of or humiliates that person, you may be sued for defamation. If you publish the same information about the person but it is true, and private, and he or she can reasonably object to its publication and is embarrassed by the disclosure of the information, you may be sued for disclosure invasion of privacy. An example of disclosure invasion of privacy will illustrate the sort of circumstances that results in this sort of suit:

> To promote the annual state fair held each year in your city, you design a newspaper ad entitled "Fun at the Fair" and use an assortment of photographs of people who attended last year's fair. Among the photos you use is one of a young woman emerging from a midway funhouse who is prevented by the stuffed animals she carries from holding down the skirt of her dress when jets of air in front of the funhouse raise it, *a la* the famous Marilyn Monroe photograph. Her entire derriere, clad only in cotton undies, is exposed to the view of the camera and several young male bystanders, who are obviously having a different kind of "fun at the fair" at the expense of the exposed woman.
>
> She sues when your ad is published, claiming disclosure invasion of privacy. Your lawyer argues at trial that since the photograph you used was taken in a public place, there were no "private facts" to disclose. The judge disagrees, stating that although the photographed incident did occur in a public place, you have increased exponentially the number of "bystanders" who witnessed the plaintiff's embarrassment and, indeed, would have never published the photograph if it did not depict her exposure. You lose, and so does your client, the state fair board.

Misappropriation Invasion of Privacy

Misappropriation invasion of privacy involves the unauthorized use, for commercial purposes, of a person's name or likeness, with resulting damage to the plaintiff's dignity and peace of mind. In fact, any invasion of privacy suit involving any use of the plaintiff's identity in an advertisement or in any commercial context will be a misappropriation invasion of privacy suit, even if other sorts of privacy claims are involved. The following illustration depicts a situation in which a misappropriation invasion of privacy claim could properly be brought:

> The winner of your city's annual marathon crosses the finish line wearing a pair of running shoes manufactured by your client. You seize the opportunity and create a poster for distribution to all retail shoe stores that stock your client's running shoes. The poster uses a photo of the winner of the race, taken from a rear angle, which does not show the runner's face but prominently pictures the runner's shoes; the headline of the poster reads "Winners Wear Whizards," and the poster copy explains that the winner of the 15th annual Santa Fe Marathon won wearing Whizard running shoes.
>
> The winner, an accountant by profession, sues for misappropriation invasion of privacy. You are astounded when your lawyer tells you that

the plaintiff can probably win his suit, because you believe the fact that the plaintiff's face was not shown in the photograph you used should eliminate the problem. It is news to you that, because the plaintiff can be identified as the runner in the photo by information in the poster other than the depiction of his face (he is the only person who won the 15th annual Santa Fe Marathon), you have, as your lawyer says, "misappropriated his identity." Your lawyer recommends that you settle the case with a cash payment to the plaintiff. You know the rest of the story.

The Right of Publicity

The right of publicity is very similar to misappropriation invasion of privacy. These rights form a sort of progression, or chain, from defamation to false-light invasion of privacy to intrusion invasion of privacy to disclosure invasion of privacy to misappropriation invasion of privacy to the right of publicity. The last link in the chain, the right of publicity, differs from all the other rights named above in one basic way. Libel or any of the sorts of invasion of privacy that we have discussed involve an assault upon someone's reputation, peace of mind, or dignity. In contrast, when you infringe someone's right of publicity you infringe a property right—that is, you may be sued because you have infringed someone's legal right to be the only one who profits from the commercial value of his or her identity.

Private individuals have privacy rights, and so do celebrities, though perhaps to a lesser extent, but in most ordinary circumstances only celebrities have the right of publicity. That is because generally only movie stars, sports figures, famous authors, and retired politicians have the sort of name recognition that makes someone's identity valuable to advertisers. When a private person's identity is used without permission for commercial purposes, that person sues for misappropriation invasion of privacy, not for infringement of the right of publicity. The right of publicity otherwise looks pretty much like misappropriation invasion of privacy. That is, an infringement of someone's right of publicity occurs when that person's name or likeness is used for commercial purposes without his or her consent. The following examples illustrate some of the features characteristic of right-of-publicity infringement disputes and suits:

- You design packaging for the newest product of your video production company, a video called *Golfing Tips of the Pros*. On the cover case, you use photos of three famous golfers, Arnold Palmer, Jack Nicklaus, and Nancy Lopez. You neglect to ask anybody's permission to do so. You figure that all the famous golfers whose photos you used are public figures, and you remember hearing something about public figures having less ability to control press coverage of their activities than private individuals.

    When the video hits the market, the representatives of Mr. Palmer, Mr. Nicklaus, and Ms. Lopez call up the video distributor, threatening to sue the distributor if the videos are not pulled from store shelves and also to find out your address in order to serve process in the lawsuits that are filed. At trial, you are forced to admit that the golfing tips embodied in the video are actually tips from the pros at the Sunnydale Golf Club and that the three famous golfers had nothing to do with creating the video. The lawyers representing the golfers argue that your use of their clients' photos on the video cover implies that those tips in the video are from the pros and constitutes a violation of the right of publicity of the three golfers.

You decide to cut your losses and settle the suit before the plaintiffs present their case. Your lawyer says you should be happy that the plaintiffs did not also claim that your actions constituted illegal unfair competition and that the video was pulled from store shelves before the Federal Trade Commission could find out that its packaging was materially misleading and commence a proceeding against your client for violation of its advertising regulations. You go home and ponder what Shakespeare said about killing lawyers.

• You are the marketing director for the Jukebox Café chain of restaurants, and you plan a "Fifties Days" promotion for all twelve locations. The centerpiece of your promotion will be a weekly Elvis look-alike contest. You will also produce souvenir Elvis coffee mugs and T-shirts for sale at the restaurants' gift shops both during and after the promotion.

For the mugs and shirts, you plan to use a vintage photo of a skinny Elvis Presley in performance with the slogan "I Saw Elvis at the Jukebox Café." The company's CEO loves the Elvis contest idea and the mug and T-shirt tie-ins, but he says he is worried that you need permission from somebody to use Elvis Presley's photograph and name in the promotion. You assure him that you remember reading that no dead person can be defamed and that, therefore, it is unnecessary to get permission from anyone before launching the planned promotion. All the Jukebox Café locations sell record quantities of cheeseburgers during the Fifties Days promotion, and you have to reprint the Elvis T-shirts twice during it in order to meet the demand.

You bask in glory until the day you get a call from the Jukebox Café legal department. The lawyer says that the Elvis Presley estate has sued the corporation for infringing Elvis Presley's right of publicity by producing and selling Elvis mugs and T-shirts. The suit asks for an injunction against further sales of the mugs and shirts, impoundment of all the unsold infringing mugs and shirts in your possession, your profits from sales of the items, and a substantial award of damages.

The Jukebox Café in-house lawyer says that you are knee-deep in cheeseburgers because you have, indeed, run roughshod over the rights of the deceased Mr. Presley. You tell him that most people believe that Elvis Presley has been dead for years and ask him if he is one of those who think differently. He tells you that, for purposes of the lawsuit, it really doesn't make much difference, because under Tennessee law, the right of publicity, under some circumstances, survives the death of the celebrity and is owned and can be enforced by the celebrity's estate. You tell him that you did not know this. He says that it is obvious that you did not and that whether you knew what you were doing is immaterial. He tells you that the corporation intends to settle the lawsuit quickly and agrees not to fire you, but says you can forget about your bonus this year.

Because right of publicity is a relatively new area of the law and has not been around long enough for all jurisdictions and courts and legal scholars to agree completely on its shape, right of publicity varies widely from one jurisdiction to another. Most states, but not all, expressly recognize the right, either by court decision or statute. It is likely that the right will be recognized in the future in most of the states that have not at this writing recognized it just as soon as appeals court decisions are handed down in appropriate suits or forward-thinking legislators pass right-of-publicity statutes in states where there are none presently.

Because right-of-publicity law varies widely from one state to another, and because you probably will not conduct an investigation prior to using a celebrity's identity to see just how much you can get away with under which statutes of which states, you are well advised either to try to stay within the narrowest right of publicity restrictions that exist anywhere in the United States or eliminate the guessing game and get the celebrity's permission to use her or his name or likeness. You may be able to get away with using without permission the identities of some celebrities who live (or lived) in certain states and never run afoul of the law, but the only way to know for sure what you can do without permission is to do it and wait to see if a lawsuit shows up in your mail, which is no way to run an airline.

Descendability of the Publicity Right

There are some other twists to right-of-publicity law that you may not expect. One of the more interesting ones is the fact that, in some states, the right of publicity is a "descendable" right; that is, if you are famous, in some states and under certain circumstances, your heirs can continue to exclusively control and profit from the commercial exploitation of your identity even after your death. This is unlike either the law of privacy or defamation. Your estate can't sue anyone for invasion of privacy or defamation if the alleged invasion or defamatory act occurred after your death. Your rights in these areas die with you because it is presumed that you no longer care, once you are dead, what anyone says about you. But a celebrity's right of publicity is a property right more like trademark ownership than a personal right to protect feelings from assault. Property can be passed to heirs and so can the right to protect the right of publicity after the celebrity's death.

Identifiability

Another peculiarity of right of publicity law is the many ways by which a celebrity's right may be infringed. Generally speaking, the standard for identifiability is the same for right-of-publicity lawsuits as for invasion of privacy suits and libel suits.

That is, if some people recognize a statement, a photo, or even a fictitious depiction as referring to the plaintiff, the defendant is in trouble.

However, since a celebrity is, by definition, a person whose appearance, voice, and personal habits are scrutinized and publicized so that they become very well known, almost anything about a celebrity can identify him or her. This means that in the usual case, if you imitate any part of a celebrity's "persona," including his or her appearance, voice, singing voice, and nickname sufficiently well that the ad that embodies the imitation "works," you have infringed that celebrity's right of publicity. Think of it this way: If somebody is capitalizing on your hard-won fame by using your well-known nickname ("When you're 'the Greatest,' you fight in Slugger boxing shorts") or distinctive singing voice and style in an ad without your permission, you probably don't care whether it really is you in the ad or not, since what is being summoned up by the imitator and stolen from you is your reputation, not just your actual performance or image.

Non-News Media Defendants

In order to avoid lawsuits, you need to understand that non-media professionals can't get away with using the names and images of citizens or celebrities in quite the ways that journalists, newspapers, and magazines (including online journals) can. Many, and perhaps most, U.S. invasion-of-privacy lawsuits are filed because of transgressions by the news media, but that doesn't mean that non-media defendants are safer from invasion-of-privacy suits than newspapers, magazines, or the broadcast media. In fact, because the courts don't allow defendants accused of invading plaintiffs' privacy in other contexts to plead the various defenses related to freedom of the press that are available to media defendants in such suits, a higher percentage of non-media defendants are found liable for invasion-of-privacy suits filed against them than are media defendants.

And practically all suits for infringement of the right of publicity are filed against defendants who are in the chain of people who market a product; First Amendment defenses are generally unavailable in those suits. This means that you, if you are not a news photographer or reporter, must pay special attention to privacy issues and to possible publicity claims, since if you invade someone's privacy or infringe his or her right of publicity, you can't get off the hook by "pleading the First."

Sometimes copyright- and trademark-infringement suits result from what are essentially business disputes; that is, two parties who have differing ideas of who is entitled to ownership of a copyright or a trademark can't work out their dispute between themselves and so resort to the courts for a resolution of the dispute. Libel suits and suits for invasion of privacy or infringement of the publicity right are seldom as dispassionate as even a fiercely fought copyright or trademark suit because, by definition, all involve somebody's stepped-on feelings or reputation or both.

Consider the fact that even lawyers, who usually speak in terms of "bringing an action" or "filing a complaint," have been heard to utter the phrase "slap those *%#@&! with a lawsuit" in contexts involving clients who have (choose any two of the following) squashed feelings, a damaged or misappropriated reputation, or a fat wallet and fire in their eyes. For any non-media defendant, there is simply nothing to be won in any of the sorts of lawsuits we have discussed so far. Furthermore, such suits are typically fought by plaintiffs as grudge matches, long past the point where prudence would dictate that they let sleeping dogs lie. And despite the facts that there is now more legal protection available for celebrities than ever before and that marketers should now be well aware of the danger of using celebrities' identities without permission, there doesn't seem to be a decline in the number of right-of-publicity infringement suits. Florence Henderson, who played the demure mom Carol Brady on the 1970s show *The Brady Bunch*, was, in recent years, forced to sue the manufacturer of T-shirts that use her picture above the caption "Porn Queen."

All this means that, with regard to privacy and publicity infringement suits, an ounce of prevention beats a whole covey of lawyers for the defense. And prevention means releases.

Releases as a Solution

A release (also sometimes called a "consent" or "consent form") is simply a written document indicating that someone has given his or her permission for his or her name, photograph, performance, or other element of his or her identity to be used for the purposes specified in the release. Releases don't have to be long or complicated to do the job. In fact, in many cases a verbal release would actually suffice, but most people don't want to rely on the memory and honesty of someone else to prove that a use of that person's name or photo was a permitted use. The Photo Release reproduced in appendix G of this book may do the trick, but it is also possible that it will need some modification. Talk to your lawyer if you are in doubt about whether it will work in your situation.

What You Can Do *Without* A Release

A release should allow you to proceed with your plans in any of the situations described so far in this chapter—or it won't. That is, if you approach someone for permission to use his or her name or photograph in any situation such as those described, you'll be granted permission to do what you want or the person will deny you permission. You'll be safe from legal action either way—if you ask for and get permission before making use of the name or photograph *or* if you refrain from doing so after permission is denied. As with the right to use someone's copyright, it's a very bad idea to proceed with plans to use the name or photograph of anyone after you have been denied permission to do so. You must learn when you need such permission and what, if anything, you can safely do without specific permission.

This chapter has so far enumerated ways in which you can get into serious trouble for using someone's name or photo without permission. Although it may seem that there are no situations in which you don't need permission to mention or depict someone, that's not the case. The following list is a guide to situations when you may be able to use another person's name or photo safely *without* a release; remember in referring to this list that small changes in the facts described can affect the need for a release:

- **You may use the names of dead people as fictional characters**. Many writers are almost superstitiously fearful about the names they use in their works, fearing that someone with the same name as the heroine of the novel will sue. Mere name-sameness is not, as a general rule, enough to allow someone to sue, and win, on the basis of invasion of privacy or defamation. However, it could be that your heroine, who is the product of your imagination, and the person suing, who you never heard of, both have red hair and that the plaintiff suing you feels that she has been defamed because readers of your novel will believe that *she* is the red-haired jewel thief you describe. You can avoid this dilemma in most cases by intentionally using for your characters the names of deceased private individuals (as opposed to celebrities). You can't defame a dead person, nor can you invade his or her privacy. Some fiction writers gather potential character names from the obituaries; this allows them to say that their jewel thief was named Marian Hunnicutt after the nice old lady down the street who died last year rather than the school board member from Iowa who is suing for defamation and invasion of privacy.

    Remember, though, that this tactic won't rescue you if there are too many points of similarity between your character and the actual person who is complaining. Naming your characters after dead people is one safeguard against lawsuits, but it offers only some protection—you should render your fictional personage as unrecognizable as possible by changing all his or her characteristics from those of whoever inspired you and/or by combining the traits of several people to produce your character. Emulate the nineteenth-century novelist Frances Trollope, who, when asked if she based her characters on real people, said, "Yes, but I pulp them first. One does not recognize the pig in the sausage."

- **You may use images and characteristics of living people as reference sources**. Illustrators and painters often use photographs to get the angle of an elbow or the curve of a neck right during the creation of a project. Similarly, fiction writers often give one person's bad temper and another person's eye color to a newly created fictitious character. This is accepted artistic practice and doesn't invade anyone's privacy or infringe anyone's right of publicity.

The trick is to truly use your models as reference sources *only* and to use more than one such model for any finished image or character. This does not mean copying without alteration any part of an existing photograph or faithfully reproducing enough traits of any one person that he or she is recognizable. Recall that the term is "reference"—which means something you refer to in the course of creating your work. Remember Mrs. Trollope and combine selected features from several sources in your finished work rather than slavishly recreating a single existing photograph or replicating the traits of one person.

- **You may truthfully refer to living or dead individuals in a news story**. You can say that Sandra Jones chaired the garden club meeting or that Harold Rich is a candidate for the city council or that little Julie Murphy was hit by a speeding car as she crossed the street in front of the school but is expected to recover. In short, if it is of any conceivable interest to the public, does not invade anyone's privacy, and does not defame anyone, you can tell it in a news story and you can use the names of the people involved.

  In addition, if you take a photograph in a public place or ask people to pose for a photo after you tell them that you are a news photographer, you can also use their photographs—either alone with a caption or to accompany news stories about them. The dividing line here between a permissible and an impermissible use is whether the publication—be it a newspaper, a television show, a magazine or newsletter, or a blog—is a legitimate journalistic effort. Thanks to the First Amendment, anyone anywhere in America can start a newspaper or other publication tomorrow without any license or permission from the government or anyone else. However, don't assume that a court will view your neighborhood newsletter as deserving the same respect and privileges as the *Washington Post* if you end up in court. People who take advantage of the First Amendment to vent their views and promote their opinions often forget that the right to free speech does not convey the right to say *anything* under *any* circumstances.

  If you expect to claim journalistic privilege, act like a journalist, however humble your publication. Educate yourself completely and thoroughly about what you can do and print or broadcast under what circumstances, and remember that you really do *not* want to ended up in court. Whether you're a big or little news outlet or commentator, conducting your activities so carelessly that you are sued is dumb and expensive. Fight to the death for freedom of speech, but don't get yourself hauled into court because you were careless in what you broadcast or posted a rumor that you couldn't verify or printed private information that you had no right to have.

- **You may quote anyone accurately in a news story.** This is like the ability to refer to people by name in news stories. The First Amendment lets you write about almost anything you learn in a legal fashion (leave the undercover reporting to the pros) that isn't private information or defamatory. This includes reporting what someone said. If you are present when the statement is made, you can quote parts of it in print, on the air, or online unless the statement invades someone's privacy. Before you publish, be very sure that your quotation is accurate, that you gained access to it legally, that it doesn't report information that the law allows the owner to keep private, and that it will not constitute the re-publishing of a defamatory statement.

Again, if you're not an actual newspaper or broadcast journalist or online newshound, leave the fine distinctions between what is legal and what is not to those whose news organizations have in-house lawyers to advise them. The fact that you're an amateur won't help you much in court if your error is egregious enough, and if it is, that error may be sufficient to keep you from ever rising above "wannabe" status.

- **You may refer truthfully to consumer products in ads or news stories, including reviews**. This even allows you to mention the product of another company, unfavorably but truthfully, in an ad for your own product. Comparative advertising isn't actionable in court if the ad makes clear that the product marketed by the other company is owned by that company ("Soapy Suds is a registered trademark of the SoftSoap Corporation") and if the comparison reported in the ad ("Crystal Clear dishwashing liquid cuts grease 40 percent faster than Soapy Suds") is supported by previously conducted legitimate research and is reported accurately.

  If you aren't a competing marketer, you may make the same sort of reference to products in news stories, even if they are critical; that is, you can say that "Crystal Clear cuts grease better than Soapy Suds, in the opinion of our consumer products reporter, and at nearly a dollar less per bottle was judged to be the better value for the shopper." But stay away from any parodies of trademarks unless you want to defend the lawsuit that will almost certainly be coming your way. Marketers invest lots of money in trademarks and don't like to see them mocked by even the wittiest jokesters. (For further information about the legalities of advertising, see *The Advertising Law Guide*, by Lee Wilson, published by Allworth Press.)

- **You may state your opinion about anyone or anything, even if it is negative**. A defamatory statement is an untrue statement of fact about someone. This is different from an opinion. An opinion is an expression of your personal judgment or taste. This exception to defamation includes statements of your opinions of people, products, works of art, events, and so forth. Opinions are the basis of every movie or book review published and of evaluations of products that depend at least partly on matters of taste for their appeal, such as fashionable clothing, home furnishings, or art. Since your opinion is only your feeling about something, rather than an assertion of fact, no one can argue with it, and free speech allows you to express it, even if others disagree.

  Be very careful in publishing, by whatever media, negative opinions of people or products. It is unlikely that a negative review of a current movie will result in a lawsuit, but a negative comment about a person could, even if you specifically couch your comment in the language of opinion ("In my opinion, Mr. Sweeney is not competent to serve on the city council"). If the comment is actually defamatory, the mere use of "opinion" language is not sufficient to save you from a lawsuit. If you habitually express your opinions in any print, broadcast, or online forum, learn the rules of defamation thoroughly and completely. If you don't express opinions regularly or don't want to learn the rules of defamation-free expression, keep your mouth shut. All it takes is one defamatory statement that you thought was merely an opinion to land you in court for libel.

- **You may take photographs in public places**. In a free country, your camera can "see" whatever you can and can record it, in most instances. This means that you can take pictures of buildings or people or the landscape from any point where you can legally stand (i.e., without trespassing on private property). The photos you take under such conditions are yours and you own the copyright in them. What you cannot do with any photo that includes the images of people who are recognizable is use them in an ad without permission from those people. In fact, it is dangerous to use a commercial building or private home in an ad without permission from the owners of the property, since any such use arguably creates an association between the business housed in the commercial building or invades the privacy of the people who live in the home.

And remember that photos taken in any private setting are subject to far more restrictions on use. Private-setting photos can easily lead to invasion-of-privacy lawsuits unless permission to take and publish them is obtained in advance. When in doubt, get permission. Otherwise, you may end up with a beautiful photo that you cannot display or publish because you fear a lawsuit. The same rules apply to paintings—if the person or property is identifiable, get permission before including him or her or it in a painting, for the same reasons. An ounce of prevention is preferable to a complaint in a lawsuit any day.

PART IV.

Appendixes

Fair Use Checklist[1]

PRELIMINARIES

Name[2]: _____ Date[3]: _____

Project

Name or title of project[4]:

_____

_____

Description of project[5]:

_____

_____

Work to Be Used[6]

Description of work to be used, including name or title:

_____

_____

Author or owner of copyright in work to be used:

_____

_____

Address and phone number of author or owner of copyright in work to be used:

_____

_____

Copyright information for work to be used[7]:

_____

_____

Copyright Status of Work to be Used
Is the work you want to use a public-domain work? ____yes ____no

If you answer "yes" and are *sure* that the work is no longer protected by copyright, no permission to use the work is necessary. If you answer "no," answer the questions below to help you determine whether your use of the work is a fair use.

EVALUATION

Factors in Fair Use

Purpose of the proposed use[8]:

_____

_____

Character of the Use[9]:

____nonprofit educational use[10]   ____**commercial use**[11]

____research use   ____**advertising use**

____scholarship use   ____**profit from use**[12]

____criticism use

____comment use

____news reporting use

____parody use[13]

____restricted use[14]

____transformative or productive use[15]

____credit will be given to author   ____**credit will not be given to author**[16]

Nature of the copyrighted work[17]:

____factual work   ____**creative work**[18]

____published work   ____**unpublished work**[19]

Amount of the portion of the work used in relation to the copyrighted work as a whole[20]:

____less than 5 percent   ____**15 percent**[21]

____5 percent   ____**more than 15 percent**

____10 percent

Substantiality[22] of the portion of the work used in relation to the copyrighted work as a whole:

____portion used is not substantial   ____**portion used is substantial**

Effect of the use upon the potential market for or value of the copyrighted work[23]:

____does not impair market for the work

____significantly impairs market for the work[24]

____will not replace a sale of the work

____could replace a sale of the work

____will not diminish market for the work

____will diminish market for the work

____does not increase exposure of the work

____significantly increases exposure of the work[25]

____use of the work limited in time

____repeated use of the work over longer period[26]

Other pertinent factors:

____you own a copy of the work[27]

____you borrowed a copy of the work

____permission to use the work is not available

____permission to use the work is readily available[28]

Conclusion

Completed Analysis[29]:

If you check more than two items in the right-hand column of answers under Factors in Fair Use (these are printed in boldface type), your proposed use is probably not a fair use. Two right-hand column answers indicate that you should further examine your planned use and, possibly, revise your plans for using the copyrighted work. One right-hand-column answer indicates that your planned use is probably a fair use, unless you checked "commercial use" under "Character of the Use." "Commercial use" is the spoiler in any fair-use evaluation. If your planned use involves earning money from your project in any way, get legal advice before you proceed with your project.

____Based on the answers to the questions above, I have determined that my use of the copyrighted work is a fair use of that work.

____Based on the answers to the questions above, I have determined that my use of the copyrighted work is not a fair use of that work. I will either obtain permission from the copyright owner before using the copyrighted work in my project, will decrease my use of the work so that my use will constitute fair use, or will abandon my plans to use the copyrighted work in my project.

NOTES:[30]

_____

_____

_____

_____

_____

_____

_____

_____

_____

_____

_____

_____

_____

_____

_____

_____

_____

_____

_____

[1] Use this checklist to help you decide whether you need permission to use a work in your own project and to keep a record of information about that work. If you don't have complete information to enter in every blank, just enter what you know; you can do the research to fill in the blanks later, if necessary. The goal in using this form is to assemble and organize the information you have, in an effort to consider the work you want to use in light of the use you want to make. Retain the completed checklist so that you can later recreate your fair-use evaluation if you need to explain how you reached the decision you made. Remember that you may have to make the fair-use evaluation again if the circumstances surrounding your project change—for instance, if a classroom use of a copyrighted work expands outside the classroom.

[2] Write your name here.

[3] This date may be important in the case of a copyright that is still valid but will expire before your project is completed. After awhile, it can also let you know that you have spent too much time trying to get permission to use a work and should give up.

[4] Write the name of your project here. Use a working title or a title that is a description—for example, "American Love Songs of the Fifties," or "Fifties Love Songs Compilation CD."

[5] Describe your project in as much detail as possible, including the medium in which you are working (a documentary film, an anthology of short stories, a musical composition, etc.).

[6] Recording the information about the work you want to use when you gather it can save a lot of time later; further, in addition to helping you make the fair-use analysis, it can also expedite the process of getting permission to use the work, if you decide that permission is necessary.

[7] If there is a copyright notice on the work you want to use, copy it here; include any other information you have about the work, such as "This play was first produced on Broadway in 1965" or "This story was published in *Good Housekeeping* magazine in 1970." Some of this information may be important in determining the copyright status of the work or the owner of copyright in it, if you do not already have that information.

[8] For example, "segment of song (music and lyrics) used in soundtrack of documentary film"; "section of photograph used in collage of images of young children"; "two lines of poem used as epigraph for magazine article." Remember, too, the uses enumerated as fair uses in the House Report that accompanied the draft copyright statute during its progress through Congress before its passage; these are fair uses, barring any unusual circumstance connected with them: "[Q]uotation of excerpts in a review or criticism for purposes of illustration or comment; quotation of short passages in a scholarly or technical work, for illustration or clarification of the author's observations; use in a parody of some of the content of the work parodied; summary of an address or article, with brief quotations, in a news report; reproduction by a library of a portion of a work to replace part of a damaged copy; reproduction by a teacher or student of a small part of a work to illustrate a lesson; reproduction of a work in legislative or judicial proceedings or reports; incidental and fortuitous reproduction, in a newsreel or broadcast, of a work located in the scene of an event being reported."

[9] Nonprofit, educational, research, criticism, and news reporting uses are almost always fair; commercial uses, such as uses in advertising, are seldom fair.

[10] Remember that although the entity making use of the copyrighted work is a legitimate nonprofit organization, the *use* itself may be a fundraising use, which makes it a commercial use.

[11] Whether a proposed use is a commercial use can be a problematic question. For instance, quoting a small section of a long poem in a short story is probably fair use, even if the short story is published by a magazine for a fee. Printing a long section of the same poem on coffee mugs or T-shirts and selling those is not a fair use and would require the permission of the poet to avoid copyright infringement.

[12] Some uses that are arguably non-commercial in the ordinary sense of that term nevertheless produce profits. For instance, sales of tickets to a performance of a copyrighted play with no remuneration to the playwright would be a for-profit use of the play and not a fair use, even if the group presenting the production was an informal group such as a little-theatre association that used all the play proceeds to pay for staging the production. The use of the play would be a fundraising use only, but fundraising uses are commercial uses even for nonprofit organizations.

[13] Parody use of a copyrighted work is risky unless done carefully. The conventional wisdom that a permissible parody takes from the underlying copyrighted work only the amount of material that is necessary to call to mind the original, copyrighted work and make the point of the parody. This generally means that attempts at parody that rely far too much on mere replication of the original, copyrighted works or significant portions of them are not fair uses. One court characterized the circumstances surrounding a permissible, fair use of a copyrighted work in a parody thusly: "the audience [is] aware that underlying the parody there is an original and separate expression, attributable to a different artist."

[14] A restricted use of a work, such as copies of one poem circulated only to students in a classroom by a teacher, argues for fair use of the work.

[15] The "transformative or productive use" question gauges whether the purported "fair" use changes the copyrighted work for a new utility or adds value to it. One court said that the question whether the alleged fair use is "transformative" is an inquiry into whether the second use "adds something new with a further purpose of different character, altering the first with new expression, meaning or message." Unlike the four factors discussed repeatedly in this book, this question is not part of the copyright statute but has, rather, been created by some court decisions on fair use. The purported "fair" uses that have been held by these courts to be "transformative or productive" are typically unusual uses of the copyrighted work and often involve some element of parody. Legitimate, fair-use parodies are transformative because they add to the underlying work by their wit and the acute observation and commentary inherent in the added expression; that is, they take only what is necessary to call to mind the parodied work and create a new work whose purpose is distinct from the parodied copyrighted work.

It is worth noting that true "transformative" works—like true, permissible parodies—are rare and hard to achieve. Because the evaluation that a use is "transformative or productive" is highly subjective and, despite being applied in a number of reported cases, somewhat ambiguous, because truly transformative uses are rare, and because most ordinary people are not equipped to make the decision that a use is "transformative or productive" with any accuracy, it is best not to rely on your own judgment that your use will qualify as a fair use on this ground. Remember, fair use is a *defense* to infringement; relying on your own evaluation that a use qualifies as a fair use because it is a "transformative or productive" use of a copyrighted work is simply asking for the opportunity to try to make that point in court, in the course of a lawsuit for copyright infringement. It is far better to be certain enough of a use before you complete your project that the risk of such a dispute is all but eliminated than to wait to see whether the owner of copyright in the work that you used in that project will claim infringement. Nevertheless, the "transformative or productive" question is given here for the sake of accuracy and completeness.

Two examples of uses ruled by courts to be "transformative" are: a photograph used in an ad of the head of actor Leslie Neilsen superimposed on a photograph of the body of a nude pregnant model, in a parody of the famous and controversial Annie Liebovitz photograph of actress Demi Moore on the cover of *Vanity Fair* magazine; and a book titled *The Seinfeld Aptitude Test*, which quizzed readers regarding characters, dialogue, and plot details of almost every episode of the television comedy series *Seinfeld*. The defendant in the first case won; those in the second case lost—the court ruled that even though they had made a "transformative" use, the other three factors of the fair-use test were against them. The court also paid attention to the fact that the authors and publishers of *The Seinfeld Aptitude Test* had used a high percentage of scripts from the show in the book.

[16] Credit should be given to the author of the material from another work that is used, if possible in the context of your project; however, it is also important to realize that giving credit to the author of the material used does *not* turn an infringing use into a non-infringing use.

[17] The permissible uses that may be made of informational works are considerably broader than permissible uses of creative works. However, the courts have yet to permit the fair use defense to infringement in a case involving an *unpublished* work, where the private nature of the work is ordinarily protected.

[18] A creative work is a work that owes its existence more to the imagination of the author than to the author's gathering of facts or information; this includes, among other creative works, stories, poems, novels, films, musical compositions, plays, and paintings. Creative works such as fiction are given more protection than factual works.

[19] Unpublished works, like creative works, are given more protection from unauthorized uses than published works, since the decision whether or not to publish is a right of the copyright owner and a use without permission of an unpublished work by definition eliminates that choice of the copyright owner, at least to the extent that the user publishes the unpublished copyrighted work.

[20] This is the quantitative part of the evaluation. Make your best guess here as to the percentage of the work you want to use. Remember that "the copyrighted work as a whole" means the whole of the individual work you want to use—for example, if you want to use part of a song off a CD, "the

copyrighted work as a whole" means the whole song, *not* the whole CD; and if you want to use part of a story, determine your estimated percentage used in relation to the story itself, *not* in relation to the book-length collection of stories that includes the story you want to use.

[21] Using more than 10 percent of a copyrighted work without permission is dangerous, but whether the use is a fair use depends also on the other factors. Any use of 10 percent or more of the copyrighted work is almost certainly going to be held to be too great a use by a court—in the case involving *The Seinfeld Aptitude Test*, the court said that 3.6 percent verbatim quoting of the original scripts was too great.

[22] This is the qualitative part of the evaluation. "Substantial" means that the portion of the work used is central or significant to the entire work. That is, did you quote the twelve-page climactic scene of a mystery novel, thereby disclosing the identity of the killer, or did you quote only a three-paragraph section that describes the city where the detective works? Even if your use is relatively small from a quantitative standpoint, if it takes the "heart" from the copyrighted work, it may not be a fair use.

[23] This evaluation is often determinative in a court's decision as to whether the use constitutes infringement. It is undoubtedly the most important of the four factors to be weighed in determining fair use. If the market for the copyrighted work is significantly diminished because of the purported fair use, then it is not a fair use. Fewer readers will want to buy a book if its most sensational and newsworthy sections have been previously excerpted in a magazine. A related factor that is considered is the effect of the purported fair use on any of the rights in the copyright of the work said to be infringed. If, without permission, one person writes and sells a screenplay based on another person's copyrighted novel, the right to prepare and sell a screen adaptation of the novel may have been lost to the author of that novel. And the questions raised under this factor are not limited to whether use of the copyrighted work will result in loss of revenue for the copyright owner. Rather, they seek to gauge the effect of the use on the entire potential market for the copyrighted work.

[24] For instance, the right of the copyright owner to sell the movie rights to his novel is impaired because you based your independent film on his book without permission.

[25] For instance, you posted the copyrighted work on the Internet, thereby making it accessible to millions of Web users.

[26] A repeated use of the copyrighted work has the effect of eroding, over time, the rights of the copyright owner, even if one use of the work does not. For instance, even if you make only ten copies of a poem for use in teaching a college literature class, if you keep those copies and use them term after term, you will expose scores of students to the poem over time; some of those students may have bought a book that contains the poem, and the fact that you eliminated the need to do so hurts the poet's and his or her publisher's sales.

[27] Check this if you or, in the case of a project prepared for your employer, your employer owns a legally acquired copy of the copyrighted work. Check it if you or your professor or college or university own a copy. In many circumstances, your actions, even if they constitute infringement, are attributable to your employer or college or university.

[28] The ability to get permission to use the copyrighted work for a reasonable price (if any) and with reasonable effort argues against a fair use, but is not, by itself, determinative.

[29] Check one of the following statements after completing this checklist.

[30] Write here any actions you take with regard to use of the copyrighted work, such as phone calls to the copyright owner, a trimming down of the portion of the copyrighted work used, or a change in the circumstances surrounding the use that will change the outcome of your fair-use analysis. Date each notation and write down phone numbers and addresses. Remember, this checklist, when completed, is your record that you made reasonable efforts to avoid committing copyright infringement and that you took reasonable action to solve any problems. Attach additional sheets with a history of your actions, if necessary.

APPENDIX B

Copyright Office Circular 22
How to Investigate the Copyright Status of a Work

Table of Contents

- For Further Information
- Search Request Form

In General Methods of Approaching a Copyright Investigation

There are several ways to investigate whether a work is under copyright protection and, if so, the facts of the copyright. These are the main ones:

1. Examine a copy of the work for such elements as a copyright notice, place and date of publication, author and publisher. If the work is a sound recording, examine the disk, tape cartridge, or cassette in which the recorded sound is fixed, or the album cover, sleeve, or container in which the recording is sold;
2. Make a search of the Copyright Office catalogs and other records; or
3. Have the Copyright Office make a search for you.

A Few Words of Caution about Copyright Investigations

Copyright investigations often involve more than one of these methods. Even if you follow all three approaches, the results may not be conclusive. Moreover, as explained in this circular, the changes brought about under the Copyright Act of 1976, the Berne Convention Implementation Act of 1988, the Copyright Renewal Act of 1992, and the Sonny Bono Copyright Term Extension Act of 1998 must be considered when investigating the copyright status of a work.

This circular offers some practical guidance on what to look for if you are making a copyright investigation. It is important to realize, however, that this circular contains only general information and that there are a number of exceptions to the principles outlined here. In many cases, it is important to consult with a copyright attorney before reaching any conclusions regarding the copyright status of a work.

How to Search Copyright Office Catalogs and Records

Catalog of Copyright Entries

The Copyright Office published the *Catalog of Copyright Entries* (CCE) in printed format from 1891 through 1978. From 1979 through 1982, the CCE was issued in microfiche format. The catalog was divided into parts according to the classes of works registered. Each CCE segment covered all registrations made during a particular period of time. Renewal registrations made from 1979 through 1982 are found in Section 8 of the catalog. Renewals prior to that time were generally listed at the end of the volume containing the class of work to which they pertained.

A number of libraries throughout the United States maintain copies of the *Catalog*, and this may provide a good starting point if you wish to make a search yourself. There are some cases, however, in which a search of the *Catalog* alone will not be sufficient to provide the needed information. For example:

- Because the *Catalog* does not include entries for assignments or other recorded documents, it cannot be used for searches involving the ownership of rights.
- The *Catalog* entry contains the essential facts concerning a registration, but it is not a verbatim transcript of the registration record. It does not contain the address of the copyright claimant.

Effective with registrations made since 1982 when the CCE was discontinued, the only method of searching outside the Library of Congress is by using the Internet to access the automated catalog. The automated catalog contains entries from 1978 to the present. Information for accessing the catalog via the Internet is provided below.

Individual Searches of Copyright Records

The Copyright Office is located in the Library of Congress, James Madison Memorial Building, 101 Independence Avenue, S.E., Washington, D.C. 20559-6000.

Most Copyright Office records are open to public inspection and searching from 8:30 a.m. to 5 p.m., eastern time, Monday through Friday, except federal holidays. The various records freely available to the public include an extensive card catalog, an automated catalog containing records from 1978 forward, record books, and microfilm records of assignments and related documents. Other records, including correspondence files and deposit copies, are not open to the public for searching. However, they may be inspected upon request and payment of a $75-per-hour search fee.

*NOTE: Copyright Office fees are subject to change. For current fees, please check the Copyright Office Web site at *www.copyright.gov*, write the Copyright Office, or call (202) 707-3000.

If you wish to do your own searching in the Copyright Office files open to the public, you will be given assistance in locating the records you need and in learning procedures for searching. If the Copyright Office staff actually makes the search for you, a search fee must be charged. The search will not be done while you wait.

In addition, the following files dating from 1978 forward are now available on the Copyright Office's Web site at *www.copyright.gov*: COHM, which includes all material except serials and documents; COHD, which includes documents; and COHS, which includes serials.

The Copyright Office does **not** offer search assistance to users on the Internet.

Searching by the Copyright Office
In General

Upon request, the Copyright Office staff will search its records at the statutory rate of $75 for each hour or fraction of an hour consumed. Based on the information you furnish, we will provide an estimate of the total search fee. If you decide to have the Office staff conduct the search, you should send the estimated amount with your request. The Office will then proceed with the search and send you a typewritten report or, if you prefer, an oral report by telephone. If you request an oral report, please provide a telephone number where you can be reached from 8:30 a.m. to 5 p.m., eastern time.

Search reports can be certified on request for an extra fee of $80 per hour. Certified searches are most frequently requested to meet the evidentiary requirements of litigation.

Your request and any other correspondence should be addressed to:

Library of Congress
Copyright Office
Reference and Bibliography Section, LM-451
101 Independence Avenue, S.E.
Washington, D.C. 20559-6000
Tel: (202) 707-6850
Fax: (202) 252-3485
TTY: (202) 707-6737

What the Fee Does Not Cover

The search fee does *not* include the cost of additional certificates, photocopies of deposits, or copies of other Office records. For information concerning these services, request Circular 6, "Obtaining Access to and Copies of Copyright Office Records and Deposits."

Information Needed

The more detailed information you can furnish with your request, the less expensive the search will be. Please provide as much of the following information as possible:

- The title of the work, with any possible variants
- The names of the authors, including possible pseudonyms
- The name of the probable copyright owner, which may be the publisher or producer
- The approximate year when the work was published or registered
- The type of work involved (book, play, musical composition, sound recording, photograph, etc.)

- For a work originally published as a part of a periodical or collection, the title of that publication and any other information, such as the volume or issue number, to help identify it
- The registration number or any other copyright data

Motion pictures are often based on other works such as books or serialized contributions to periodicals or other composite works. **If you desire a search for an underlying work or for music from a motion picture, you must specifically request such a search. You must also identify the underlying works and music and furnish the specific titles, authors, and approximate dates of these works**.

Searches Involving Assignments and Other Documents Affecting Copyright Ownership

For the standard hourly search fee, the Copyright Office staff will search its indexes covering the records of assignments and other recorded documents concerning ownership of copyrights. The reports of searches in these cases will state the facts shown in the Office's indexes of the recorded documents but will offer no interpretation of the content of the documents or their legal effect.

Limitations on Searches

In determining whether or not to have a search made, you should keep the following points in mind:

No Special Lists

The Copyright Office does not maintain any listings of works by subject or any lists of works that are in the public domain.

Contributions Not Listed Separately in Copyright Office Records

Individual works such as stories, poems, articles, or musical compositions that were published as contributions to a copyrighted periodical or collection are usually not listed separately by title in our records.

No Comparisons

The Copyright Office does not search or compare copies of works to determine questions of possible infringement or to determine how much two or more versions of a work have in common.

Titles and Names Not Copyrightable

Copyright does not protect names and titles, and our records list many different works identified by the same or similar titles. Some brand names, trade names, slogans, and phrases may be entitled to protection under the general rules of law relating to unfair competition. They may also be entitled to registration under the provisions of the trademark laws. Questions about the trademark laws should be addressed to the Commissioner of Patents and Trademarks, Washington, D.C. 20231. Possible protection of names and titles under common law principles of unfair competition is a question of state law.

No Legal Advice

The Copyright Office cannot express any opinion as to the legal significance or effect of the facts included in a search report.

Some Words of Caution
Searches Not Always Conclusive

Searches of the Copyright Office catalogs and records are useful in helping to determine the copyright status of a work, but they cannot be regarded as conclusive in all cases. The complete absence of any information about a work in the Office records does not mean that the work is unprotected. The following are examples of cases in which information about a particular work may be incomplete or lacking entirely in the Copyright Office:

· Before 1978, unpublished works were entitled to protection under common law without the need of registration.

· Works published with notice prior to 1978 may be registered at any time within the first 28-year term.

· Works copyrighted between January 1, 1964, and December 31, 1977, are affected by the Copyright Renewal Act of 1992, which automatically extends the copyright term and makes renewal registrations optional.

· For works under copyright protection on or after January 1, 1978, registration may be made at any time during the term of protection. Although registration is not required as a condition of copyright protection, there are certain definite advantages to registration. For further information, request Circular 1, "Copyright Basics."

· Since searches are ordinarily limited to registrations that have already been cataloged, a search report may not cover recent registrations for which catalog records are not yet available.

· The information in the search request may not have been complete or specific enough to identify the work.

· The work may have been registered under a different title or as part of a larger work.

Protection in Foreign Countries

Even if you conclude that a work is in the public domain in the United States, this does not necessarily mean that you are free to use it in other countries. Every nation has its own laws governing the length and scope of copyright protection, and these are applicable to uses of the work within that nation's borders. Thus, the expiration or loss of copyright protection in the United States may still leave the work fully protected against unauthorized use in other countries.

Other Circulars

For further information, request Circular 6, "Obtaining Access to and Copies of Copyright Office Records and Deposits"; Circular 15, "Renewal of Copyright"; Circular 15a, "Duration of Copyright"; and Circular 15t, "Extension of Copyright Terms," from:

> Library of Congress
> Copyright Office
> Publications Section, LM-455
> 101 Independence Avenue, S.E.
> Washington, D.C. 20559-6000

You may call the Forms and Publications Hotline (202) 707- 9100 at any time, day or night, to leave a recorded request for forms or circulars. Requests are filled and mailed promptly.

Impact of Copyright Act on Copyright Investigations

On October 19, 1976, the President signed into law a complete revision of the copyright law of the United States (title 17 of the United States Code). Most provisions of this statute came into force on January 1, 1978, superseding the Copyright Act of 1909. These provisions made significant changes in the copyright law. Further important changes resulted from the Berne Convention Implementation Act of 1988, which took effect March 1, 1989; the Copyright Renewal Act of 1992 (P.L. 102-307) enacted June 26, 1992, which amended the renewal provisions of the copyright law; and the Sonny Bono Copyright Term Extension Act of 1998 (P.L. 105-298) enacted October 27, 1998, which extended the term of copyrights for an additional twenty years.

If you need more information about the provisions of either the 1909 or the 1976 law, write or call the Copyright Office. For information about the Berne Convention Implementation Act, request Circular 93, "Highlights of U.S. Adherence to the Berne Convention." For information about renewals, request Circular 15, "Renewal of Copyright." For information about the Sonny Bono Copyright Term Extension Act, request SL-15, "New Terms for Copyright Protection." For copies of the law ($24.00 each), request "Copyright Law, Circular 92" (stock number is changed to 030-002-00197-7) from:

Superintendent of Documents
P.O. Box 371954
Pittsburgh, PA 15250-7954
Tel: (202) 512-1800
Fax: (202) 512-2250

For copyright investigations, the following points about the impact of the Copyright Act of 1976, the Berne Convention Implementation Act of 1988, and the Copyright Renewal Act of 1992 should be considered.

A Changed System of Copyright Formalities

Some of the most sweeping changes under the 1976 Copyright Act involve copyright formalities, that is, the procedural requirements for securing and maintaining full copyright protection. The old system of formalities involved copyright notice, deposit and registration, recordation of transfers and licenses of copyright ownership, and United States manufacture, among other things. In general, while retaining formalities, the 1976 law reduced the chances of mistakes, softened the consequences of errors and omissions, and allowed for the correction of errors.

The Berne Convention Implementation Act of 1988 reduced formalities, most notably making the addition of the previously mandatory copyright notice optional. It should be noted that the amended notice requirements are not retroactive.

The Copyright Renewal Act of 1992, enacted June 26, 1992, automatically extends the term of copyrights secured between January 1, 1964, and December 31, 1977, making renewal registration optional. Consult Circular 15, "Renewal of Copyright," for details. For additional information, you may contact the Renewals Section.
Tel: (202) 707-8180
Fax: (202) 707-3849

Automatic Copyright

Under the present copyright law, copyright exists in original works of authorship created and fixed in any tangible medium of expression, now known or later developed, from which they can be perceived, reproduced, or otherwise communicated, either directly, or indirectly with the aid of a machine or device. In other words, copyright is an incident of creative authorship not dependent on statutory formalities. Thus, registration with the Copyright Office generally is not required, but there are certain advantages that arise from a timely registration. For further information on the advantages of registration, write or call the Copyright Office and request Circular 1, "Copyright Basics."

Copyright Notice

The 1909 Copyright Act and the 1976 Copyright Act as originally enacted required a notice of copyright on published works. For most works, a copyright notice consisted of the symbol ©, the word "Copyright," or the abbreviation

"Copr.," together with the name of the owner of copyright and the year of first publication. For example: "© Joan Crane 1994" or "Copyright 1994 by Abraham Adams."

For sound recordings published on or after February 15, 1972, a copyright notice might read "℗ 1994 XYZ Records, Inc." See below for more information about sound recordings.

For mask works, a copyright notice might read "Ⓜ SDR Industries." Request Circular 100, "Federal Statutory Protection for Mask Works," for more information.

As originally enacted, the 1976 law prescribed that all visually perceptible published copies of a work, or published phonorecords of a sound recording, should bear a proper copyright notice. This applies to such works published before March 1, 1989. After March 1, 1989, notice of copyright on these works is optional. Adding the notice, however, is strongly encouraged and, if litigation involving the copyright occurs, certain advantages exist for publishing a work with notice.

Prior to March 1, 1989, the requirement for the notice applied equally whether the work was published in the United States or elsewhere by authority of the copyright owner. Compliance with the statutory notice requirements was the responsibility of the copyright owner. Unauthorized publication without the copyright notice, or with a defective notice, does not affect the validity of the copyright in the work.

Advance permission from, or registration with, the Copyright Office is not required before placing a copyright notice on copies of the work or on phonorecords of a sound recording. Moreover, for works first published on or after January 1, 1978, through February 28, 1989, omission of the required notice, or use of a defective notice, did not result in forfeiture or outright loss of copyright protection. Certain omissions of, or defects in, the notice of copyright, however, could have led to loss of copyright protection if steps were not taken to correct or cure the omissions or defects. The Copyright Office has issued a final regulation (37 CFR 201.20) that suggests various acceptable positions for the notice of copyright. For further information, write to the Copyright Office and request Circular 3, "Copyright Notice," and Circular 96, Section 201.20, "Methods of Affixation and Positions of the Copyright Notice on Various Types of Works."

Works Already in the Public Domain

Neither the 1976 Copyright Act, the Berne Convention Implementation Act of 1988, the Copyright Renewal Act of 1992, nor the Sonny Bono Copyright Term Extension Act of 1998 will restore protection to works that fell into the public domain before the passage of the laws. However, the North American Free Trade Agreement (NAFTA) Implementation Act and the Uruguay Round Agreements Act (URAA) may restore copyright in certain works of foreign origin that were in the public domain in the United States. Under the copyright law in effect prior to January 1, 1978, copyright could be lost in several situations. The most common were publication without the required notice of copyright, expiration of the first

28-year term without renewal, or final expiration of the second copyright term. The Copyright Renewal Act of 1992 automatically renews first-term copyrights secured between January 1, 1964, and December 31, 1977.

Scope of Exclusive Rights under Copyright

The present law has changed and enlarged in some cases the scope of the copyright owner's rights. The new rights apply to all uses of a work subject to protection by copyright after January 1, 1978, regardless of when the work was created.

Duration of Copyright Protection

Works Originally Copyrighted on or after January 1, 1978

A work that is created and fixed in tangible form for the first time on or after January 1, 1978, is automatically protected from the moment of its creation and is ordinarily given a term enduring for the author's life plus an additional 70 years after the author's death. In the case of "a joint work prepared by two or more authors who did not work for hire," the term lasts for 70 years after the last surviving author's death. For works made for hire and for anonymous and pseudonymous works (unless the author's identity is revealed in the Copyright Office records), the duration of copyright will be 95 years from publication or 120 years from creation, whichever is less.

Works created before the 1976 law came into effect but neither published nor registered for copyright before January 1, 1978, have been automatically brought under the statute and are now given federal copyright protection. The duration of copyright in these works will generally be computed in the same way as for new works: the life-plus-70 or 95/120-year terms will apply. However, all works in this category are guaranteed at least 25 years of statutory protection.

Works Copyrighted before January 1, 1978

Under the law in effect before 1978, copyright was secured either on the date a work was published with notice of copyright or on the date of registration if the work was registered in unpublished form. In either case, copyright endured for a first term of 28 years from the date on which it was secured. During the last (28th) year of the first term, the copyright was eligible for renewal. The copyright law extends the renewal term from 28 to 67 years for copyrights in existence on January 1, 1978.

However, for works copyrighted prior to January 1, 1964, the copyright still must have been renewed in the 28th calendar year to receive the 67-year period of added protection. The amending legislation enacted June 26, 1992, automatically extends this second term for works first copyrighted between January 1, 1964, and December 31, 1977. For more detailed information on the copyright term, write or call the Copyright Office and request Circular 15a, "Duration of Copyright," and Circular 15t, "Extension of Copyright Terms."

Works First Published before 1978: The Copyright Notice

General Information about the Copyright Notice

In investigating the copyright status of works first published before January 1, 1978, the most important thing to look for is the notice of copyright. As a general rule under the previous law, copyright protection was lost permanently if the notice was omitted from the first authorized published edition of a work or if it appeared in the wrong form or position. The form and position of the copyright notice for various types of works were specified in the copyright statute. Some courts were liberal in overlooking relatively minor departures from the statutory requirements, but a basic failure to comply with the notice provisions forfeited copyright protection and put the work into the public domain in this country.

Absence of Copyright Notice

For works first published before 1978, the complete absence of a copyright notice from a published copy generally indicates that the work is not protected by copyright. For works first published before March 1, 1989, the copyright notice is mandatory, but omission could have been cured by registration before or within 5 years of publication and by adding the notice to copies published in the United States after discovery of the omission. Some works may contain a notice, and others may not. The absence of a notice in works published on or after March 1, 1989, does not necessarily indicate that the work is in the public domain.

Unpublished Works

No notice of copyright was required on the copies of any unpublished work. The concept of "publication" is very technical, and it was possible for a number of copies lacking a copyright notice to be reproduced and distributed without affecting copyright protection.

Foreign Editions

In the case of works seeking *ad interim* copyright, copies of a copyrighted work were exempted from the notice requirements if they were first published outside the United States. ["*Ad interim* copyright" refers to a special short term of copyright available to certain pre-1978 books and periodicals.] Some copies of these foreign editions could find their way into the United States without impairing the copyright.

Accidental Omission

The 1909 statute preserved copyright protection if the notice was omitted by accident or mistake from a "particular copy or copies."

Unauthorized Publication

A valid copyright was not secured if someone deleted the notice and/ or published the work without authorization from the copyright owner.

Sound Recordings

Reproductions of sound recordings usually contain two different types of creative works: the underlying musical, dramatic, or literary work that is being performed or read and the fixation of the actual sounds embodying the performance or reading. For protection of the underlying musical or literary work embodied in a recording, it is not necessary that a copyright notice covering this material appear on the phonograph records or tapes on which the recording is reproduced. As noted above, a special notice is required for protection of the recording of a series of musical, spoken, or other sounds that were fixed on or after February 15, 1972. Sound recordings fixed before February 15, 1972, are not eligible for federal copyright protection. The Sound Recording Act of 1971, the present copyright law, and the Berne Convention Implementation Act of 1988 cannot be applied or be construed to provide any retroactive protection for sound recordings fixed before February 15, 1972. Such works, however, may be protected by various state laws or doctrines of common law.

The Date in the Copyright Notice

If you find a copyright notice, the date it contains may be important in determining the copyright status of the work. In general, the notice on works published before 1978 must include the year in which copyright was secured by publication or, if the work was first registered for copyright in unpublished form, the year in which registration was made. There are two main exceptions to this rule.

1. For pictorial, graphic, or sculptural works (Classes F through K under the 1909 law), the law permitted omission of the year date in the notice.
2. For "new versions" of previously published or copyrighted works, the notice was not usually required to include more than the year of first publication of the new version itself. This is explained further under "Derivative Works" below.

The year in the notice usually (though not always) indicated when the copyright began. It is, therefore, significant in determining whether a copyright is still in effect; or, if the copyright has not yet run its course, the year date will help in deciding when the copyright is scheduled to expire. For further information about the duration of copyright, request Circular 15a, "Duration of Copyright."

In evaluating the meaning of the date in a notice, you should keep the following points in mind:

Works Published and Copyrighted before January 1, 1978

A work published before January 1, 1978, and copyrighted within the past 75 years may still be protected by copyright in the United States if a valid renewal registration was made during the 28th year of the first term of the copyright. If renewed by registration or under the Copyright Renewal Act of 1992 and if still valid under the other provisions of the law, the copyright will expire 95 years from the end of the year in which it was first secured.

Therefore, the U. S. copyright in any work published or copyrighted prior to January 1, 1923, has expired by operation of law, and the work has permanently fallen into the public domain in the United States. For example, on January 1, 1997, copyrights in works first published or copyrighted before January 1, 1922, have expired; on January 1, 1998, copyrights in works first published or copyrighted before January 1, 1923, have expired. Unless the copyright law is changed again, no works under protection on January 1, 1999 will fall into the public domain in the United States until January 1, 2019.

Works First Published or Copyrighted between January 1, 1923, and December 31, 1949, but Not Renewed

If a work was first published or copyrighted between January 1, 1923, and December 31, 1949, it is important to determine whether the copyright was renewed during the last (28th) year of the first term of the copyright. This can be done by searching the Copyright Office records or catalogs as explained previously. If no renewal registration was made, copyright protection expired permanently at the end of the 28th year of the year date it was first secured.

Works First Published or Copyrighted between January 1, 1923, and December 31, 1949, and Registered for Renewal

When a valid renewal registration was made and copyright in the work was in its second term on December 31, 1977, the renewal copyright term was extended under the latest act to 67 years. In these cases, copyright will last for a total of 95 years from the end of the year in which copyright was originally secured. Example: Copyright in a work first published in 1925 and renewed in 1953 will expire on December 31, 2020.

Works First Published or Copyrighted between January 1, 1950, and December 31, 1963

If a work was in its first 28-year term of copyright protection on January 1, 1978, it must have been renewed in a timely fashion to have secured the maximum term of copyright protection. If renewal registration was made during the 28th calendar year of its first term, copyright would endure for 95 years from the end of the year copyright was originally secured. If not renewed, the copyright expired at the end of its 28th calendar year.

Works First Published or Copyrighted between January 1, 1964, and December 31, 1977

If a work was in its first 28-year term of copyright protection on June 26, 1992, renewal registration is now optional. The term of copyright for works published or copyrighted during this time period has been extended to 95 years by the Copyright Renewal Act of 1992 and the Sonny Bono Term Extension Act of 1998. There is no need to make the renewal filing to extend the original 28-year copyright term to the full 95 years.

However, there are several advantages to making a renewal registration during the 28th year of the original term of copyright. If renewal registration is made during the 28th year of the original term of copyright, the renewal copyright vests in the name of the renewal claimant on the effective date of the renewal registration; the renewal certificate constitutes *prima facie* evidence as to the validity of the copyright during the renewed and extended term and of the facts stated in the certificate; and, the right to use the derivative work in the extended term may be affected. Request Circular 15, "Renewal of Copyright," for further information.

Unpublished, Unregistered Works

Before 1978, if a work had been neither "published" in the legal sense nor registered in the Copyright Office, it was subject to perpetual protection under the common law. On January 1, 1978, all works of this kind, subject to protection by copyright, were automatically brought under the federal copyright statute. The duration of copyright for these works can vary, but none of them will expire before December 31, 2002.

Derivative Works

In examining a copy (or a record, disk, or tape) for copyright information, it is important to determine whether that particular version of the work is an original edition of the work or a "new version." New versions include musical arrangements, adaptations, revised or newly edited editions, translations, dramatizations, abridgments, compilations, and works republished with new matter added. The law provides that derivative works, published or unpublished, are independently copyrightable and that the copyright in such a work does not affect or extend the protection, if any, in the underlying work. Under the 1909 law, courts have also held that the notice of copyright on a derivative work ordinarily need not include the dates or other information pertaining to the earlier works incorporated in it. This principle is specifically preserved in the present copyright law. Thus, if the copy (or the record, disk, or tape) constitutes a derivative version of the work, these points should be kept in mind:

- The date in the copyright notice is not necessarily an indication of when copyright in all the material in the work will expire. Some of the material may already be in the public domain, and some parts of the work may expire sooner than others.
- Even if some of the material in the derivative work is in the public domain and free for use, this does not mean that the "new" material added to it can be used without permission from the owner of copyright in the derivative work. It may be necessary to compare editions to determine what is free to use and what is not.
- Ownership of rights in the material included in a derivative work and in the preexisting work upon which it may be based may differ, and permission obtained from the owners of certain parts of the work may not authorize the use of other parts.

The Name in the Copyright Notice

Under the copyright statute in effect before 1978, the notice was required to include "the name of the copyright proprietor." The present act requires that the notice include "the name of the owner of copyright in the work, or an abbreviation by which the name can be recognized, or a generally known alternative designation of the owner." The name in the notice (sometimes in combination with the other statements on the copy, records, disk, tape, container, or label) often gives persons wishing to use the work the information needed to identify the owner from whom licenses or permission can be sought. In other cases, the name provides a starting point for a search in the Copyright Office records or catalogs, as explained at the beginning of this circular.

In the case of works published before 1978, copyright registration is made in the name of the individual person or the entity identified as the copyright owner in the notice. For works published on or after January 1, 1978, registration is made in the name of the person or entity owning all the rights on the date the registration is made. This may or may not be the name appearing in the notice. In addition to its records of copyright registration, the Copyright Office maintains extensive records of assignments, exclusive licenses, and other documents dealing with copyright ownership.

Ad Interim

Ad interim copyright was a special short-term copyright that applied to certain books and periodicals in the English language that were first manufactured and published outside the United States. It was a partial exception to the manufacturing requirements of the previous U.S. copyright law. Its purpose was to secure temporary U.S. protection for a work, pending the manufacture of an edition in the United States. The ad interim requirements changed several times over the years and were subject to a number of exceptions and qualifications.

The manufacturing provisions of the copyright act expired on July 1, 1986, and are no longer a part of the copyright law. The transitional and supplementary provisions of the act provide that for any work in which ad interim copyright was subsisting or capable of being secured on December 31, 1977, copyright protection would be extended for a term compatible with the other works in which copyright was subsisting on the effective date of the new act. Consequently, if the work was first published on or after July 1, 1977, and was eligible for ad interim copyright protection, the provisions of the present copyright act will be applicable to the protection of these works. Anyone investigating the copyright status of an English-language book or periodical first published outside the United States before July 1, 1977, should check carefully to determine:

- Whether the manufacturing requirements were applicable to the work; and
- If so, whether the *ad interim* requirements were met.

For Further Information

Information via the Internet

Frequently requested circulars, announcements, regulations, other related materials, and all copyright application forms are available via the Internet. You may access these via the Copyright Office Web site at *www.copyright.gov.*

Information by fax

Circulars and other information (but not application forms) are available by Fax-on-Demand at (202) 707-2600.

Information by telephone

For general information about copyright, call the Copyright Public Information Office at (202) 707-3000. The TTY number is (202) 707-6737. Information specialists are on duty from 8:30 a.m. to 5:00 p.m., eastern time, Monday through Friday, except federal holidays. Recorded information is available 24 hours a day. Or, if you know which application forms and circulars you want, request them from the Forms and Publications Hotline at (202) 707-9100, 24 hours a day. Leave a recorded message.

Information by regular mail

Write to:
Library of Congress
Copyright Office
Publications Section, LM-455
101 Independence Avenue, S.E.
Washington, D.C. 20559-6000

APPENDIX C

Copyright Statute Sections 106 and 106A, Rights of Copyright

106. Exclusive rights in copyrighted works

Subject to sections 107 through 122, the owner of copyright under this title has the exclusive rights to do and to authorize any of the following:

(1) to reproduce the copyrighted work in copies or phonorecords;
(2) to prepare derivative works based upon the copyrighted work;
(3) to distribute copies or phonorecords of the copyrighted work to the public by sale or other transfer of ownership, or by rental, lease, or lending;
(4) in the case of literary, musical, dramatic, and choreographic works, pantomimes, and motion pictures and other audiovisual works, to perform the copyrighted work publicly;
(5) in the case of literary, musical, dramatic, and choreographic works, pantomimes, and pictorial, graphic, or sculptural works, including the individual images of a motion picture or other audiovisual work, to display the copyrighted work publicly; and
(6) in the case of sound recordings, to perform the copyrighted work publicly by means of a digital audio transmission.

§ 106A. Rights of certain authors to attribution and integrity

(a) RIGHTS OF ATTRIBUTION AND INTEGRITY.—Subject to section 107 and independent of the exclusive rights provided in section 106, the author of a work of visual art —
(1) shall have the right—
(A) to claim authorship of that work, and
(B) to prevent the use of his or her name as the author of any work of visual art which he or she did not create;

(2) shall have the right to prevent the use of his or her name as the author of the work of visual art in the event of a distortion, mutilation, or other modification of the work which would be prejudicial to his or her honor or reputation; and

(3) subject to the limitations set forth in section 113(d), shall have the right —

    (A) to prevent any intentional distortion, mutilation, or other modification of that work which would be prejudicial to his or her honor or reputation, and any intentional distortion, mutilation, or modification of that work is a violation of that right, and

    (B) to prevent any destruction of a work of recognized stature, and any intentional or grossly negligent destruction of that work is a violation of that right.

(b) SCOPE AND EXERCISE OF RIGHTS.—Only the author of a work of visual art has the rights conferred by subsection (a) in that work, whether or not the author is the copyright owner. The authors of a joint work of visual art are coowners of the rights conferred by subsection (a) in that work.

(c) EXCEPTIONS.—

(1) The modification of a work of visual art which is the result of the passage of time or the inherent nature of the materials is not a distortion, mutilation, or other modification described in subsection (a)(3)(A).

(2) The modification of a work of visual art which is the result of conservation, or of the public presentation, including lighting and placement, of the work is not a destruction, distortion, mutilation, or other modification described in subsection (a)(3) unless the modification is caused by gross negligence.

(3) The rights described in paragraphs (1) and (2) of subsection (a) shall not apply to any reproduction, depiction, portrayal, or other use of a work in, upon, or in any connection with any item described in subparagraph (A) or (B) of the definition of "work of visual art" in section 101, and any such reproduction, depiction, portrayal, or other use of a work is not a destruction, distortion, mutilation, or other modification described in paragraph (3) of subsection (a).

(d) DURATION OF RIGHTS.—

(1) With respect to works of visual art created on or after the effective date set forth in section 610(a) of the Visual Artists Rights Act of 1990, the rights conferred by subsection (a) shall endure for a term consisting of the life of the author.

(2) With respect to works of visual art created before the effective date set forth in section 610(a) of the Visual Artists Rights Act of 1990, but title to which has not, as of such effective date, been transferred from the author, the rights conferred by subsection (a) shall be coextensive with, and shall expire at the same time as, the rights conferred by section 106.

(3) In the case of a joint work prepared by two or more authors, the rights conferred by subsection (a) shall endure for a term consisting of the life of the last surviving author.

(4) All terms of the rights conferred by subsection (a) run to the end of the calendar year in which they would otherwise expire.

(e) TRANSFER AND WAIVER.—

(1) The rights conferred by subsection (a) may not be transferred, but those rights may be waived if the author expressly agrees to such waiver in a written instrument signed by the author. Such instrument shall specifically identify the work, and uses of that work, to which the waiver applies, and the waiver shall apply only to the work and uses so identified. In the case of a joint work prepared by two or more authors, a waiver of rights under this paragraph made by one such author waives such rights for all such authors.

(2) Ownership of the rights conferred by subsection (a) with respect to a work of visual art is distinct from ownership of any copy of that work, or of a copyright or any exclusive right under a copyright in that work. Transfer of ownership of any copy of a work of visual art, or of a copyright or any exclusive right under a copyright, shall not constitute a waiver of the rights conferred by subsection (a). Except as may otherwise be agreed by the author in a written instrument signed by the author, a waiver of the rights conferred by subsection (a) with respect to a work of visual art shall not constitute a transfer of ownership of any copy of that work, or of ownership of a copyright or of any exclusive right under a copyright in that work

APPENDIX D

Copyright Statute Section 108, *Libraries and Archives Exemptions from Infringement for Certain Uses by Libraries and Archives of Copyrighted Works*

Because fair use means a use of a copyrighted work that would otherwise constitute infringement but is permitted because of its brevity or because it furthers some goal of society such as news reporting or education, the exemptions in described below are not, per se, varieties of fair use. Rather, they are specifically mentioned right in the copyright statute as uses that are not infringements, which is, legally speaking, much different. If your use of a copyrighted work falls into one of these exemptions, you are not guilty of infringement because of making that use. Remember, however, that the exemptions described are specific and that your use must meet the conditions listed precisely—all of them—or your use may constitute copyright infringement after all. The language of the statute is not hard to understand if you take it slowly and work your way through each exempt situation—maybe with a pencil to check off each condition your use meets. (The "sections" mentioned are sections of the U.S. copyright statute; you may read the entire statute online at *www.copyright.gov/title17.*)

§ 108. Limitations on exclusive rights: Reproduction by libraries and archives

(a) Except as otherwise provided in this title and notwithstanding the provisions of section 106, it is not an infringement of copyright for a library or archives, or any of its employees acting within the scope of their employment, to reproduce no more than one copy or phonorecord of a work, except as provided in subsections (b) and (c), or to distribute such copy or phonorecord, under the conditions specified by this section, if —

(1) the reproduction or distribution is made without any purpose of direct or indirect commercial advantage;

(2) the collections of the library or archives are (i) open to the public, or (ii) available not only to researchers affiliated with the library or archives or with the institution of which it is a part, but also to other persons doing research in a specialized field; and

(3) the reproduction or distribution of the work includes a notice of copyright that appears on the copy or phonorecord that is reproduced under the provisions of this section, or includes a legend stating that the work may be protected by copyright if no such notice can be found on the copy or phonorecord that is reproduced under the provisions of this section.

(b) The rights of reproduction and distribution under this section apply to three copies or phonorecords of an unpublished work duplicated solely for purposes of preservation and security or for deposit for research use in another library or archives of the type described by clause (2) of subsection (a), if —

(1) the copy or phonorecord reproduced is currently in the collections of the library or archives; and

(2) any such copy or phonorecord that is reproduced in digital format is not otherwise distributed in that format and is not made available to the public in that format outside the premises of the library or archives.

(c) The right of reproduction under this section applies to three copies or phonorecords of a published work duplicated solely for the purpose of replacement of a copy or phonorecord that is damaged, deteriorating, lost, or stolen, or if the existing format in which the work is stored has become obsolete, if —

(1) the library or archives has, after a reasonable effort, determined that an unused replacement cannot be obtained at a fair price; and

(2) any such copy or phonorecord that is reproduced in digital format is not made available to the public in that format outside the premises of the library or archives in lawful possession of such copy.

For purposes of this subsection, a format shall be considered obsolete if the machine or device necessary to render perceptible a work stored in that format is no longer manufactured or is no longer reasonably available in the commercial marketplace.

(d) The rights of reproduction and distribution under this section apply to a copy, made from the collection of a library or archives where the user makes his or her request or from that of another library or archives, of no more than one article or other contribution to a copyrighted collection or periodical issue, or to a copy or phonorecord of a small part of any other copyrighted work, if —

(1) the copy or phonorecord becomes the property of the user, and the library or archives has had no notice that the copy or phonorecord would be used for any purpose other than private study, scholarship, or research; and

(2) the library or archives displays prominently, at the place where orders are accepted, and includes on its order form, a warning of copyright in accordance with requirements that the Register of Copyrights shall prescribe by regulation.

(e) The rights of reproduction and distribution under this section apply to the entire work, or to a substantial part of it, made from the collection of a library or archives where the user makes his or her request or from that of another library or archives, if the library or archives has first determined, on the basis of a reasonable investigation, that a copy or phonorecord of the copyrighted work cannot be obtained at a fair price, if —

(1) the copy or phonorecord becomes the property of the user, and the library or archives has had no notice that the copy or phonorecord would be used for any purpose other than private study, scholarship, or research; and

(2) the library or archives displays prominently, at the place where orders are accepted, and includes on its order form, a warning of copyright in accordance with requirements that the Register of Copyrights shall prescribe by regulation.

(f) Nothing in this section —

(1) shall be construed to impose liability for copyright infringement upon a library or archives or its employees for the unsupervised use of reproducing equipment located on its premises: *Provided,* That such equipment displays a notice that the making of a copy may be subject to the copyright law;

(2) excuses a person who uses such reproducing equipment or who requests a copy or phonorecord under subsection (d) from liability for copyright infringement for any such act, or for any later use of such copy or phonorecord, if it exceeds fair use as provided by section 107;

(3) shall be construed to limit the reproduction and distribution by lending of a limited number of copies and excerpts by a library or archives of an audiovisual news program, subject to clauses (1), (2), and (3) of subsection (a); or

(4) in any way affects the right of fair use as provided by section 107, or any contractual obligations assumed at any time by the library or archives when it obtained a copy or phonorecord of a work in its collections.

(g) The rights of reproduction and distribution under this section extend to the isolated and unrelated reproduction or distribution of a single copy or phonorecord of the same material on separate occasions, but do not extend to cases where the library or archives, or its employee —

(1) is aware or has substantial reason to believe that it is engaging in the related or concerted reproduction or distribution of multiple copies or phonorecords of the same material, whether made on one occasion

or over a period of time, and whether intended for aggregate use by one or more individuals or for separate use by the individual members of a group; or

(2) engages in the systematic reproduction or distribution of single or multiple copies or phonorecords of material described in subsection (d): *Provided,* That nothing in this clause prevents a library or archives from participating in interlibrary arrangements that do not have, as their purpose or effect, that the library or archives receiving such copies or phonorecords for distribution does so in such aggregate quantities as to substitute for a subscription to or purchase of such work.

(h) (1) For purposes of this section, during the last 20 years of any term of copyright of a published work, a library or archives, including a nonprofit educational institution that functions as such, may reproduce, distribute, display, or perform in facsimile or digital form a copy or phonorecord of such work, or portions thereof, for purposes of preservation, scholarship, or research, if such library or archives has first determined, on the basis of a reasonable investigation, that none of the conditions set forth in subparagraphs (A), (B), and (C) of paragraph (2) apply.

(2) No reproduction, distribution, display, or performance is authorized under this subsection if —

(A) the work is subject to normal commercial exploitation;

(B) a copy or phonorecord of the work can be obtaincd at a reasonable price; or

(C) the copyright owner or its agent provides notice pursuant to regulations promulgated by the Register of Copyrights that either of the conditions set forth in subparagraphs (A) and (B) applies.

(3) The exemption provided in this subsection does not apply to any subsequent uses by users other than such library or archives.

(i) The rights of reproduction and distribution under this section do not apply to a musical work, a pictorial, graphic or sculptural work, or a motion picture or other audiovisual work other than an audiovisual work dealing with news, except that no such limitation shall apply with respect to rights granted by subsections (b) and (c), or with respect to pictorial or graphic works published as illustrations, diagrams, or similar adjuncts to works of which copies are reproduced or distributed in accordance with subsections (d) and (e).

APPENDIX E

Copyright Statute Section 110 Nonprofit Educational Institutions Exemptions from Infringement for Certain Performances by Nonprofits of Copyrighted Works

Because fair use means a use of a copyrighted work that would otherwise constitute infringement but is permitted because of its brevity or because it furthers some goal of society such as news reporting or education, the exemptions described below are not, per se, varieties of fair use. Rather, they are specifically mentioned right in the copyright statute as uses that are not infringements, which is, legally speaking, much different. If your use of a copyrighted work falls into one of these exemptions, you are not guilty of infringement because of making that use. Remember, however, that the exemptions described are specific and that your use must meet the conditions listed precisely—all of them—or your use may constitute copyright infringement after all. The language of the statute is not hard to understand if you take it slowly and work your way through each exempt situation—maybe with a pencil to check off each condition your use meets. (The "sections" mentioned are sections of the U.S. copyright statute; you may read the entire statute online at *www.copyright.gov/title17/*.)

§ 110. Limitations on exclusive rights: Exemption of certain performances and displays

Notwithstanding the provisions of section 106, the following are not infringements of copyright:

(1) performance or display of a work by instructors or pupils in the course of face-to-face teaching activities of a nonprofit educational institution, in

a classroom or similar place devoted to instruction, unless, in the case of a motion picture or other audiovisual work, the performance, or the display of individual images, is given by means of a copy that was not lawfully made under this title, and that the person responsible for the performance knew or had reason to believe was not lawfully made;

(2) except with respect to a work produced or marketed primarily for performance or display as part of mediated instructional activities transmitted via digital networks, or a performance or display that is given by means of a copy or phonorecord that is not lawfully made and acquired under this title, and the transmitting government body or accredited nonprofit educational institution knew or had reason to believe was not lawfully made and acquired, the performance of a nondramatic literary or musical work or reasonable and limited portions of any other work, or display of a work in an amount comparable to that which is typically displayed in the course of a live classroom session, by or in the course of a transmission, if —

(A) the performance or display is made by, at the direction of, or under the actual supervision of an instructor as an integral part of a class session offered as a regular part of the systematic mediated instructional activities of a governmental body or an accredited nonprofit educational institution;

(B) the performance or display is directly related and of material assistance to the teaching content of the transmission;

(C) the transmission is made solely for, and, to the extent technologically feasible, the reception of such transmission is limited to —

(i) students officially enrolled in the course for which the transmission is made; or

(ii) officers or employees of governmental bodies as a part of their official duties or employment; and

(D) the transmitting body or institution —

(i) institutes policies regarding copyright, provides informational materials to faculty, students, and relevant staff members that accurately describe, and promote compliance with, the laws of the United States relating to copyright, and provides notice to students that materials used in connection with the course may be subject to copyright protection; and

(ii) in the case of digital transmissions —

(I) applies technological measures that reasonably prevent —

(aa) retention of the work in accessible form by recipients of the transmission from the transmitting body or institution for longer than the class session; and

(bb) unauthorized further dissemination of the work in accessible form by such recipients to others; and

(II) does not engage in conduct that could reasonably be expected to interfere with technological measures used by copyright owners to prevent such retention or unauthorized further dissemination;

(3) performance of a nondramatic literary or musical work or of a dramatico-musical work of a religious nature, or display of a work, in the course of services at a place of worship or other religious assembly;

(4) performance of a nondramatic literary or musical work otherwise than in a transmission to the public, without any purpose of direct or indirect commercial advantage and without payment of any fee or other compensation for the performance to any of its performers, promoters, or organizers, if —

(A) there is no direct or indirect admission charge; or

(B) the proceeds, after deducting the reasonable costs of producing the performance, are used exclusively for educational, religious, or charitable purposes and not for private financial gain, except where the copyright owner has served notice of objection to the performance under the following conditions:

  (i) the notice shall be in writing and signed by the copyright owner or such owner's duly authorized agent; and

  (ii) the notice shall be served on the person responsible for the performance at least seven days before the date of the performance, and shall state the reasons for the objection; and

  (iii) the notice shall comply, in form, content, and manner of service, with requirements that the Register of Copyrights shall prescribe by regulation;

(5) (A) except as provided in subparagraph (B), communication of a transmission embodying a performance or display of a work by the public reception of the transmission on a single receiving apparatus of a kind commonly used in private homes, unless —

  (i) a direct charge is made to see or hear the transmission; or

  (ii) the transmission thus received is further transmitted to the public;

(B) communication by an establishment of a transmission or retransmission embodying a performance or display of a nondramatic musical work intended to be received by the general public, originated by a radio or television broadcast station licensed as such by the Federal Communications Commission, or, if an audiovisual transmission, by a cable system or satellite carrier, if —

  (i) in the case of an establishment other than a food service or drinking establishment, either the establishment in which the communication occurs has less than 2,000 gross square feet of space (excluding space used for customer parking and for no other purpose), or the establishment in which the communication occurs has 2,000 or more gross square feet of space (excluding space used for customer parking and for no other purpose) and —

    (I) if the performance is by audio means only, the performance is communicated by means of a total of not more than 6 loudspeakers, of which not more than 4 loudspeakers are located in any 1 room or adjoining outdoor space; or

(II) if the performance or display is by audiovisual means, any visual portion of the performance or display is communicated by means of a total of not more than 4 audiovisual devices, of which not more than 1 audiovisual device is located in any 1 room, and no such audiovisual device has a diagonal screen size greater than 55 inches, and any audio portion of the performance or display is communicated by means of a total of not more than 6 loudspeakers, of which not more than 4 loudspeakers are located in any 1 room or adjoining outdoor space;

(ii) in the case of a food service or drinking establishment, either the establishment in which the communication occurs has less than 3,750 gross square feet of space (excluding space used for customer parking and for no other purpose), or the establishment in which the communication occurs has 3,750 gross square feet of space or more (excluding space used for customer parking and for no other purpose) and —

(I) if the performance is by audio means only, the performance is communicated by means of a total of not more than 6 loudspeakers, of which not more than 4 loudspeakers arc located in any 1 room or adjoining outdoor space; or

(II) if the performance or display is by audiovisual means, any visual portion of the performance or display is communicated by means of a total of not more than 4 audiovisual devices, of which not more than 1 audiovisual device is located in any 1 room, and no such audiovisual device has a diagonal screen size greater than 55 inches, and any audio portion of the performance or display is communicated by means of a total of not more than 6 loudspeakers, of which not more than 4 loudspeakers are located in any 1 room or adjoining outdoor space;

(iii) no direct charge is made to see or hear the transmission or retransmission;

(iv) the transmission or retransmission is not further transmitted beyond the establishment where it is received; and

(v) the transmission or retransmission is licensed by the copyright owner of the work so publicly performed or displayed;

(6) performance of a nondramatic musical work by a governmental body or a nonprofit agricultural or horticultural organization, in the course of an annual agricultural or horticultural fair or exhibition conducted by such body or organization; the exemption provided by this clause shall extend to any liability for copyright infringement that would otherwise be imposed on such body or organization, under doctrines of vicarious liability or related infringement, for a performance by a concessionnaire, business establishment, or other person at such fair or exhibition, but shall not excuse any such person from liability for the performance;

(7) performance of a nondramatic musical work by a vending establishment open to the public at large without any direct or indirect admission charge, where the sole purpose of the performance is to promote the retail sale of copies or phonorecords of the work, or of the audiovisual or other devices utilized in such performance, and the performance is not transmitted beyond the place where the establishment is located and is within the immediate area where the sale is occurring;

(8) performance of a nondramatic literary work, by or in the course of a transmission specifically designed for and primarily directed to blind or other handicapped persons who are unable to read normal printed material as a result of their handicap, or deaf or other handicapped persons who are unable to hear the aural signals accompanying a transmission of visual signals, if the performance is made without any purpose of direct or indirect commercial advantage and its transmission is made through the facilities of: (i) a governmental body; or (ii) a noncommercial educational broadcast station (as defined in section 397 of title 47); or (iii) a radio subcarrier authorization (as defined in 47 CFR 73.293-73.295 and 73.593-73.595); or (iv) a cable system (as defined in section 111 (f));

(9) performance on a single occasion of a dramatic literary work published at least ten years before the date of the performance, by or in the course of a transmission specifically designed for and primarily directed to blind or other handicapped persons who are unable to read normal printed material as a result of their handicap, if the performance is made without any purpose of direct or indirect commercial advantage and its transmission is made through the facilities of a radio subcarrier authorization referred to in clause (8) (iii), *Provided,* That the provisions of this clause shall not be applicable to more than one performance of the same work by the same performers or under the auspices of the same organization; and

(10) notwithstanding paragraph (4), the following is not an infringement of copyright: performance of a nondramatic literary or musical work in the course of a social function which is organized and promoted by a nonprofit veterans' organization or a nonprofit fraternal organization to which the general public is not invited, but not including the invitees of the organizations, if the proceeds from the performance, after deducting the reasonable costs of producing the performance, are used exclusively for charitable purposes and not for financial gain. For purposes of this section, the social functions of any college or university fraternity or sorority shall not be included unless the social function is held solely to raise funds for a specific charitable purpose.

The exemptions provided under paragraph (5) shall not be taken into account in any administrative, judicial, or other governmental proceeding to set or adjust the royalties payable to copyright owners for the public performance or display of their works. Royalties payable to copyright owners for any public performance or display of their works other than such performances or displays as are exempted under paragraph (5) shall not be diminished in any respect as a result of such exemption.

In paragraph (2), the term "mediated instructional activities" with respect to the performance or display of a work by digital transmission under this section refers to activities that use such work as an integral part of the class experience, controlled by or under the actual supervision of the instructor and analogous to the type of performance or display that would take place in a live classroom setting. The term does not refer to activities that use, in 1 or more class sessions of a single course, such works as textbooks, course packs, or other material in any media, copies or phonorecords of which are typically purchased or acquired by the students in higher education for their independent use and retention or are typically purchased or acquired for elementary and secondary students for their possession and independent use. For purposes of paragraph (2), accreditation —

(A) with respect to an institution providing post-secondary education, shall be as determined by a regional or national accrediting agency recognized by the Council on Higher Education Accreditation or the United States Department of Education; and

(B) with respect to an institution providing elementary or secondary education, shall be as recognized by the applicable state certification or licensing procedures.

For purposes of paragraph (2), no governmental body or accredited nonprofit educational institution shall be liable for infringement by reason of the transient or temporary storage of material carried out through the automatic technical process of a digital transmission of the performance or display of that material as authorized under paragraph (2). No such material stored on the system or network controlled or operated by the transmitting body or institution under this paragraph shall be maintained on such system or network in a manner ordinarily accessible to anyone other than anticipated recipients. No such copy shall be maintained on the system or network in a manner ordinarily accessible to such anticipated recipients for a longer period than is reasonably necessary to facilitate the transmissions for which it was made.

APPENDIX F

Sample Permission Letters

When a Permission Is Requested From the Owner of the Copyright in a Published Work

Because copyright law does not require nonexclusive licenses of copyright to be written and because most permissions to use copyrighted works fall into this category, most permissions don't need to be in writing. However, a written permission is an excellent idea, if for no other reason than that the person requesting the permission and the one granting it will have, in writing, documentation of the scope of the permission. The sample permission request letter that follows allows the would-be user of a work to request and receive permission to use the work in one document. Use a letter similar to this one to request permission to use any work that is not a public-domain work. Refer to the permissions checklist in chapter 12 to make sure you cover all the bases.

[1]**Helen Brewster**
4209 Candler Street
Farmington, AL 21987

June 25, 2005

[2]Miss Geraldine Hambrick
Permissions Administrator
Modern Textbook Company
3351 Old Tannery Lane
Tarrant, NH 09231

Dear [3]Ms. Hambrick,

I am writing regarding [4]the chart on page 243 of Professor John Malcolm's book *Return to the Wild*, which your company publishes. As you will recall, [5]I spoke to you on the phone yesterday regarding obtaining permission to use Professor Malcolm's chart in an article for *Southern Wildlife*. You told me at that time that you would allow me to use the chart without charge if I would mention Professor Malcolm's book and include in my article directions for buying it.

[6]My article is scheduled for publication in the September 2005 issue of *Southern Wildlife*. I plan to reprint Professor Malcolm's chart in it. Unless you let me know that you want some change, I will include [7]the following language in the caption for the chart: "This chart is reprinted from *Return to the Wild* by John Malcolm, published in 2005 by the Modern Textbook Company; copies may be purchased for $29.95 direct from the publisher by calling (800) 443-9821."

Please counter-sign both copies of this letter, in the spaces indicated, in the presence of a [8]notary and return one signed copy to me [9]at your earliest convenience to evidence that I have your permission[10]to use the chart from Professor John Malcolm's book in the way described in this letter in return for printing in the projected article, as a caption to that chart, the language set out above. [11]I am sending two copies of this letter so that you may retain a copy for your files. I have also enclosed a self-addressed, stamped envelope for your convenience.

[12]Please call me at (992) 745-6377 if you have questions. Thank you for your kindness.

Sincerely,

[13] (signed) Helen Brewster

[14]My signature below evidences my agreement and consent to everything foregoing in this letter:

[15]Modern Textbook Company

By Geraldine Hambrick, [16]an authorized signatory

[17]_____   _____

Signature   Date of Signature

[18]Verification:

Signed before me this _____ day of _____ by

_____, who is personally known to me:

_____

Signature of Notary Public

_____

Printed Name of Notary Public

My commission expires on _____. (Seal of Notary Public)

---

[1] Insert your name and address here, or use stationery preprinted with your name and address.

[2] Insert the name of the owner of the copyright in the work or works you want permission to use. This person may be the author of those works, as in this example, or may instead be the publisher, heir, or executor of the estate of the author. In cases where a publisher is involved, as in this example, the publisher may have acquired ownership of the copyright from the author or merely have acquired the exclusive right to publish the work from the author; in either case, the publisher controls any uses of the work.

[3] Insert the name of the person to whom the letter is addressed.

[4] Since the chart for which permission to use is sought appears in a published book, this reference is sufficient to identify it and no attachment of a copy of the chart is necessary, as it would be in the case of an unpublished work.

[5] State your reason for writing right away. In this example, this paragraph serves to remind the recipient of a recent phone call regarding the use of the copyrighted work and the outcome of that phone call—namely, the granting of permission to use the work.

[6] Letting the permissions person know that there is a time factor involved in securing the permission is important, as well as mentioning the publication in which the chart will be republished.

[7] It's important to specify the proposed language for a credit line, especially if, as in this example, that language will also serve as the compensation for the use of the chart. This eliminates the possibility that the credit line will appear with a mistake in it or for some other reason does not satisfy the needs of the textbook company.

[8] Having the person to whom you address the letter counter-sign both copies of it in front of a notary should eliminate any later question as to whether he or she really did grant the permission you request.

[9] It's a good idea to specify a reasonably short deadline by which the copyright owner should respond, to eliminate delays.

[10] It is important to repeat here the specific terms of the permission, both to clarify them and to state what the counter-signature is intended to signify.

[11] It is best to make it as easy as possible for the person from whom the permission is requested to say "yes" to your request. This means that you should not expect the person to whom you address your letter to have to photocopy it or type an envelope to return it to you.

[12] It is always possible that there must be further negotiations or that some important term in the permission request letter must be revised to reflect the permission correctly. In the interests of eliminating any such problem quickly, it is far better to include a phone number or e-mail address in the letter to facilitate further communication than to simply expect the copyright owner to write back by regular mail.

[13] Your signature on the letter will serve to demonstrate your agreement to abide by whatever conditions on the use of the copyrighted work you have proposed to abide by.

[14] By counter-signing the letter, the copyright owner agrees to grant the permission requested on the terms mentioned.

[15] Insert the name of the owner of the copyright in the work or works you want permission to use. This person may be the author of those works or, as in this example, may have acquired from the author the exclusive right to publish the work.

[16] In any situation where the person who will sign the permission request letter is not the author of the copyrighted work, it is important to include this language, which constitutes a representation that the named person is authorized to grant the permission his or her signature evidences.

[17] Leave this space blank for the signature of the person who counter-signs the letter. The signature of that person at the bottom of the letter transforms your proposal (to use a certain work, under the conditions stated) into an agreement between you.

[18] Everything under the "Verification:" heading relates to the verification of the counter-signature by the notary public who witnesses it. All of the signatures should occur on the same page of the letter to eliminate any question of validity of the permission.

When a Permission Is Requested from the Author of an Unpublished Work

Because copyright law does not require nonexclusive licenses of copyright to be written and because most permissions to use copyrighted works fall into this category, most permissions don't need to be in writing. However, a written permission is an excellent idea, if for no other reason than that the person requesting the permission and the one granting it will have, in writing, documentation of the scope of the permission. The sample permission request letter that follows allows the would-be user of a work to request and receive permission to use the work in one document. Use a letter similar to this one to request permission to use any work that is not a public-domain work. Refer to the permissions checklist in chapter 12 to make sure you cover all the bases.

[1]**Terrence Allison**
655 Garland Avenue
Ocean City, CA 67209

January 30, 2006

[2]Ms. Morgan Harrell
Sunnyside Retirement Manor
7751 Briarcliff Lane
Grove Park, IL 82340

Dear [3]Ms. Harrell,

[4]Your nephew, Morgan Mitchell, was kind enough to give me your address. I am writing [5]because I am preparing to open a restaurant, to be called Terrence's by the Sea, here in Ocean City, a town I am told you know well. I want to use as a major element in the décor of my restaurant an enlarged photographic copy of one of your paintings, [6]a snapshot of which I enclose. I inherited this painting from my aunt Julia Farris, who summered in Ocean City for many years; [7]perhaps you knew her. I never knew the name of the painter until [8]your old friend Mrs. Eileen Parker, the librarian here, gave me your name and the phone number for your nephew. [9]However, I have treasured your painting since it came into my possession and for nearly fifteen years have moved it from one apartment to another, where it was always given a place of honor.

[10]Would you consider allowing me to use your painting to make a mural for the front lobby of my restaurant? [11]I am well aware that you own the copyright in your painting and that I cannot use it in any way other than displaying it unless I have your permission. [12]I will pay you $500 for the right to turn your painting, through a [13]photographic process that will not damage the original painting, into a [14]single mural to be [15]permanently affixed to an interior wall of the building I own here at 723 Shell Avenue, which will become the location for my restaurant.

[16]I agree that I will not create more than one finished copy of your painting, to be used as the mural described above, and that I will not allow others to make any further copies of your painting without your permission.

If you will agree to allow me to create a single mural for my restaurant from the painting depicted in the attached snapshot, please [17]counter-sign both copies of this letter, in the spaces indicated, in the presence of a [18]notary and return one signed copy to me [19]by February 28, 2006. [20]I am sending two copies of this letter and its attachment so that you may retain a copy for your files. I have also enclosed a self-addressed, stamped envelope for your convenience. [21]I will send you my check for $500 as soon as you return one signed copy of this letter to me.

[22]I would also be happy to discuss this matter further with you or your nephew. [23]Either you or he may call me at (783) 887-5523 if you have questions. Thank you for [24]considering my request.

Sincerely,

[25](signed) Terrence Allison

[26]My signature below evidences my agreement and consent to everything foregoing in

this letter:

Ms. Morgan Harrell:

[27] _____   _____

Signature   Date of Signature

[28]Verification:

Signed before me this _____ day of _____ by

_____, who is personally known to me:

_____

Signature of Notary Public

_____

Printed Name of Notary Public

My commission expires on _____. (Seal of Notary Public)

---

[1] Insert your name and address here, or use stationery preprinted with your name and address.

[2] Insert the name of the owner of the copyright in the work or works you want permission to use. This person may be the author of those works, as in this example, or may instead be the publisher or heir or executor of the estate of the author.

[3] Insert the name of the person to whom the letter is addressed.

[4] Tell the recipient of the letter how you located her or him, especially if he or she is a private individual or if you are directed to him or her by a mutual friend or acquaintance. Remember, you are the supplicant here and any fact that could create good feeling between you and the person to whom you are writing should be used to do so.

[5] State your reason for writing early in the letter.

[6] Here a snapshot of the painting must serve to identify the copyrighted work for which permission to use is sought, since the painting itself cannot be attached to the letter requesting permission. Any such identifying material should be stapled to each copy of the permission request letter in order that it remains a part of everyone's record of the permission.

[7] If you have or may have a mutual friend or acquaintance, mention this circumstance to the person to whom the letter is addressed.

[8] Again, if you have a mutual friend or acquaintance, mention this circumstance to the person to whom the letter is addressed.

[9] If you can honestly state a circumstance that is likely to flatter the person to whom the letter is addressed, do so. Such aboveboard ingratiation is called diplomacy.

[10] Remember that your letter is a request and phrase the portion of it that outlines what you want to do as such. Be as clear as possible about what you want to do, how it would be achieved, how long you want to do it, and what payment, if any, would be given to the owner of the copyright you want to use.

[11] Acknowledging the rights of the copyright owner is smart because it lets her or him know that you know that your rights in the work are limited.

[12] If you are offering to pay for the right to do what you want to do, state the amount you would pay clearly.

[13] Make it clear just how your goal will be accomplished and that the work you want to use will not be damaged.

[14] Make sure that you specify the extent of the use you want permission to make; one mural is far different from multiple murals or other copies.

[15] This is also important; anything other than a permanent attachment to a wall would turn the mural contemplated in this letter into, essentially, a moveable larger version of the painting.

[16] It may be important to represent that you will not exceed the permission you ask for and that you will not facilitate a similar use of the copyrighted work by others who do not have permission to use it. Here, it would be easy to create numerous copies of the painting from the photograph of the painting that is necessary to turn it into a mural; the copyright owner would certainly want assurances that nothing of the sort would be permitted.

[17] This turns your letter into a binding agreement.

[18] Having the person to whom you address the letter counter-sign both copies of it in front of a notary should eliminate any later question whether he or she really did grant the permission you request.

[19] It's a good idea to specify a reasonably short deadline by which the copyright owner should respond. Such a deadline gives some urgency to your request and diminishes the possibility that a copyright owner who is inclined to give you the permission you want will simply file your letter and forget about it. A deadline also serves to let you know fairly quickly whether you can proceed with the project for which you need the requested permission.

[20] It is best to make it as easy as possible for the person from whom the permission is requested to say "yes" to your request. This means that you should not expect the person to whom you address your letter to have to photocopy it or type an envelope to return it to you.

[21] Let the copyright owner know that she or he will not have to wait for the fee you promise and make sure that you do, indeed, send it along promptly; non-payment or delayed payment could call into question the validity of the agreement you reached.

[22] If you have phrased your request correctly and answered the questions that he or she would likely have, the copyright owner may simply counter-sign your letter and return it. However, it is a very good idea to leave the possibility of further negotiation open, if for no other reason than that most people don't like to feel that the terms of agreements have been dictated to them.

[23] Include contact information for more speedy communication than by return letter, since lots of people would simply file and forget a request letter that required a letter in return.

[24] Again, acknowledging that the copyright owner has a choice whether or not to grant your request is good psychology.

[25] Your signature on the letter will serve to demonstrate your agreement to abide by whatever conditions on the use of the copyrighted work you have proposed to abide by.

[26] By counter-signing the letter, the copyright owner agrees to grant the permission requested on the terms mentioned.

[27] Leave this space blank for the signature of the person who counter-signs the letter. The signature of that person at the bottom of the letter transforms your proposal (to use the copyrighted work, under the conditions stated) into an agreement between you.

[28] Everything under the "Verification:" heading relates to the verification of the counter-signature by the notary public who witnesses it. All of the signatures should occur on the same page of the letter, to eliminate any question of validity of the permission.

When a Permission Is Requested From the Heir of the Creator of an Unpublished Work and a Waiver of Any Invasion-of-Privacy Claim Is Sought

Because copyright law does not require nonexclusive licenses of copyright to be written and because most permissions to use copyrighted works fall into this category, most permissions don't need to be in writing. However, a written permission is an excellent idea, if for no other reason than that the person requesting the permission and the one granting it will have, in writing, documentation of the scope of the permission. The sample permission request letter that follows allows the would-be user of a work to request and receive permission to use the work in one document. Use a letter similar to this one to request permission to use any work that is not a public-domain work. Refer to the permissions checklist in chapter 12 to make sure you cover all the bases.

[1]Anne Clifford
325 Shoreview Street
Madison, MN 98034

December 8, 2005

[2]Mrs. Marjorie Simpson Atkins
1081 Creekside Road
Madison, MN 98035

Dear [3]Mrs. Atkins,

[4]This letter, when counter-signed below by you, will evidence your consent and permission to the publication of my book *Twentieth-Century Madison: From Village to City*, which is attached hereto in the form of a 250-page manuscript, which you agree you [5]have examined. By your signature below, you represent that

you are the [6]owner of copyright in the unpublished journal of your grandmother Matilda Simpson and assent to the use and publication in my book [7]of the portions of that journal that are contained in the attached manuscript. Furthermore, by your signature below you waive any claim for [8]invasion of privacy based on such publication of the aforementioned portions of the Matilda Simpson journal. In addition, you agree that [9]you will receive no payment or royalty of any kind from the publication of my book or any future project based on the attached manuscript and that you make the grants contained herein in return for the sum of $100 and five copies of my book as and when it is published.

If you will agree to allow me to use sections of your grandmother's journal as described above, [10]counter-sign both copies of this letter, in the spaces indicated, in the presence of a [11]notary and [12]return one signed copy to me [13]by January 31, 2006. I am submitting to you two copies of this letter and its attachment so that you may retain a copy for your files. I have also enclosed a [14]self-addressed, stamped envelope for your convenience. [15]I will send you my check for $100 as soon as you return one signed copy of this letter to me and will send you five copies of my book if and when it is published.

[16]Call me at (882) 978-3213 if you have any questions. Thank you for [17] considering my request.

Sincerely,

[18](signed) Anne Clifford

[19]My signature below evidences my agreement and consent to everything foregoing in this letter:

Marjorie Simpson Atkins:

_____   _____

Signature   Date of Signature

[20]Verification:

Signed before me this _____ day of _____ by

_____, who is personally known to me:

_____

Signature of Notary Public

_____

Printed Name of Notary Public

My commission expires on _____. (Seal of Notary Public)

[1] Insert your name and address here, or use stationery preprinted with your name and address.

[2] Insert the name of the owner of the copyright in the work or works you want permission to use. This person may be the author of those works or, as in this example, the heir or executor of the estate of the author.

[3] Insert the name of the person to whom the letter is addressed.

[4] In a situation such as this example, where the owner of copyright in the material to be used has objected to the use of the material without permission and the person who wants to use the material seeks a meeting with the copyright owner in order to convince her to allow the use, circumstances may not permit negotiation. In such a case, the best course may be to draft a letter specifying the permission that is needed on the chance that the copyright owner will be convinced during the meeting to allow the use; the letter in such a case is an embodiment of the offer the person seeking the permission is willing to make. That person can present the letter to the copyright owner at the end of the meeting, if it has gone well, or can re-draft it after the meeting to conform to the terms that are negotiated during the meeting. This may be troublesome, but it is far better to spend time getting the permission you need documented in the right form than to have to abandon the project because you can't obtain that permission.

[5] Give the copyright owner plenty of time to determine what he or she is agreeing to allow; if there is a meeting, it may be necessary for the copyright owner to take time to scan through a long work such as the manuscript in this example.

[6] It's important to make sure that the person you approach is the owner of the copyright you want to use; otherwise, the permission you request would be useless.

[7] An alternate way of handling this would be to prepare a list of only the portions of the journal to be used; this list of excerpts would then be attached to the permission request letter in the same manner and referred to in the letter in the same way so as to make them part of the ultimate agreement.

[8] Even though, in this example, the only mentions of the copyright owner are journal entries by her grandmother about her as a child, she could still sue for invasion of privacy if segments of the journal that mention her were published without her permission. It's a very good idea to get the consent of any living person who is mentioned in any textual work or depicted in any photograph before you use his or her name or image in your own work. It may not be easy to find out whether a person is still living or to get permission to use his or her name or image, but it may be necessary to do so to eliminate suits for invasion of privacy. Get a lawyer to evaluate your specific proposed use of someone's name or image if you are in doubt on this point. It may be that you can eliminate any possibility of dispute by approaching the person named or depicted in advance of the publication of your project, even if the material you want to use is not inherently embarrassing to the person. People who are caught by surprise often sue in situations that may not have angered them if they had known in advance about the use.

[9] In any situation where the proposed use of the copyrighted work may produce income over a period of time, it is advisable to state that the person whose permission you seek is not entitled to any of that future income and instead will receive a one-time payment in the amount stated and given the copies of the published book as his or her only compensation.

[10] This turns your letter into a binding agreement.

[11] Having the person to whom you address the letter countersign both copies of it in front of a notary should eliminate any later question whether he or she really did grant the permission you request.

[12] In a situation where a permission is negotiated in a face-to-face meeting, the person seeking the permission can either leave both copies of the letter with the copyright owner for the owner to read and sign later in the presence of a notary. If there is any hurry or if the meeting settles an incipient dispute, it may be better to accompany the copyright owner to a notary immediately after the meeting so that the letter can be counter-signed right away.

[13] It's a good idea to specify a reasonably short deadline by which the copyright owner should respond. Such a deadline gives some urgency to your request and diminishes the possibility that a copyright owner who is inclined to give you the permission you want will simply file your letter and forget about it. A deadline also serves to let you know fairly quickly whether you can proceed with the project for which you need the requested permission.

[14] It is best to make it as easy as possible for the person from whom the permission is requested to say "yes" to your request. This means that you should not expect her or him to have to photocopy it or type an envelope to return it to you. Make sure that the self-addressed envelope is large enough to hold the permission letter and its attachment.

[15] Let the copyright owner know that she or he will not have to wait for the fee you promise and make sure that you do, indeed, send it along promptly; non-payment or delayed payment could call into question the validity of the agreement you reached. Similarly, send the copies of the published book you promise as soon as it is available.

[16] Include contact information for more speedy communication than by return letter, since lots of people would simply file and forget a request letter that required a letter in return.

[17] Acknowledging that the copyright owner has a choice whether or not to grant your request is good psychology.

[18] Your signature on the letter will serve to demonstrate your agreement to abide by whatever conditions on the use of the copyrighted work you have proposed to abide by.

[19] By counter-signing the letter, the copyright owner agrees to grant the permission requested on the terms mentioned.

[20] Everything under the "Verification:" heading relates to the verification of the counter-signature by the notary public who witnesses it. All of the signatures should occur on the same page of the letter to eliminate any question of validity of the permission.

When Permission for the Use of a Published Work Has Already Been Negotiated and/or Was Granted after the Use Was Made

Because copyright law does not require nonexclusive licenses of copyright to be written and because most permissions to use copyrighted works fall into this category, most permissions don't need to be in writing. However, a written permission is an excellent idea, if for no other reason than that the person requesting the permission and the one granting it will have, in writing, documentation of the scope of the permission. The sample permission request letter that follows allows the would-be user of a work to request and receive permission to use the work in one document. Use a letter similar to this one to request permission to use any work that is not a public-domain work.

[1]Samuel Renegar
923 Sutton Avenue
Franklin, OH 41098

May 23, 2006

[2]Estate of Dr. Martin Luther King, Jr.
Intellectual Properties Management
One Freedom Plaza
449 Auburn Avenue NE
Atlanta, GA 30312
Attention: Mr. Thomas Baker

Dear [3]Mr. Baker,

[4]I am writing on behalf of the Benjamin Franklin High School debate team; I am chairman of the parents' committee for that team. I understand that you spoke yesterday to Ms. Marilyn Jones, the lawyer for the school board here in Hill County. I am writing in regard to the matter about which Ms. Jones called you.

As Ms. Jones mentioned to you, the Franklin High debate team has been selling Great American Speeches, printed in a form suitable for framing, in order to raise enough money to finance a trip for the debate team members and two parent-chaperons to a national debate convention. [5]One of the speeches in the set we have been selling is Dr. Martin Luther King, Jr.'s "I have a dream" speech; for your reference, [6]I have attached a copy of that speech in the form in which we have marketed it. [7]You wrote to tell us that Dr. King's estate owns the copyright in his speech, that we did not have the right to sell copies of it, and to ask us to stop selling it as part of our set of Great American Speeches. However, when Ms. Jones called and explained what we had been doing, you were kind enough to say that you would allow us to keep the money we had made from the sales of Dr. King's speech so long as we did not again sell the speech in any form without your permission.

[8]We sold 150 copies of Dr. King's speech; our proceeds attributable to that speech total $750. Our fundraiser is finished, all the sets of our Great American Speeches have been sold, and there are no remaining copies of Dr. King's speech in our possession. I can guarantee that as long as I am associated with it, the Franklin High debate team will not again make any use of Dr. King's speech without your prior consent. Thank you for allowing us to keep the money we have raised through our sale of Dr. King's speech—your kindness will allow the debate team to make the trip to the debate convention.

Please counter-sign both copies of this letter, in the spaces indicated, in the presence of a [9]notary and return one signed copy to me [10]at your earliest convenience to evidence that we have your permission (granted after the fact), [11]to make and sell 150 copies of Dr. King's speech as described in this letter without payment to you for the right to do so and that you have agreed to allow us to keep the money we made from selling those copies. [12]I am sending two copies of this letter so that you may retain a copy for your files. I have also enclosed a self-addressed, stamped envelope for your convenience.

[13]Please call me at (763) 778-0998 if you have questions. Thank you for your kindness.

Sincerely,

[14](signed) Samuel Renegar

Agreed and accepted:

[15]Estate of Dr. Martin Luther King, Jr.

By Thomas Baker, [16]an authorized signatory

[17] _____   _____

Signature   Date of Signature

[18]Verification:

Signed before me this _____ day of _____ by

_____, who is personally known to me:

_____

Signature of Notary Public

_____

Printed Name of Notary Public

My commission expires on _____. (Seal of Notary Public)

---

[1] Insert your name and address here, or use stationery preprinted with your name and address.

[2] Insert the name of the owner of the copyright in the work or works you want permission to use. This person may be the author of those works or, as in this example, may be executor of the estate of the author.

[3] Insert the name of the person to whom the letter is addressed.

[4] Identify yourself and state your reason for writing right away. In this example, this paragraph serves to remind the recipient of a recent phone call regarding the use without permission of the copyrighted work and the outcome of that phone call—namely, the granting of permission to use the work.

[5] In any letter in which permission is sought to use a copyrighted work, including a situation in which permission is requested after the fact of the use, it is important to describe the use with some specificity.

[6] It is important to identify the work used and the specific use that has been made of it in such a way that there can be little chance later of a misunderstanding. Here, identifying a famous speech by name is enough because its content is a matter of historical record; the attachment serves to show exactly what use was made of the speech.

[7] This sentence and the next tell the story of the copyright owner's actions and the response of the user of the copyrighted work. One of the goals of this sort of permission letter is to set down the sequence of events that have transpired and to make clear that even though there was originally an objection from the copyright owner to the use of the copyrighted work, that objection has been eliminated; a brief recounting of the history of the dealings between the parties helps achieve that goal.

[8] This sentence adds to a full statement of the history of the use of the copyrighted work; it is also necessary to the permission—how can the copyright owner here fully consent to the (originally unpermitted) use of the speech and allow the debate team to retain the money raised by its sale unless both the number of copies sold and the money produced by those sales are specified?

[9] Having the person to whom you address the letter counter-sign both copies of it in front of a notary should eliminate any later question whether he or she really did grant the permission you request.

[10] It's a good idea to specify a reasonably short deadline by which the copyright owner should respond, but in a situation such as this example, in which the person requesting permission and documentation of that permission is doing so only after a complaint by the copyright owner, it would be unwise to dictate a time limit for a response. Further, in the situation outlined, the use has already occurred, so a delay in documenting the permission would not impede the use.

[11] It is important to repeat here the specific terms of the permission, both to clarify them and to state what the counter-signature is intended to signify.

[12] It is best to make it as easy as possible for the person from whom the permission is requested to say "yes" to your request. This means that you should not expect the person to whom you address your letter to have to photocopy it or type an envelope to return it to you.

[13] It is always possible that there must be further negotiations or that some important term in the permission request letter must be revised to reflect the permission correctly. In the interests of eliminating any such problem quickly, it is far better to include a phone number or e-mail address in the letter to facilitate further communication than to simply expect the copyright owner to write back by regular mail.

[14] Your signature on the letter will serve to demonstrate your agreement to abide by whatever conditions on the use of the copyrighted work you have proposed to abide by.

[15] Insert the name of the owner of the copyright in the work or works you want permission to use. This person may be the author of those works or, as in this example, may be executor of the estate of the author.

[16] In any situation where the person who will sign the permission request letter is not the author of the copyrighted work, it is important to include this language, which constitutes a representation that the named person is authorized to grant the permission his or her signature evidences.

[17] Leave this space blank for the signature of the person who countersigns the letter. The signature of that person at the bottom of the letter transforms your proposal (to use a certain work, under the conditions stated) into an agreement between you.

[18] Everything under the "Verification:" heading relates to the verification of the counter-signature by the notary public who witnesses it. All of the signatures should occur on the same page of the letter to eliminate any question of validity of the permission.

Sample Forms

Nonexclusive License of Copyright

Although exclusive licenses of copyright must be in writing; it is not necessary that *nonexclusive* licenses of copyright be written. However, a written nonexclusive license is an excellent idea, if for no other reason than that the parties to the agreement will have, in a written license, documentation of the duration and scope of the license as well as of other important terms of their agreement. This form agreement allows the author of a work to license it to another person or a company on a nonexclusive basis—that is, others may be granted the same rights to use the copyright. Use this form as a model for any license you grant or request.

Nonexclusive License of Copyright

This agreement is made between _____[1] (hereinafter referred to as "the Author"[2]) and _____[3] (hereinafter referred to as "the Licensee"), with reference to the following facts:

That the Author, an independent contractor,[4] is the creator of and owner of the copyright in a certain unpublished[5] _____ (hereinafter referred to as "the Work"), which may be more fully described as follows: _____
_____,[6]
a photocopy[7] of which is attached hereto and made a part of this agreement by this reference.

The Author and the Licensee agree as follows:

1. That the Author hereby grants to the Licensee the nonexclusive right to reproduce, publish, prepare derivative works of and from, combine with other materials, display publicly, and otherwise use and exploit the Work[8] for a period of _____ (_____)[9]months from the date written below.
2. That, during the term of this License of Copyright, the Licensee shall have the nonexclusive right to exercise the rights granted herein throughout the United States and Canada.[10]

3.   That the Licensee shall have the right to crop, edit, alter, or otherwise modify the Work to the extent that the Licensee, in the sole discretion of the Licensee, deems necessary to suit it to such uses as the Licensee may choose to make of the Work.[11]

4.   That the Licensee will pay to the Author the sum of _____ ($_____), which amount it is agreed will constitute Author's only compensation for the grant of rights made herein.[12]

5.   That the Author warrants that he or she is the owner of copyright in the Work and possesses full right and authority to convey the rights herein conveyed. The Author further warrants that the Work does not infringe the copyright in any other work, and does not invade any privacy, publicity, trademark, or other rights of any other person.[13] The Author further agrees to indemnify and hold the Licensee harmless in any litigation in which a third party challenges any of the warranties made by the Author in this paragraph if any such litigation results in a judgment adverse to the Author in a court of competent jurisdiction.[14]

6.   That this agreement shall be governed by the laws of the State of _____[15] applicable to contracts made and to be performed therein and shall be construed according to the Copyright Law of the United States, Title 17, Section 101, *et seq.*, United States Code.

7.   That this agreement shall enure to the benefit of and bind the parties and their respective heirs, representatives, successors, and assigns.[16]

In witness whereof, the Author and the Licensee have executed this document in _____ (___) counterpart originals[17] as of[18] the _____day of _____, 20__.[19]

_____[20]	_____[21]
Author	Licensee
_____[22]	_____[23]
_____	_____
Address	Address
_____[24]	By: _____[25]
Social Security number	
	_____[16]
	Title

---

[1] Insert the name of the author of the work. If two or more people created the work as co-authors, insert all their names here and add enough spaces for their signatures, etc., at the end of the agreement.

[2] If you want to be more specific, use "Photographer," "Writer," "Songwriter," "Composer," "Illustrator," etc.; use the same designation throughout the document everywhere the word "Author" appears here. If two or more people created the work as co-authors, use the following language: (hereinafter jointly referred to as "the Author")

[3] Insert the name of the person or company to whom the copyright in the work is being licensed.

[4] This form license agreement is inappropriate for use by anyone who is *not* an independent contractor. The works created by employees as part of their jobs are works-for-hire; no written agreement is necessary to document the work-for-hire situation in such a circumstance because the relationship of the employee and employer determines, as a matter of law, the ownership of the copyright in any work created on the job by the employee. However, even someone who works at a full-time job is an independent contractor with regard to any activity outside his or her job responsibilities. This language makes clear that the Author is not an employee of the Licensee.

[5] If the Work has been published, use language similar to the following to specify the year of first publication of the Work: "a certain drawing, first published in 2005." One of the three elements of copyright notice is the year date of first publication of the work.

[6] Insert a detailed description of the Work sufficient to allow the parties to the license and everyone else to determine just which particular work, out of all similar works, is the subject of the license, i.e., "a photograph of three-year-old twin girls, each holding a black Labrador puppy," "a poem titled *Midsummer's Eve*," "a musical composition titled 'Wind Dance,' " "an essay titled 'High Hopes,'" "a non-fiction magazine article titled 'Trends in Consumer Electronics Purchases,'" etc.

[7] If it is practicable, attach a copy of the Work, similar to the sort of copies required for registration of copyright, to each original of the Nonexclusive License of Copyright document. If it is not practicable to do so, omit this language and use a much more detailed description of the Work or use photographs (for three-dimensional works such as sculptures) or other identifying material, such as the script for a film, and change the language describing the attached materials.

[8] These are the exclusive rights of copyright given to copyright owners by the U.S. copyright statute and the copyright statutes of other countries. However, since this is a nonexclusive license, the Author may also grant the right to other parties to exercise these rights; further, the Author retains the right to exercise these rights simultaneously with any licensee.

[9] When they draft agreements, lawyers traditionally use both words and figures to specify important numbers and sums of money one party must pay the other. This is done to diminish the possibility that a typographical error will lead to a misunderstanding of some important provision of the agreement, such as its duration, or the underpayment of one party or overpayment by the other. This is a good practice to adopt in modifying this form agreement for your own use. The period of the license may be as short or as long (up to a maximum of the remainder of the term of copyright protection for the Work) as the parties wish. Use "for the full term of copyright protection" to license the copyright for the remainder of the term of copyright protection; otherwise, specify the number of months or years the license will endure.

[10] Specify the territory to which the license applies. If the Author's intent is to grant a nonexclusive license for the entire world, use this language: "That the Licensee shall have the nonexclusive right to exercise the rights granted herein throughout the world . . ."

[11] Unless permission to alter the work is given by the author of the work, anyone who significantly modifies it may be legally liable to the author for distorting his or her work. The right to alter a work may be important to an advertising agency or company that intends to use the work in various formats. This paragraph may be omitted if the Author objects to any modification of the Work. Or, any such modification may be made dependent upon the prior written approval of the Author: "That the Licensee shall not have the right to crop, edit, alter, or otherwise modify the work without the prior written consent of the Author to any such modification." Ordinarily, nonexclusive licensees, as opposed to those who acquire ownership of the copyright in a work they want to use or the exclusive right to use it, are granted only limited rights to alter a work unless that work is of no real artistic importance to the author.

[12] If payment is to be made in installments, use language similar to the following: "That the Licensee will pay to the Author the sum of _____ ($_____), which amount it is agreed will constitute the Author's only compensation for the grant of rights made herein and which shall be paid according to the following schedule: _____
($_____) shall be paid upon the execution of this agreement; _____
($_____) shall be paid on a date not later than _____ (___) days after the date of execution of this agreement; and _____ _____ ($_____)

shall be paid on a date not later than sixty days after the date of execution of this agreement." The phrase "only compensation" refers to the fact that this agreement does not provide for the periodic payment of royalties to the Author, as do many agreements in which authors license copyrights to others, such as book publishers or music publishers. This simple Nonexclusive License of Copyright form is inadequate to document a license of copyright made in return for the promise of the payment of royalties.

[13] This sort of provision is common in licenses of copyright to protect the person or company acquiring the license of copyright from lawsuits for infringement based on actions of the Author. This seems reasonable if you consider that licensees usually have no knowledge of the circumstances surrounding the creation of the work of others and need to make sure that they are buying only rights in copyrights, *not* lawsuits.

[14] This is called a "hold harmless" clause and is very common in book publishing, music publishing and other agreements in which one party acquires rights in the copyright in a work created by an independent contractor. This is a fairly mild example of a "hold harmless" clause. Authors should expect to see provisions similar to those made in Paragraph 5 of this agreement in any document that licenses a copyright for any substantial period of time; no licensee should agree to acquire a license of copyright unless the author of the work will make, in writing, promises similar to these in the document that grants the license of copyright.

[15] Insert the name of the state where you live here. It is an advantage to a litigant to be able to file or defend a suit in his or her home state. However, it may be that each party to the agreement will want any suit concerning it be filed in his or her home state. This is a point of negotiation but, as a practical matter, the more powerful of the two parties to the agreement will prevail.

[16] This allows the Author to assign any sums due under the agreement to a third party or the estate of an Author who dies to collect any such sums on his or her behalf. It also permits the Licensee to in turn assign its nonexclusive license to another person or company. However, under some circumstances, especially those where the license is granted in return for the periodic payment of royalties, the author will not want the licensee to assign its nonexclusive license to any other party; the usual reason for this objection is that the author may not know and trust this secondary licensee and may have no confidence in the ability of any such secondary licensee to exploit the copyright in the licensed work. In such an event, add this language to limit the right of the licensee to assign the license of copyright to another entity: "However, the Licensee shall not attempt to convey any of the rights granted herein to the Licensee to any third party without the prior written consent of the Author."

[17] Specify how many original copies of the agreement (i.e., copies of the agreement, even if they are photocopies, that bear the original signatures of the parties)

[18] In agreements, "as of" means: "We are signing this agreement today, but we mean for it to take effect *as of* two weeks ago", or "next month." A date specified that is before or after the agreement is actually signed is referred to as the "effective date" of the agreement.

[19] If you want the agreement to become effective on the date it is signed, use that date here. If you want it to be effective as of a previous date, use that date. If you want to postpone the time when the agreement becomes operative until a later date, use that future date.

[20] Leave this space blank for the signature of the Author.

[21] Leave this space blank for the signature of the Licensee.

[22] Insert the Author's address here.

[23] Insert the Licensee's address here.

[24] Leave this space blank for the Author's Social Security Number. It may be necessary for the Licensee to file a report of the Licensee's payments to the Author with the Internal Revenue Service; if so, the Author's Social Security Number will be necessary for any such filings.

[25] Insert here the name of the person who is acting on behalf of his or her company when that company is the Licensee. If the Licensee is an individual, this line may be omitted.

[26] Insert here the title of the person who is acting on behalf of his or her company when that company is the Licensee. If the Licensee is an individual, this line may be omitted.

Exclusive License of Copyright

To be legally effective, exclusive licenses of copyright must be in writing and must be signed by at least the owner of the copyright licensed; this form agreement allows the author of a work to license it exclusively to another person or company. Use this form as a model for any exclusive license you grant or request.

Exclusive License of Copyright

This agreement is made between _____[1] (hereinafter referred to as "the Author"[2]) and _____[3] (hereinafter referred to as "the Licensee"), with reference to the following facts:

A. That the Author, an independent contractor,[4] is the creator of and owner of the copyright in a certain unpublished[5] _____ (hereinafter referred to as "the Work"), which may be more fully described as follows: _____,[6] a photocopy[7] of which is attached hereto and made a part of this agreement by this reference.

B. That the Work was completed during 20__.[8]

C. That the Author's date of birth is _____, _____.[9]

The Author and the Licensee agree as follows:

1. That the Author hereby grants to the Licensee the sole and exclusive right to reproduce, publish, prepare derivative works of and from, combine with other materials, display publicly, and otherwise use, control the use of, and exploit the Work[10] for a period of _____ (___)[11] months from the date written below.

2. That, during the term of this License of Copyright, the Licensee shall have the right to exercise the rights granted herein throughout the United States and Canada.[12]

3. That the Licensee shall have the right to crop, edit, alter, or otherwise modify the Work to the extent that the Licensee, in the sole discretion of the Licensee, deems necessary to suit it to such uses as the Licensee may choose to make of the Work.[13]

4. That the Licensee will pay to the Author the sum of _____ ($_____), which amount it is agreed will constitute the Author's only compensation for the grant of rights made herein.[14]

5. That the Author warrants that he or she is the owner of copyright in the Work and possesses full right and authority to convey the rights herein conveyed. The Author further warrants that the Work does not infringe the copyright in any other work and does not invade any privacy, publicity, trademark, or other rights of any other person.[15]

The Author further agrees to indemnify and hold the Licensee harmless in any litigation in which a third party challenges any of the warranties made by the Author in this paragraph if any such litigation results in a judgment adverse to the Author in a court of competent jurisdiction.[16]

6. That this agreement shall be governed by the laws of the State of _____[17] applicable to contracts made and to be performed therein and shall be construed according to the Copyright Law of the United States, Title 17, Section 101, *et seq.*, United States Code.

7. That this agreement shall enure to the benefit of and bind the parties and their respective heirs, representatives, successors, and assigns.[18]

In witness whereof, the Author and the Licensee have executed this document in _____ (___) counterpart originals[19] as of [20] the _____ day of _____, 20____.[21]

_____[20]
Author

_____[22]

_____
Address

_____[24]
Social Security number

_____[21]
Licensee

_____[23]

_____
Address

By: _____[25]

_____[16]
Title

---

[1] Insert the name of the author of the work. If two or more people created the work as co-authors, insert all their names here and add enough spaces for their signatures, etc., at the end of the agreement.

[2] If you want to be more specific, use "Photographer," "Writer," "Songwriter," "Composer," "Illustrator," etc.; use the same designation throughout the document everywhere the word "Author" appears here. If two or more people created the work as co-authors, use the following language: (hereinafter jointly referred to as "the Author")

[3] Insert the name of the person or company to whom the copyright in the work is being licensed.

[4] This form license agreement is inappropriate for use by anyone who is *not* an independent contractor. The works created by employees as a part of their jobs are works-for-hire; no written agreement is necessary to document the work-for-hire situation in such a circumstance because the relationship of the employee and employer determines, as a matter of law, the ownership of the copyright in any work created on the job by the employee. However, even someone who works at a full-time job is an independent contractor with regard to any activity outside his or her job responsibilities. This language makes clear that the Author is not an employee of the Licensee.

[5] If the Work has been published, use language similar to the following to specify the year of first publication of the Work: "a certain drawing, first published in 2005." One of the three elements of copyright notice is the year date of first publication of the work.

[6] Insert a detailed description of the Work sufficient to allow the parties to the license and everyone else to determine just which particular work, out of all similar works, is the subject of the license,

i.e., "a photograph of three-year-old twin girls, each holding a black Labrador puppy," "a poem titled *Midsummer's Eve*," "a musical composition titled 'Wind Dance,'" "an essay titled 'High Hopes,'" "a non-fiction magazine article titled 'Trends in Consumer Electronics Purchases,'" etc.

[7] If it is practicable, attach a copy of the Work, similar to the sort of copies required for registration of copyright, to each original of the Exclusive License of Copyright document. If it is not practicable to do so, omit this language and use a much more detailed description of the Work or use photographs (for three-dimensional works such as sculptures) or other identifying material, such as the script for a film, and change the language describing the attached materials.

[8] Specify the year during which the Work was finished by the Author. (The Copyright Office permits exclusive licensees to register with the Copyright Office their interests in the copyrights they license; the year date the Work was completed is required on any application for copyright registration

[9] Insert the correct date. (The author's date of birth is also required on any application for copyright registration.)

[10] These are the exclusive rights of copyright given to copyright owners by the U.S. copyright statute and the copyright statutes of other countries.

[11] When they draft agreements, lawyers traditionally use both words and figures to specify important numbers and sums of money one party must pay the other. This is done to diminish the possibility that a typographical error will lead to a misunderstanding of some important provision of the agreement, such as its duration, or the underpayment of one party or overpayment by the other. This is a good practice to adopt in modifying this form agreement for your own use. The period of the license may be as short or as long (up to a maximum of the remainder of the term of copyright protection for the Work) as the parties wish. Use "for the full term of copyright protection" to license the copyright for the remainder of the term of copyright protection; otherwise, specify the number of months or years the license will endure.

[12] Since a copyright owner may grant simultaneous exclusive licenses to a copyright in different geographic areas, specify the territory to which the license applies. If the Author's intent is to grant an exclusive license for the entire world, use this language: "That the Licensee shall have the right to exercise the rights granted herein throughout the world . . ."

[13] Unless permission to alter the work is given by the Author of the work, anyone who significantly modifies it may be legally liable to the Author for distorting his or her work. The right to alter a work may be important to an advertising agency or company that intends to use the work in various formats. This paragraph may be omitted if the Author objects to any modification of the Work. Or, any such modification may be made dependent upon the prior written approval of the Author: "That the Licensee shall not have the right to crop, edit, alter, or otherwise modify the work without the prior written consent of the Author to any such modification."

[14] If payment is to be made in installments, use language similar to the following: "That the Licensee will pay to the Author the sum of _____ ($_____), which amount it is agreed will constitute the Author's only compensation for the grant of rights made herein and which shall be paid according to the following schedule: _____ ($_____) shall be paid upon the execution of this agreement; _____ ($_____) shall be paid on a date not later than thirty days after the date of execution of this agreement; and _____ ($_____) shall be paid on a date not later than _____ (___) days after the date of execution of this agreement."

The phrase "only compensation" refers to the fact that this agreement does not provide for the periodic payment of royalties to the Author, as do many agreements in which authors license copyrights to others, such as book publishers or music publishers. This simple form Exclusive License of Copyright is inadequate to document a license of copyright made in return for the promise of the payment of royalties; while the *license* provisions of this agreement are adequate for such an arrangement, agreements that provide for the payment of royalties universally make many other provisions, such as a provision specifying the right of the author to occasionally examine the books of the Licensee.

[15] This sort of provision is common in licenses of copyright to protect the person or company acquiring the license of copyright from lawsuits for infringement based on actions of the Author.

This seems reasonable if you consider that licensees usually have no knowledge of the circumstances surrounding the creation of the work of others and need to make sure that they are buying only rights in copyrights, *not* lawsuits.

[16] This is called a "hold harmless" clause and is very common in book publishing, music publishing, and other agreements in which one party acquires rights in the copyright in a work created by an independent contractor. This is a fairly mild example of a "hold harmless" clause. Authors should expect to see provisions similar to those made in Paragraph 5 of this agreement in any document that exclusively licenses a copyright for any substantial period of time; no licensee should agree to acquire an exclusive license of copyright unless the author of the work will make, in writing, promises similar to these in the document that grants the license of copyright.

[17] Insert the name of the state where you live here. It is an advantage to a litigant to be able to file or defend a suit in his or her home state. However, it may be that each party to the agreement will want any suit concerning it be filed in his or her home state. This is a point of negotiation but, as a practical matter, the more powerful of the two parties to the agreement will prevail.

[18] This allows the Author to assign any sums due under the agreement to a third party or the estate of an Author who dies to collect any such sums on his or her behalf. It also permits the Licensee to in turn assign its exclusive license to another person or company. However, under some circumstances, especially those where the license is granted in return for the periodic payment of royalties, the author will not want the licensee to assign its exclusive license to any other party; the usual reason for this objection is that the author may not know and trust this secondary licensee and may have no confidence in the ability of any such secondary licensee to exploit the copyright in the work. In such an event, add this language to limit the right of the licensee to assign the license of copyright to another entity: "However, the Licensee shall not attempt to convey any of the rights granted herein to the Licensee by the Author to any third party without the prior written consent of the Author."

[19] Specify how many original copies of the agreement (i.e., copies of the agreement, even if they are photocopies, that bear the original signatures of the parties)

[20] In agreements, "as of" means: "We are signing this agreement today, but we mean for it to take effect *as of* two weeks ago", or "next month." A date specified that is before or after the agreement is actually signed is referred to as the "effective date" of the agreement.

[21] If you want the agreement to become effective on the date it is signed, use that date here. If you want it to be effective as of a previous date, use that date. If you want to postpone the time when the agreement becomes operative until a later date, use that future date.

[22] Leave this space blank for the signature of the Author.

[23] Leave this space blank for the signature of the Licensee.

[24] Insert the Author's address here.

[25] Insert the Licensee's address here.

[26] Leave this space blank for the Author's Social Security Number. It may be necessary for the Licensee to file a report of the Licensee's payments to the Author with the Internal Revenue Service; if so, the Author's Social Security Number will be necessary for any such filings.

[27] Insert here the name of the person who is acting on behalf of his or her company when that company is the Licensee. If the Licensee is an individual, this line may be omitted.

[28] Insert here the title of the person who is acting on behalf of his or her company when that company is the Licensee. If the Licensee is an individual, this line may be omitted.

Photo Release

If you ever use photographs of private individuals in any project, written releases should be a part of your standard operating procedure, a routine part of your business that you *never* neglect. This is true even if, or perhaps especially if, you are a cottage industry, spare-bedroom entrepreneur. If you use the name or even a recognizable description of a living individual in any literary project, you may need a similar release; check with a lawyer regarding your specific project. The form release below is *not* sufficient for right-of-publicity licensing; if you want to use the name, likeness, or performance of any celebrity or public figure in any advertisement or to sell any product, you need a license from that celebrity to avoid a suit.

In addition to getting a signed release, there are a few rules to remember in using releases. Here they are:

- Have a lawyer prepare a release that is designed to work for you. Generally, the broader the release, the better. That is, the less specific your release in stating the uses to which your subject agrees his or her photo can be put, the more leeway you have later.
- However, if the intended use for the photo is something that the model could object to if she or he is not made aware of it, such as use of the photograph in a book with highly sexual content or in an ad for guns or cigarettes, include the specific purpose contemplated in a handwritten addition to the general release. This handwritten addition should be made on the same piece of paper as the general release, preferably in a space reserved for such additions, even if it must be made on the reverse of the page, and should be initialed by the person who signs the release at the same time he or she signs.
- Your release should give you permission to alter the photo, since only having permission to use it "as is" may make it unusable for your purposes. (The release reproduced here may do the trick, but it also may need modification to work for you. Talk to your lawyer if you are in doubt about whether it will suffice in your situation.)
- Have your release printed on your letterhead and carry a supply of blank release forms with you so that you will have them whenever you need them. Any employee of yours who is involved in your project should take the same care with releases; make sure your employees and any freelancers you hire know that you expect them to secure signed releases on your behalf.
- Get a signed release from everyone who appears in any photo you may use in an ad or publication or in any other way. Make *no* exceptions. Get releases even from people in the background of street shots, party shots, or other group shots, unless their faces are not visible and their own mothers wouldn't recognize the set of their shoulders and the color of their hair. Get releases even from paid models. And be especially sure to get releases from private individuals who are not paid for their services.
- Make sure that you get mom, dad, or a legal guardian, not just Aunt Linda or the child's agent or chaperone, to sign a release for anyone under twenty-one, the upper-limit age of majority (in some states), since the signature of a minor may invalidate the release.
- Never obtain a release by trickery or in any circumstances that could lead to a later challenge that the subject of the photograph or ad copy was misled as to the use that would be made of it. If you don't tell the truth, or the whole

truth, about the uses that will be made of the photograph or copy that depicts or mentions the person who signs a release, how can he or she validly agree to allow that use?

- Keep a central file of all releases you obtain for any project, arranged alphabetically by the names of the people who sign releases. Or, even better, keep one copy of each release with the negatives for the photos of the person to whom the release applies and one in a central file, for insurance against loss.

- It is also best to give a copy of the release to the person signing it, but that person probably won't keep his or her copy and, anyway, you are the one who needs proof that the release was signed, not the model or subject.

- Make sure that you indicate, on the back of contact sheets or on negative envelopes or in some other reliable way, the name of each subject of each group of photos. Otherwise, things may get mixed up and Jim may sue you for using his photo, because the only permission you had to use it was, in reality, a signed release from Paul.

- Never vary from your firm policy to obtain releases from everyone whose photo you take or hire taken. And never use a photo or copy from a freelancer without seeing and keeping a copy of the release from the subject of the photo or copy. Never.

Release for Photographs[1]

I hereby grant to _____ [2]
and its[3] assigns, licensees, and successors the irrevocable and unlimited right and permission to use, publish, and disseminate my name and any of the photographs (hereinafter called "the Photographs") taken on _____,
20__ [4] by _____ [5] that include my image, in a
book [tentatively] titled _____, to be
published by _____ [6] and in other
print publishing projects and in all media in connection with that book or any other publishing projects, for advertising, trade, or any other lawful purpose.

I further grant to _____ [7]
and its[8] assigns, licensees, and successors the right to crop, modify, and otherwise alter the aforementioned Photograph or Photographs, including preparing composite or distorted representations, and to combine it or them with any written copy, photographs, or illustrations. I waive my right to inspect that Photograph or Photographs as so altered or combined with other elements.

In return for the grants made herein, I agree that I shall receive as my only compensation _____ (__) copy of the book _____,
when such book is published.[9] However, I understand that, in the sole discretion of _____,[10] the book may not contain
any photograph of me.[11]

I understand that by signing this Release, I am waiving any claim I might otherwise make for invasion of privacy or infringement of the right of publicity. Furthermore, I represent that I have read this Release before signing it and understand its provisions.

I affirm and warrant that I have reached the age of majority and have full authority to make the grants herein contained.[12]

_____   _____
Signature   Date of Signature

_____   _____
Print Name[13]   Signature of Witness[14]

_____   _____
Mailing Address[15]   Address of Witness[16]

_____   _____

or

I am the parent or legal guardian of _____[17], a minor, and hereby make the grants and representations set out above on behalf of him or her.

_____   _____
Signature   Date of Signature

_____   _____
Print Name[18]   Signature of Witness[19]

_____   _____
Mailing Address[20]   Address of Witness[21]

_____   _____

---

[1] This Release for Photographs is suitable for use in a situation where a photograph is taken of a private individual and used as a book illustration; it does not really suffice as a release for use of a photograph of a celebrity in marketing any product or service. Further, because uses of a private individual's photograph for any purpose but as a book illustration may involve questions and rights that are not contemplated in this Release, get legal advice regarding your specific situation before using or adapting this Release for different purposes.

[2] Insert the name of the publishing company here, or use the name of the photographer if no publishing company is involved. If the publishing company is a corporation, use its legal name, i.e., Bifocal Books, Inc. If it is a partnership, use something like this: "John Jones and Sam Smith, doing

business as Jones and Smith." If it is a sole proprietorship using a trade name, use something like this: "John Jones doing business as Jones Photography."

[3] If the entity obtaining the release is a person rather than a corporation or partnership or sole proprietorship, use "his" or "her" instead of "its."

[4] Insert the date the photographs were taken.

[5] Insert the name of the photographer.

[6] Insert a broad description of the project that will include the photographs.

[7] Insert the name of the publishing company here, or use the name of the photographer if no publishing company is involved. If the publishing company is a corporation, use its legal name, i.e., Bifocal Books, Inc. If it is a partnership, use something like this: "John Jones and Sam Smith, doing business as Jones and Smith." If it is a sole proprietorship using a trade name, use something like this: "John Jones doing business as Jones Photography."

[8] If the entity obtaining the release is a person rather than a corporation or partnership or sole proprietorship, use "his" or "her" instead of "its."

[9] In the case of this project, the models would be working for publicity and the chance of being featured in a book of photography. In the case of paid models, insert language such as "I agree that I shall receive _____ ($_____) as my only compensation."

[10] Insert the name of the publishing company here, or use the name of the photographer if no publishing company is involved.

[11] This language is necessary to make clear that the final decision whether the photograph including this model will be included in the book as published is a decision of the editor of the book and that no promise is made that the model will appear in the final book.

[12] This space for the model's signature should be used if the model is of legal age (sometimes this is eighteen, sometimes twenty-one). If the model is not of legal age in the state where the photograph is taken, the parent or guardian of the model must sign in the subsequent signature space. In some cases, professional models have been declared "emancipated minors" by going to court and requesting to be treated as adults for purposes of pursuing a profession. However, never believe that a minor has been emancipated and is able to be treated as an adult in making binding contracts without credible proof that this is so, such as seeing the court decree yourself.

[13] Get the model to print his or her name in order to file this release correctly in your files and also so that the model's name in any credit line in any publication that includes the photographs of this model may be correctly spelled.

[14] Get someone to witness the model's signature in order to avoid any later claim that the signature is not that of the model. Having the signature notarized by a notary public would be a very good way to ensure that the signature is never questioned, but notaries are not always available in situations in which photo releases are used and, in most cases, the signature of a witness who can be located later will suffice.

[15] It may never be necessary to communicate with the model, but having the model's address is a good idea.

[16] If you ever need to be able to call on the witness to the model's signature, you will need to know where to find him or her.

[17] Insert the name of the minor who is the model for the photographs.

[18] Get the parent or guardian to print his or her name so that you will have its correct spelling.

[19] Get someone to witness the parent or guardian's signature in order to avoid any later claim that the signature is not that of the parent or guardian.

[20] It may never be necessary to communicate with the parent or guardian, but having the parent or guardian's address is a good idea.

[21] If you ever need to be able to call on the witness to the parent or guardian's signature, you will need to know where to find him or her.

INDEX

(Actual entities and persons are given index entries; fictitious entities and persons are not.)

Books from Allworth Press

Allworth Press
is an imprint
of Allworth
Communications, Inc.
Selected titles are
listed below.

The Copyright Guide: A Friendly Handbook for Protecting & Profiting from Copyrights, Third Edition
by Lee Wilson (paperback, 6 × 9, 256 pages, $19.95)

The Trademark Guide: A Friendly Handbook for Protecting & Profiting from Trademarks, Second Edition
by Lee Wilson (paperback, 6 × 9, 272 pages, $19.95)

The Advertising Law Guide: A Friendly Desktop Reference for Advertising Professionals
by Lee Wilson (paperback, 6 × 9, 272 pages, $19.95)

The Patent Guide: A Friendly Guide to Protecting & Profiting from Patents
by Carl W. Battle (paperback, 6 × 9, 224 pages, $19.95)

Turn You Idea or Invention into Millions
by Don Kracke (paperback, 6 × 9, 224 pages, $18.95)

Legal Guide for the Visual Artist, Fourth Edition
by Tad Crawford (paperback, 8 1/2 × 11, 272 pages, $19.95)

Business and Legal Forms for Photographers, Third Edition
by Tad Crawford (paperback, 8 1/2 × 11, 192 pages, $29.95, includes CD-ROM)

Business and Legal Forms for Illustrators, Third Edition
by Tad Crawford (paperback, 8 1/2 × 11, 160 pages, $29.95, includes CD-ROM)

Business and Legal Forms for Authors and Self-Publishers, Third Edition
by Tad Crawford (paperback, 8 3/8 × 10 7/8, 272 pages, $29.95, includes CD-ROM)

Starting Your Career as a Freelance Illustrator or Graphic Designer, Revised Edition
By Michael Fleishman (paperback, 6 × 9, 80 b&w illus., 272 pages, $19.95)

Please write to request our free catalog. To order by credit card, call 1-800-491-2808 or send a check or money order to Allworth Press, 10 East 23rd Street, Suite 510, New York, NY 10010. Include $6 for shipping and handling for the first book ordered and $1 for each additional book. Ten dollars plus $1 for each additional book if ordering from Canada. New York State residents must add sales tax.

To see our complete catalog on the World Wide Web, or to order online, you can find us at *www.allworth.com*.